"If you are looking for a book that am̶ matches over 'Christian nationalism,' Miles Smith's Religion & Republic is not for you. But if you want an even-handed and illuminating assessment of the actual role Christianity played in the American founding and early republic, I can't think of a better choice than this book."

—THOMAS S. KIDD
Midwestern Baptist Theological Seminary

"Much of the conversation about a Christian America has been marked by either ideological nonsense or historical superficiality — or worse. In this book Miles Smith offers a corrective that is both timely and deeply thoughtful. In Religion & Republic, Smith argues for a distinctively Protestant understanding that corrects much of the confusion that surrounds so many of the historical assertions made by evangelicals. This is a really important book that arrives at a critical moment in the American experience and will greatly illuminate many contemporary debates."

—R. ALBERT MOHLER
The Southern Baptist Theological Seminary

"The early American republic, Miles Smith argues persuasively in this learned study, was a nation of Christians who, notwithstanding commitments to nonestablishment and religious liberty, maintained social, political, legal, and educational institutions aligned with Protestant Christian traditions thought necessary to preserve social order and nourish the civic virtues required for republican government to succeed. Religion & Republic explores often overlooked chapters in American history and bristles with fresh insights that will inform and challenge scholars and polemicists inclined to see the early republic as the denouement of either Christian nationalism or secular liberalism."

—DANIEL L. DREISBACH
Professor in the School of Public Affairs at American University in Washington, D.C.

RELIGION
& REPUBLIC

RELIGION & REPUBLIC

Christian America from the
Founding to the Civil War

MILES SMITH

DAVENANT PRESS 2024

ISBN: 1-949716-31-7
ISBN-13: 978-1-949716-31-3

Cover design and typesetting by Rachel Rosales, Orange Peel Design
Proofread by John Barach

TABLE OF CONTENTS

FOREWORD

Recently I came across this astute observation, made in 1963, from the right-wing populist Willmoore Kendall, writing about the relationship between American Conservatism and religion:

> The problem, put briefly, is this: the United States is—has been down to now anyhow—a Christian society governed, or rather self-governed, under a secular Constitution; nothing short of the sea-change I mentioned a moment ago, is likely to deprive Judaeo-Christian religious beliefs of the special status, approximating that of a public truth, that they enjoy within it. But, also, nothing short of such a sea-change is likely, in the foreseeable future, to gain for them a *more* privileged status than they now enjoy. Attempts to resolve the religious-society-secular-Constitution tension in the United States, in either the one direction or the other, are not only divisive, but contrary to the American tradition itself.[1]

---

1. Willmoore Kendall, *The Conservative Affirmation* (Washington, DC: Regnery Gateway, 2022), xlvi.

As much as any observation I've come across in the past several years, these three (run-on) sentences explain the confused and combustible situation American Christians find themselves in as we enter the second quarter of the twenty-first century. While the tension began to unravel after World War II, Kendall could still plausibly argue in 1963 that the enduring "problem" of a religious society with a secular Constitution had not been resolved in one direction or the other. Six decades later, Kendall would not, I trust, make the same claims. In most parts of the country, in most elite institutions, and in most public debates, Christianity is no longer "a public truth." If anything, opposition to Christian beliefs—especially related to ethics and morality—is, in the most powerful quarters of the country anyway, the *new* public truth.

Part of what makes Kendall's observation relevant is that he was speaking explicitly about American *conservatism*. Progressives are happy to cut the religious-society-secular-Constitution tension by reshaping America into a thoroughly secular, if not positively anti-Western and anti-Christian, nation. Conservatives, on the other hand, know that such a reshaping not only misunderstands the American past but is poison for the American future. And yet, because so much of our culture, our laws, and our society's general assumptions about meaning and morality have become anti-Christian, there is an understandable impulse among many conservatives that the only solution is to break the tension hard in the other direction. For many Christians, the answer to Ross Douthat's question "How should contemporary Christians react to the decline of their churches, the secularization of the culture, the final loss of Christendom?" is a loud call to establish a Medieval-style Christendom or to reframe a continent-sized country of 330 million people along the lines of sixteenth-century

Geneva.[2] Whether these bold visions prove courageous or merely Quixotic remains to be seen. After all, we cannot know the future.

But we *can* know the past, and throughout our history as a country America was neither a repristination of Calvinist Geneva or Constantine's Rome nor a secular *novus ordo seclorum*. Kendall's warning explains why we live in such divisive times. From 1789 onward, there existed a sometimes contentious but often complementary set of convictions that (1) America would never have a federally established Christian Church *and* that (2) America was and always had been an obviously Christian country. That is to say, from the end of the eighteenth century until the second half of the twentieth century, and *especially* in the nineteenth century, America could be fairly described as a nation held together—in law, in culture, and in shared assumptions—by a broadly Christian order that privileged Protestant Christianity while also tolerating religious minorities.

If this reading of history becomes more well known and more widely accepted in the years ahead, I'm confident that we will have this book to thank. *Religion and Republic* is a deeply researched work, written with verve and lucidity by Hillsdale professor Miles Smith—an excellent historian, a man of many opinions (!), and, I should also say, a friend. Miles's argument is straightforward: "What this volume proposes is that the United States Constitution's disestablishment did not secularize society, nor did it remove institutional Christianity from the civic, state educational, or political spheres." Elegantly simple. And, I'm convinced, true.

---

2. The question in quotation marks is the first sentence in Douthat's piece "A Gentler Christendom" in *First Things* (June 2022).

As I write this Foreword, public theology (at least on the internet) is dominated by arguments for and against Christian Nationalism. I agree wholeheartedly with Miles that historians and ministers would do well to set aside the term, whether one wants to wave Christian Nationalism as a banner or employ it as a bogeyman. The fact is that the term is of recent vintage and that no one agrees on what it means. Is Christian Nationalism shorthand for theocracy, Catholic integralism, Trumpist Republicans, church establishments, the necessity of a strong-armed Christian prince, the views of the magisterial Reformers, Christian discipleship, Christian laws, Christian influence, or something else? As Miles points out in the book, it is all too easy for one side to label everything they don't like as Christian Nationalism, and the other side to label everything they *do* like as Christian Nationalism. *Religion and Republic* makes a convincing case that Christian Nationalism does not represent the best of the disestablished liberal Protestant tradition as it came to flourish in the American republic.

The importance of Miles's work is that he demonstrates so fully and so convincingly what disestablishment did and did not mean in the nineteenth century. On the one hand, American republicanism, enamored as it was with liberty, was always allergic to any hint of Erastianism, suspicious of any notion that the government had a right to interfere in church business. America's version of liberalism was the liberalism of tolerance, of limited government, of civil and religious liberty. The Constitution enshrined the principle (on the federal level) that there could be no establishment of religion—a principle that worked its way through the states over the next forty years. Unlike almost all of Europe, there would be no state church in America.

But disestablished did not mean disentangled. American Christians went along with disestablishment, and often were champions of it, not out of a position of weakness, but of strength. Protestant Christianity did not need a state church to maintain its privileged position in the American civil, political, and social order. Even as the individual states continued down the road of disestablishment, Christian institutions proliferated, Christian beliefs were resolutely defended, and the American people were often warned against ignoring the Christian foundations of their republican experiment in self-government. Disestablishment was not the same as secularism, or even religious pluralism. True, everyone agreed that government should not be sectarian, but this did not mean government ought to be anti-religious or irreligious, or even had to be strictly neutral on religious questions. Virtually no one in America in the nineteenth century conceived of a political and social order devoid of religion. What's more, the religion which they assumed was necessary and ought to be protected and promoted was Protestant Christianity.

Religion & Republic is a history book first and foremost. Unlike some contemporary historians, Miles refrains from using history as a (rather obvious) Trojan horse for political and theological agendas. Miles wants to show us what was, not lay out a plan for what ought to be. And yet, if there is an implicit exhortation in the book, it is to consider again the wisdom of "Christian institutionalism." In good conservative fashion, Miles reminds us that too often evangelicals have prioritized the individual or the nation-state, without giving much thought to the intermediate institutions that sustain human civilization. Christians can start by taking civil and social institutions seriously, not confusing them with the church or confusing the church's mission with their mission, but taking them seriously nonetheless.

American Protestants should not be fooled into thinking they can turn back the clock to the consensus that existed in the Early Republic. For better or worse, their world is not our world. But that doesn't mean we can ignore the way we were, for any political project seeking to renew the future of America must be grounded in the realities of the American tradition. And that means initiating people into a tradition that was something other than Christian Nationalism or anti-Christian secularism or mere libertarian proceduralism. It means teaching our own history as people who once conceived of themselves as both a religious people and as a republic

Kevin DeYoung
January 2024

ACKNOWLEDGMENTS

This book has been first and foremost an outgrowth of friendships. C.S. Lewis wrote in *The Four Loves* that friendship is "born at the moment when one man says to another 'What! You too? I thought that no one but myself . . .'" Throughout my academic life, I've been able to find the sorts of kindred spirits who have sharpened me intellectually, encouraged me vocationally, and lifted me up spiritually. Mine is a life truly blessed with friendship, and this book could not have been written without the help and support of friends, scholars, mentors, and pastors, all of whom I'm thankful to call friends.

I must start with thanking profusely the editorial team at the Davenant Press. Brad Littlejohn has been a friend for years, and gave this project life when, in a moment of my vocal exasperation, he calmy suggested, "why don't you send it to us." Davenant is what it is because of Brad. Colin Redemer built on Brad's suggestion and urged me to find my actual voice and not take the easy way out by just writing something merely for the academy. Mark Hamilton has been faithfully laboring behind the scenes. Rhys Lavery has been remarkable—this project has been made infinitely better under his steady hand. Thank you Rhys; thank you.

My years at the College of Charleston and at the Citadel made me the scholar I am today. David Gleeson, now of the University of Northumbria, forced me to take historiography seriously. Edmund Drago forced me to be a writer, and to think creatively. Bernard Powers was a model gentleman scholar. Tim Coates gave me the best possible advice on how to pursue the academy as a vocation. Brig. General Michael B. Barrett modeled academic integrity. Irina Gigova-Ganaway got me thinking about nations.

At TCU I made lifelong friends, and became part Texan. Sam Negus and Mitchell Klingenberg have become friends that stick as close as brothers. Jeff Wells, Keith Altavilla, Brooke Poston, Joe Stoltz, and Jamie Harp are all working in the academy, and all made my graduate life better. Ken Stevens was the best advisor I could have asked for. His kindness and willingness to give of his time made a dissertation a more pleasant experience than it might have otherwise been. Gene Smith dragged me kicking and screaming in to becoming a better writer, and I'm profoundly grateful for it. Steven Woodworth's willingness to be a public Christian and a public scholar gave me courage in my vocation I might not have otherwise had.

My time at Regent and in Virginia returned me, if only for a short time, to the South Atlantic states I grew up in. Bill Reddinger, Kevin Grimm, Eric Jones, Danny Hitchock, Steve Webb, Jim and Nick Higgins, Josh McMullen, and Bob Herron all made my time in Virginia a blessing. Micah Mattix was a respite in hard times. Bob McDonnell was kind enough to pinch hit for me several times, which is about as much as I'd ask a former governor to do. Micah Meadowcroft, Michael Lucchese, and Chris McCaffrey came from DC to see me for birthdays, which I loved. Jeff

Elliott remains the ideal Presbyterian minister, and one of the godliest men I've ever known. Johnny Napier, Steve Dickens, Betsy Barrows, and Zach Kuenzli all let me share their lives and families. Mark Jumper is a big brother I lean on still.

No institution has marked me professionally as much as Hillsdale College has. David Whalen, then Provost, graciously took a chance on untried and untested twenty-nine year old from a textile town in the North Carolina Piedmont to fill a one year job. Chris VanOrman gave me my dream job. Larry Arnn welcomed me back after four years away. Mark Kalthoff treated me like a valued member of the history department from the moment I set foot on campus. Mark has been there for me at my best, and at my worst. When I needed his help, he always gave it. I don't know what I could have done without him. Darryl Hart sharpens me and tests me; he also is a big brother who has been there to pick me up when I needed it most. Brad Birzer is a constant encouragement. Korey Maas is the essence of steady friendship and leadership. Eric Hutchinson has been someone to bounce ideas off of. Dave Stewart fills my head with images of battlefield success. Bill McClay always is cheerfully available to shoot the breeze over a pint. Adam Carrington is that truly best of friends. Jason Gerhke, Matt Gaetano, Richard Gamble, Paul Moreno, Mark Moyar, Steve Naumann, Anna Vicenza, Don Westblade, Jason Peters, Catherine Kuiper, Paul Rahe, Elizabeth Fredericks, Cody Strecker, Ian Church, Christina Lambert, Tripp Young, Calvin Stockdale, Jeanette White, Pete Jennings, James Strausburg, Dan and Katie O'Toole, and Scot Bertram all make life the joy that it is. I miss John Somerville very much, but I'm happy he's back in our home state of North Carolina. Andrew Fink is a friend, a Christian, and a statesman. Tim Walberg and his staff have been responsive and prompt every time

I've needed something from them. My students at Hillsdale College are my pride and joy; I'm devoted to you all, and I am reminded that you are friends as much as anyone else.

Glen Moots and Mark Hall saw early versions of this work. A phone call to Mark started the project, and he has been a friend throughout the process. Brad Birzer has been there with me every step of the way, offering guidance over lunch or a beer at our local brewery. Craig Smith, Dan Gullotta, and I have litigated the Early Republic through text for years.

Pastor-scholars from different traditions have unselfishly offered me their own stocks of friendship, wisdom, and erudition. Kevin DeYoung, Derek Rishmawy, Jake Meador, James Anderson, D. Blair Smith, and James Wood represent a broad but convicted Reformed tradition in the PCA. Sean Willman is a model Lutheran, and a good friend. Southern Baptists Jordan Steffaniak, Andrew Walker, Brandon Ayescue, Jake Stone, and Buster Brown remind me why a healthy Protestantism in the USA needs a healthy SBC. Jordan Ballor and Micah Watson make me take a break from Dutch jokes to praise their work at Calvin University. In my own Anglican tradition Rev. Steven Wedgeworth, Rev. Bart Gingrich, Rev. Richard Tarsinato, Rev. Drew Collins, and Rev. Clay Thompson are model churchmen.

I could not do what I do without my church home at Holy Trinity Parish. I have been delighted to serve on vestry with Sam Knecht, Eric Coykendoll, Jeremiah Regan, Pai Ringenberg, Jeremiah Regan, Renee Young, Jon Gregg, Blake McAlister, and John Novak IV. Adam Rick guided our parish ably through Covid, and has taken on the perhaps even weightier role of being chaplain at Hillsdale College. Wendy Coykendoll keeps our church running. Bishop Bill Love is always a text or phone call away. Julian Dobbs is unquestionably my reverend father in God, and he has been so in good times and in bad.

My pastor, The Ven. Alan R. Crippen II, has become a trusted advisor, counselor, and priest. He had said kind words, firm words, hard words, and fun words, all in Christ-like love. I could not have completed this project without him, nor could I have had the motivation to do so without his encouragement.

I miss my friends back "home" in North Carolina every day, especially Eric Tornfelt, Alex Farmartino, Brian Williams, Josh Baker and his brothers, and Michael Parker. I know we will all see Steve Baker again, but not yet. My brother Aaron brings me back to lighthearted joys from our shared childhood and is always kind enough to let me watch TV at his place at Christmas, given my long-time absence in owning one of my own. Jaime Boerema has been patient with me, and has taken care of me when I was undoubtedly difficult to take care of. Her joyful constancy and selfless care for others impress me daily.

My greatest temporal gratitude is for my parents, Cathy and Miles Smith III. I won the life lottery; I was raised in the world of Southern Presbyterians who took the Bible, church, and history seriously. Our home life was loving, and at an early age I found out that Jesus loved me and died for me. I can call my parents at any time. They have loved me and cared for me over forty years. This book is dedicated to them, precisely because I will never be able to thank them enough for the completely wonderful life I have been able to live through no merit of my own.

PREFACE

"There are two opposite errors into which those who study the annals of our country are in constant danger of falling, the error of judging the present by the past, and the error of judging the past by the present. The former is the error of minds prone to reverence whatever is old, the latter of minds readily attracted by whatever is new. The former error may perpetually be observed in the reasonings of conservative politicians on the questions of their own day. The latter error perpetually infects the speculations of writers of the liberal school when they discuss the transactions of an earlier age. The former error is the more pernicious in a statesman, and the latter in a historian."

—Lord Macaulay[1]

In *Was America Founded as a Christian Nation?* John Fea confidently asserts that "If the United States was ever a 'Christian nation,' it was so during the period between the

---

1. Thomas Babington Macaulay, *The History of England from the Accession of James II* (Chicago: Donohue, Henneberry & Co, 1890), vol. 2, 217.

ratification of the Constitution (1789) and the start of the Civil War (1861)."[2] Although the Constitution, Fea argues, mandated that "there would be no official or established religion in America, and the states were gradually removing religious requirements for officeholders, Christianity, and particularly Protestant evangelicalism, defined the culture." The Constitution, of course, precluded only a federally established religion, and state churches lingered on until Massachusetts finally got rid of its Congregationalist establishment in 1833. But Fea is right on the merits. In many ways the United States was a Christian nation between 1789 and 1861, and few if any major Protestant divines or intellectuals wasted their efforts denouncing the Christian nation they lived in. Charles Hodge (1797–1898), principal of Princeton Seminary and perhaps the best known Presbyterian of the nineteenth century, wanted to keep America Christian for the sake of the Sabbath. Anglo-Americans "are a sabbath-keeping people," he said, a religious habit that was to be "highly prized and sedulously guarded; and in this country especially, we should be watchful lest the influx of immigrants of other nationalities deprive us of this great distinction and its blessings."[3] Baptist luminary Isaac Backus (1724–1806) was "convinced America was not only a Christian nation, but a Protestant one."[4] Episcopal bishop George Washington Doane (1799–1859) told his parishioners frequently that the United States was a "free,

2. John Fea, *Was America Founded As a Christian Nation?* (Louisville: Westminster John Knox, 2011), Chap. 1, Kindle.

3. Charles Hodge, *Systematic Theology*, vol. 3, *Soteriology* (Grand Rapids, MI: Eerdmans, 1940), XIX.8, 335.

4. William G. McLoughlin, "Isaac Backus and the Separation of Church and State in America," *American Historical Review* 73, no. 5 (1968): 1392–413.

intelligent, and Christian nation."[5] Immigrant Protestants joined the chorus of their Anglophone co-religionists. C. F. W. Walther (1811–1887), the leader of Saxon Lutheran immigrants who formed what is now the Lutheran Church Missouri Synod in 1847, was no friend of Calvinism or theocracy; he came to the United States fleeing the syncretic Prussian Union, a state church formed in 1817 that forced Calvinist innovation upon Prussian Lutherans. Nonetheless, even Walther could sound like a militant Protestant establishmentarian. He complained of the United States that "Here, under the cover of religious freedom, even the principles of natural religion, which sets man apart as human, are often trampled and they even proclaim: 'There is no God!'"[6] The Constitution of the American republic, said Walther, "permits no atheist the right of citizenship. It grants freedom *of* religion not freedom *from* religion." Neither Hodge, Backus, Doane, nor Walther were particularly theocratic extremists in the era. All four were well known, and respected.

Fast forward to 2016; there is a general election, and Donald Trump has thrown out the playbook of Republican orthodoxy in order to gain a new type of voter. He's also thrown out the evangelical leaders that George W. Bush relied on. Other Christians unused to power or status welcome

---

5. George Washington Doane, "Influence Without Intervention, The Duty of our Nation to the World," in *The Life and Writings of George Washington Doane*, vol. 4, *The Educational Writings of George Washington Doane*, ed. William Croswell Doane (New York: D. Appleton, 1861), 268.

6. C. F. W. Walther, "Fourth of July Address Presented at a Christian Youth Group," in *From Our Master's Table: Sermons and Addresses Already Appearing Since 1847 Partly in Pamphlet Form and Partly in Periodicals Newly Offered in a Single Volume of Dr. C. F. W. Walther*, ed. Joel Basely (Dearborn: Mark V, 2008), 175.

the chance to have their voices heard on the national stage. And they aren't afraid to talk about Christian America. The dispossessed evangelical leaders of the Bush Republican Party—many but not all Southern Baptists—use the moment to indict the so-called "court evangelicals"[7] who have them replaced them as unprincipled hacks. But they're not only unprincipled hacks. They're also a fundamental threat to the liberal order. They are—scary music—Christian Nationalists. A half decade later the evangelical civil war over Trump has led numerous politically minded evangelicals to gladly embrace the term "Christian Nationalist"; in 2022 two books, one popular, one intellectual, were published within months of each other.[8] And so there is confusion about the nature of religion and its relationship to the United States' political order. To be fair, the relationship between church and state has never been crystal clear, but in the United States in the third decade of the twenty-first century, the question of religion's relationship to the civil order is more controversial than it has been in some time.

Over the past several years the topic of so-called "Christian Nationalism" has occupied the minds of evangelical intellectuals and pastors, as well as those outside of evangelicalism. At the time of writing, in late 2023, no less than half a dozen books have been written on the subject in the past year. Three of them have been published in the past six months.[9] Yet for all the talk, I have yet to see a uni-

---

7. For a fuller treatment of the term "Court Evangelicals," see Fea, *Believe Me.*

8. At the popular level, see Andrew Torba and Andrew Isker, *Christian Nationalism: A Biblical Guide for Taking Dominion and Discipling Nations* (self-published, 2022). At the intellectual level, see Stephen Wolfe, *The Case for Christian Nationalism* (Moscow: Canon, 2022).

9. The aforementioned books by Torba and Isker and Wolfe advance

form definition of the term. For some, "Christian Nationalism" refers to the movement by Trumpist Revivalists to take over so-called "evangelicalism." For others, any conservative Christian socio-political commitment is "Christian Nationalism." Because of this confusion, I fear the term has become essentially meaningless, even for those who wish to own it in good faith, and so I feel it should be set aside by both historians and ministers alike. I do not say this dismissively—I have been reluctant to dismiss the term entirely, for several reasons. The primary one is that while I am a historian by vocation, I'm also a vestryman in the Anglican Church in North America. When prominent evangelicals label "Christian Nationalism"—whatever the deuce it is—as a heresy, I bristle. The cornerstone of my communion is the Book of Common Prayer, which was designed very literally to Christianize—more accurately to Protestantize—the

---

positive cases for Christian Nationalism. However, they have been accompanied by a wave of negative assessments, such as Andrew L. Whitehead, *American Idolatry: How Christian Nationalism Betrays the Gospel and Threatens the Church* (Grand Rapids: Brazos, 2023); Lerone Martin, *The Gospel of J. Edgar Hoover: How the FBI Aided and Abetted the Rise of White Christian Nationalism* (Princeton: Princeton University Press, 2023); Pamela Cooper-White, *The Psychology of Christian Nationalism: Why People Are Drawn In and How to Talk Across the Divide* (Minneapolis: Fortress, 2022); Bradley Onishi, *Preparing for War: The Extremist History of White Christian Nationalism—and What Comes Next* (Minneapolis: Broadleaf, 2023). The list could go on, and more books with "Christian Nationalism" in their titles are forthcoming. Credit must go to the likes of Andrew Seidel, whose *The Founding Myth: Why Christian Nationalism Is Un-American* (New York: Union Square) came out in 2019, somewhat ahead of the curve; others include Samuel L. Perry, *The Flag and the Cross: White Christian Nationalism and the Threat to American Democracy* (Oxford: Oxford University Press, 2022); David P. Gushee, *Defending Democracy from its Christian Enemies* (Grand Rapids: Eerdmans, 2023); and Katherine Stewart, *The Power Worshippers: The Dangerous Rise of Religious Nationalism* (New York: Bloomsbury, 2020).

early modern English nation. On some level, the Christian national roots of Anglicanism seem hard to escape. Similar historical developments among Reformation-era Calvinists and Lutherans might lead observers to label Thomas Cranmer, John Calvin, and Martin Luther "Christian Nationalists." So inasmuch as the term might be used to denote historic Protestantism, I have not wanted to cede it entirely to those who use it as a pejorative.[10]

Still, whatever historic usefulness the term "Christian Nationalist" might have had in describing the early American republic, however, seems immaterial once we inquire who is using it now. Increasingly it is being used on all sides to denote *any* Christian political involvement. This seems to me so broad as to be entirely useless. Donald Trump's administration *and* conservatives on the Supreme Court *and* Right to Life *and* soup kitchens run by urban Catholic churches *and* a very anti-lottery Presbyterian Church cannot all be "Christian Nationalism" if the term is to have any substantive meaning. Whatever usefulness the term "Christian Nationalism" might have historically through its connections to Protestant political theology, its primary use today by both its detractors and its proponents bears little, if any, relation to the historic usage. What is left is one side labeling anything they *don't* like as "Christian Nationalism," and the other side labeling everything they *do* like as "Christian Nationalism." Neither group's understanding of the relationship between Christianity and the state seems sustainable or desirable. Neither revivalist folk

---

10. See my articles "Would That It Really Were 'Christian Nationalism,'" (*The American Conservative*, March 8, 2021, https://www.theamericanconservative.com/would-it-really-were-christian-nationalism/) and "The Uselessness of 'Christian Nationalism'" (*Mere Orthodoxy*, July 18, 2022, https://mereorthodoxy.com/the-uselessness-of-christian-nationalism).

Christianity nor *en masse* progressive deconstruction are worthy successors to historic Protestant political thought passed down from the Reformers to the conservative older mainline churches. "Christian Nationalism," as it's used currently, represents neither the Reformers nor the best of the disestablished liberal Protestant tradition of the American republic. The term is at best probably useless, and more likely cartoonishly silly altogether. Whatever energy spent trying to rescue the term could be better spent on more substantive Christian socio-political pursuit, and I'm thankful that the Davenant Institute is one such organization less interested in grandstanding labels and more interested in doing the hard scholarly work of Protestant resourcement.

The ultimate purpose of this history is to wed Protestant resourcement with a relatively scholarly history of the Early Republic that posits the history of the United States within a continuing Protestant tradition and not an evangelical one. Evangelicals are Protestants who understand themselves to be, according to Thomas S. Kidd, "born-again Protestants who cherish the Bible as the Word of God and who emphasize a personal relationship with Jesus Christ through the Holy Spirit." British historian David Bebbington defined four hallmarks of evangelicals: they are committed to biblicism, a particular hermeneutic regarding Christian scriptures; crucicentrism, or prioritizing atonement as the major thematic priority of preaching and teaching; conversionism, a dialectic regarding Christian conversion largely at odds with historic Lutheran, Anglican, and Reformed understandings of baptism's efficacy; and activism, or the belief that true Christianity needs to be shown through efforts at moral and social reform. In Kidd and Bebbington's definitions, evangelical Christianity is highly personal and wedded to subjective experience. Institutions are of second-ary importance in the Christian life.[11]

The distinction between evangelical and Protestant is crucial. Evangelical historians tell the story of religion in the United States as one of socio-moral transformation, typically centering around the Great Awakening, Jonathan Edwards, George Whitfield, moral reformers in the Second Great Awakening, Dwight Moody, Charles Spurgeon, and other popular ministers in the Gilded Age, the Fundamentalist/Modernist controversy, the works of Carl F. H. Henry, the rise of the Moral Majority, and most recently evangelical support for Donald Trump. The religious commitments of civil and political institutions are generally ignored. Andrew Wilson's recent *Remaking the World: How 1776 Created the Post-Christian West* posits that 1776 and the advent of the American republic, among other things, remade the world, and in many ways remade North American Protestant Christianity into "evangelicalism."[12] Nathan Finn noted in his review of the book that evangelicals needed to "remember that the same century that gave rise to our modern world also gave rise to the modern evangelical movement. The earliest generations of evangelicals flourished in the dawning days of the world in which contemporary evangelicals now live."[13] Mark Noll, the dean of evangeli-

---

11. Thomas S. Kidd, *Who is An Evangelical? The History of a Movement in Crisis* (New Haven: Yale University Press, 2019), 5; David W. Bebbington, *Evangelicalism in Modern Britain: A History from the 1730s to the 1980s* (London: Unwin Hyman, 1989), 2–17.

12. Andrew Wilson, *Remaking the World: How 1776 Created the Post-Christian West* (Wheaton: Crossway, 2023).

13. Nathan A. Finn, "1776: The Year That Shaped the Post-Christian West," *The Gospel Coalition*, November 9, 2023, https://www.thegospelcoalition.org/reviews/remaking-world/.

cal-identifying historians, wrote of the era between 1750 and 1850 as one of almost complete theological and civil transformation. His *America's God* "describes a shift away from European theological traditions, descended directly from the Protestant Reformation, toward a Protestant evangelical theology, decisively shaped by its engagement with revolutionary and post-revolutionary America."[14] Noll proposed that "nineteenth-century protestant evangelicalism differed from the religion of the Protestant Reformation as much as sixteenth-century century Reformation Protestantism differed from the Roman Catholic theology from which it emerged."[15]

For Noll, American religion was created by older "expectations for church and theology inherited from Europe" giving way. The process that "ended with an intimate union between evangelical and Revolutionary politics began with disruption in the historic colonial churches."[16] That disruption, for Noll, lay in the Great Awakening and in ministers like Jonathan Edwards and George Whitfield. Noll sees religion in this context as a set of social and intellectual propositions; he has little to say on the connection between colonial religion and colonial socio-political institutions. Indeed, the complete absence of the deep connection between seventeenth-century religion and English ideas of commonwealth are, as one reviewer of *America's God* noted, conspicuously absent.[17] English Protestant—Anglican

---

14. Mark A. Noll, *America's God: From Jonathan Edwards to Abraham Lincoln* (Oxford: Oxford University Press, 2002), 3.

15. Noll, *America's God*, 3.

16. Noll, *America's God*, 46–47.

17. Francis J. Bremer, "Faith and Society: The Making of a Christian America," *Reviews in American History* 32, no. 1 (2004): 7–13.

and Puritan—notions of government and religion and the symbiosis between the two were built into American political and social institutions. Religious society might change, but institutionalized Protestantism was embedded in the American order in ways that mere social-religious revivals could not and did not change easily. Perhaps unintentionally, evangelical historians have implied that the American Revolution was far more radical than it actually was regarding religion. Two-time Pulitzer Prize-winning historian Bernard Bailyn famously noted that "the primary goal of the American Revolution...was not the overthrow or even the alteration of the existing social order but the preservation of political liberty." [18] Religion, undoubtedly a part of the social order, was never meant to be revolutionized, nor was its place in the civil and political realms meant to be transformed.

The history presented in this volume ultimately sees Protestant continuity in the Early Republic where evangelicals see transformation. Where they see a religious *novus ordo seclorum*, I see a lingering Protestant *ancien regime* built into American institutions like colleges and state laws and diplomatic practice, among other things. That this Protestant order was disestablished and not theocratic did not make it any less Protestant, any less an order, or any less institutional. American Protestants did not recreate the Calvinist oligarchy of Geneva or Lutheran monarchies of Germany, but neither did they recreate Protestantism or become something other than Protestant. John Jay (1745–1829) saw an essential Protestant continuity and commonality in the new American republic when he told the people of New York in 1787 that "Providence has been pleased to give this

---

18. Bernard Bailyn, *The Ideological Origins of the American Revolution* (Cambridge: Harvard University Press, 1967), 94.

one connected country to one united people—a people descended from the same ancestors, speaking the same language, professing the same religion."[19] Jay, and many other Early Republic statesmen and divines, saw a continuity between the British Protestant milieu they were born in and the new American nation they constituted in 1789.

Since roughly 1980 the history of religion, and particularly Protestantism, in the United States has been litigated along a series of binaries: evangelical v. mainline, theocratic v. secular, liberal v. conservative, etc. While these binaries are not artificial in themselves, they are particularly problematic if they are applied retroactively to the Early Republic or any point in history that precedes the so-called evangelical historiography created in the latter part of the twentieth century. Consequently, Americans have little understanding of religion in the nineteenth century and, more importantly, they have no idea how the fundamental laws of the United States reconciled Protestantism to a disestablished republican order. This book is an attempt to explain that reconciliation or lack thereof, and my broad thesis is that there actually wasn't any reconciliation that needed to take place. The American Revolution wasn't deistic or even Lockean, and it certainly wasn't secular. It was a conservative revolution led by generally Protestant Anglophone North Americans. The laws of the colonies were not remade wholesale or stripped of their Christian foundations. In fact, Christianity was baked into the American republic's diplomatic, educational, judicial, and legislative regimes, and institutional Christianity in states' apparatuses coexisted comfortably with a disestablishmentarian order.

19. John Jay, "Federalist 2," in Alexander Hamilton, John Jay, James Madison, *The Federalist: A Commentary on the Constitution of the United States* (New York: M. Walter Dunne, 1901), 15.

This book is not an endorsement of the Early Republic's socio-religious order; neither is it a polemical condemnation. It's an offering to modern evangelical Protestants who have not dealt with the history of religion in the United States on historically useful terms. The Fundamentalist/Modernist controversy of the early twentieth century and the rise of so-called evangelicalism in its aftermath convinced evangelical Protestants that they had a sort of religious *tabula rasa* by which they could carve a new—typically triumphalist—story of evangelicalism in America. The problem is that "evangelicalism" doesn't have much of a history, unless you think that history started in Wheaton in the 1940s. But Protestantism does, and it is important for evangelical Protestants to ask hard questions about their own rhetoric and their philosophy of history and their historical antecedents. That we might disagree with the political theology of historical Christian figures should not lead us to anathematize them.

The long-documented individualism and anti-traditionalism of evangelicalism has risen to the point of dogma for figures like Russell Moore, who see the historic Christian idea of discipling the nations as heretical. "Christian nationalism," he argued in 2023, is dangerous "for the witness of the church, because Christian nationalism is fundamentally, at its core, anti-evangelical. If what the Gospel means is for people to come before God, person by person, not nation by nation or village by village or tribe by tribe, then Christian nationalism is heretical."[20] If Christian Nationalism is simply the idea that nations and tribes can be saved as well as individuals, we have a problem on our hands, because most Christians before the twentieth century made space for communitarian conceptions of salvation. Does Russell

---

20. Russell Moore, "The State of Evangelical America," *New York Times*, July 30, 2023.

Moore think that St Paul, the church fathers, John Calvin, Thomas Cranmer, Martin Luther, and the Protestants of the Early Republic were heretics? I doubt it. So why the conversation about Christian Nationalism? It's all about politics and Trump, and you didn't buy this book to read about that. You do probably want to know more about Protestants, religion, and the civil and social order in the United States between 1789 and 1860, however.

This book does not purport to posit that the United States was a Christian nation in the early nineteenth century, despite it being described that way perhaps with good purpose. My own belief is that the United States was a republic of Christians that were committed to what I have chosen to call "Christian institutionalism." Early Republic Protestants wanted to maintain Christian principles in their nation's various social and political institutions without sacralizing those principles or subordinating the American republic to a church. Christianity and the Christian church are not synonyms. There are Christian nurses, Christian artists, and, yes, even Christian politicians. My state representative, for example, is a devout Lutheran. That he is not a theocrat does not annihilate his Lutheranism or his Christianity. Orestes Brownson (1803–1876) wrote in the introduction to his *The American Republic*: "I write throughout as a Christian, because I am a Christian; as a Catholic, because all Christian principles, nay, all real principles are catholic.... I could not write otherwise if I would, and would not if I could. I have not obtruded my religion."[21] Likewise I write in this work as a Christian and as an Anglican, and while that does not factor into my analysis *per se*, it does mean that I have chosen to write on religion in a way that reflects the irenic

---

21. Orestes Brownson, *The American Republic: Its Constitution, Tendencies, and Destiny* (New York: P. O'Shea, 1866), xiii.

Protestant disposition I believe Anglicanism reflects. Christianity is more than merely the Sunday worship hour, and to suppose that the church is the only Christian institution is to impose a twentieth-century clericalist dogma on Early Republic Americans who believed Christianity permeated almost every aspect of their lives.

Church and state in the United States is well-trod historiographic territory. Since 1980 professional Christian historiography has often been done by evangelicals seeking to disprove hagiographies associated with historical tropes utilized for political purposes. John Fea's *Was America Founded as a Christian Nation?* and the works of D. G. Hart are necessary correctives to the hagiographies of non-professionals such as D. James Kennedy or David Barton. Mark David Hall, James Kabala, and Daniel Dreisbach have offered works that make a compelling case for what the aims of the Constitution's writers were regarding the national settlement on church and state. Carl Esbeck and Jonathan Den Hartog recently published the authoritative account of state disestablishment. Mark Noll's *America's God* and *America's Book* are excellent accounts of religious culture but rely on a sort of retroactive taxonomy of "evangelical" that limits understanding of how Protestants viewed themselves, how they exercised political and social power, and how they saw their ability to shape society and the state. A plethora of books on southern religion exist, but with the noted exception of Robert Elder's *The Sacred Mirror*—which convincingly argues that Southern evangelicals were not individualistic or proponents of merely spiritual Christianity—most deal with chattel slavery. The work in your hands does not spend a significant amount of time on the relationship of southern slaveholding to the American republic's state apparatus or to North American churches—not because slavery's relationship to those institutions is insignificant or unimportant, but because there are already excellent works on those respective subjects in print. Charles Iron's *Proslavery Christianity* and David Ericson's *Slavery in the American Republic*, for example, are two good books to consider for those respective topics. Given the amount of intellectual energy given to slavery over the last two decades and the multitudes of books that have been published on slavery, I have very purposefully not made it the focus of this study.

Christian, and more specifically Protestant, socio-civil foundations of the United States are historically incontrovertible, and I lay out what evidence I can in this work. My main addendum would be to note that what is variously called "secularism" or "pluralism," or what might be more accurately described as "the right to be irreligious" (but not necessarily anti-religious) has a time-honored and legally protected place in American civil life and should continue to have that place. That is not, however, because secularism or pluralism are unmitigated goods on their own terms. In the nineteenth century, Presbyterian divines rightly celebrated the Protestant foundation of the United States, but they understood that Protestantism guaranteed liberties that included the right of the individual to live without religion in the American order. The federal union was never meant to create a secular state or states, but it also was not meant to create a specific *type* of religious citizenry.

Protestant religion and broad civil liberty—including the liberty to not be Protestant—went hand in hand. In an 1852 sermon, the pastor of Pittsburgh's First Presbyterian Church, Nathaniel West, proposed that the United States was indeed a Protestant nation. God had appointed the republic to be the new protective Protestant "Ark of God" for religious liberty. The very name Protestant, said West, "associates with it whatever is held sacred as to genuine religion and civil liberty."[22] Pure religion, and well-regulated civil liberty were "the strong instrumental arms of sure protection to a nation. Where they are, God is, and where he is, there spiritual and temporal salvation are." Religion and civil liberty were all any nation required for "safety and prosperity." "Give these two blessings to any people, and they must flourish. Take them away, and all that is debasing, demoralizing, and enslaving, must follow." West listed the denominations he believed bore testimony against Old World tyranny in the form of monarchy, aristocracy, and the Roman Catholic hierarchy. His list was ecumenical but nonetheless still Protestant. He denominated Lutherans, the Church of England, Scottish Presbyterians, Methodists, and various other Protestant sects as friends of God's Ark—the United States—but also noted that there were enemies to the Ark as well. "With the Ark," West exclaimed, "is associated every thing sacred and venerable, in religion and civil liberty."[23]

Religious historians and political scientists rightly push back against the notion of a de-churched, de-Christianized, and anti-religious advent for the United States. Yet the Protestant Founders—fifty-two of the fifty-five signers of the Declaration of Independence were Protestants, as were the majority of the Constitution's signers—very purposefully rejected religious tests to sustain a specific type of religiosity. This rejection was not to actualize *en masse* secularism, but to establish a broad-based religious order that included Jews, Catholics, Muslims, and others. Their inclusion nonetheless rested on the Anglo-Protestant foundation of

22. Nathaniel West, *The Ark of God: The Safe-guard of the Nation. A Discourse in Defense of Protestantism* (Pittsburgh: J.T. Shyrock, 1852), 3.

23. West, *Ark of God*, 50.

civil liberty. The United States' religious order would understandably become more than Protestant, but it would never be anything less than Protestant either.

CHAPTER I

INTRODUCTION

The argument that this book puts forth is not revolutionary, but it is a thesis still largely inaccessible (or unknown) to evangelical Protestant intellectuals, laypeople, and pastors in a scholarly form. What this volume proposes is that the United States Constitution's disestablishment did not secularize society, nor did it remove institutional Christianity from the civic, state educational, or political spheres. That occurred nearly a century later. Likewise, the Constitution did not create a unitary social or semi-sacralized Christian nation as some conservative evangelicals and neo-theocrats argue. Instead, the Constitution enacted a religious order designed to perpetuate the civil building blocks of liberal society informed by the English Whig and later late eighteenth-century American republican tradition. This order was liberal in its views on establishmentarianism and at the same time conservative on its conceptualization of Christianity's place in the civil and social orders and in its intellectual influences.

This book posits that the Early Republic United States, a period that broadly extends from 1790 to 1860,[1] in fact remained committed to disestablishment while simultaneously protecting and even perpetuating institutional—usually but not always Protestant—Christianity through federal and state courts, state colleges and institutions, state legislatures, and executive proclamations from governors and presidents, and through state cooperation with religious institutions and Protestant divines. These were not attempts to create a pseudo-state church, precisely because most politicians, Protestant intellectuals, and ministers did not believe that Protestant Christianity needed a state church or churches to maintain its institutional position in the American civil, political, and social order. Almost every major Protestant denomination and intellectual rejected the perceived Erastianism of historic Protestant and Roman Catholic Christianity and affirmed federal disestablishment.[2] Disestablishment disconnected church and state, but it did not separate them from their mutual purpose of creating and upholding a moral order committed to historically Christian conceptions of virtue. Christians in the United States historically

---

1. In this this book I have chosen to use the term "Early Republic" in its broadest sense; the term "Early National" is used to denote the era that ends with the rise of democracy and Andrew Jackson's presidency. "Antebellum" is largely a synonym of Early Republic, and will be used that way in this work.

2. Specifically, Erastianism is the view that sins committed by Christians should be punished by the state, and that the church should not withhold sacraments as a form of punishment. The position was advanced by the Swiss Calvinist Thomas Erastus (1524–1583) and eventually debated at the Westminster Assembly, although the position was ultimately rejected and not incorporated into the Confession. However, the term is often used more loosely to simply refer to the civic enforcement of religion in a Protestant setting.

believed that their faith had a necessary and salutary effect on law, politics, and society that deserved to be preserved and perpetuated by the civil magistrate. This did not preclude a belief in religious liberty.

This book is not meant to address controversies over contemporary Christian engagement in politics, nor is it intended to be a blueprint for liturgical, theological, or social action. The point of this work is not to call into question the liberal order. Nor is it to answer the question of how, at the chronological apex of the cultural and social Christian nation, cultural Christianity became so obviously a chief conduit for social progressivism. Rather, the point is to argue that the foundations of the United States were committed to liberalism and not secularism and to provide an accurate and scholarly picture of the United States religious settlement in the Early Republic for Christian scholars, ministers, and interested laypeople. Disestablishment was, and is, the law of the land, and it has served the United States and Christianity well. What disestablishment means and meant, however, remains a source of confusion and controversy for evangelical Protestants even in the early twenty-first century. But it hasn't always been that way.

Protestants in the Early Republic affirmed disestablishment, but generally broke with Jefferson and Madison, who sought to remove institutional religion's influence. Simultaneously Protestants believed that disestablishment was good, and that only a society of pious Christians could properly create a disestablishmentarian order and make it work. Christianity, in their minds, was a necessary foundation for disestablishment.

Methodist intellectual leader, journalist, and theologian Nathan Bangs (1778–1862) summarized the position shared broadly by Protestants in 1850. The history of the world, "from the sin of Adam nearly to the present time," showed that "generally wickedness prevailed," and that "the principles of intolerance were incorporated in all the religious establishments then existing."[3] Intolerance via religious establishments, Bangs argued, began to gradually improve at the beginning of the eighteenth century, and in the nineteenth century "the principles of religious toleration [were] more generally understood and exemplified in practice among the several nations of the earth." Bangs, and most American Protestants, did not perceive disestablishment as a rejection of Christianity's place in society, but as its culmination. Disestablishment did not assign the church to a merely spiritual role in society but elevated it above political meddling. Disestablishment was the apotheosis of a Christian society, not its termination.

The effect of the Christian gospel, and not its rejection, brought about disestablishment according to Bangs. He wrote that the "the influence of Gospel truth upon the understandings and consciences of mankind—that influence which penetrates the heart, converts the sinner into a saint, and makes him 'a new creature'" led Americans Christians to see the wrongness of coercing consciences.[4] When sinners were created new, "the laws of God" were written on their hearts, "and that law which requires us to do as we would be done by." God's law exerts "a controlling effect upon the conscience." A population governed by God's law could "no more oppress their fellow-men, abridge any of their rights, or inflict pains and penalties for difference of opinion, than they can wish those acts of injustice should be visited on themselves." Bangs argued that the "light of this truth, re-

---

3. Nathan Bangs, *The Present State, Prospects and Responsibilities of the Methodist Episcopal Church, With an Appendix of Ecclesiastical Statistics* (New York: Lane & Scott, 1850), 176.

4. Bangs, *The Present State*, 177.

flected from the throne of God on the renewed Christian's heart, is not confined there; its rays shoot forth in every direction, and the world around him becomes enlightened." Consequently, "the principles of civil as well as religious liberty have been widely diffused among the nations, by which means the bands of sectarian jealousy have been broken, denominational pride and bigotry have been, in a great measure, destroyed." Across the globe in the nineteenth century the influence of the gospel meant that "civil despotism has lost its hold in many places, and is fast losing its hold in others." It was from true Christianity's "benign influence" that "minds of statesmen have been enlightened, religious and civil bigotry has been weakened, and the principles of civil liberty have imbedded themselves in the human heart." Bangs believed that the testament of disestablishment allowed for the "folly of religious intolerance" to be "seen in its own odious and hateful character." Like many Early Republic Protestants, Bangs averred that is was easy to "trace the hand of God in bringing about these delightful results."

Bangs's enthusiasm for disestablishment did not entail the belief that the maintenance of public Christianity was *adiaphora* to the maintenance of disestablishment. He followed his adulatory paragraph on the American settlement with a plea for American missionaries to Christianize—or more precisely Protestantize—the rest of the globe.[5] Disestablishment was not synonymous with notions of religious pluralism. American missionaries, as Emily Conroy-Krutz has noted, turned to proselytize North America and, like their British counterparts, remained committed to sharing the Protestant faith, but with key socio-religious differences that affected where and why they shared their faith. "The

---

5. Bangs, *The Present State*, 177.

British were imperial and global; the Americans were republican and continental."[6]

Continental reform lay at the heart of evangelical Protestantism in the early nineteenth century. Missionary work joined with political forces and a Christian-influenced state educational regime to perpetuate Protestantism piety in society. Protestants of the North American republic gave up the principle of religious establishment, argues Mark Noll, but that did not mean "giving up life in society."[7] They simply renounced "traditional mechanisms by which Christian churches (including almost all of the European state churches of the eighteenth century) still protected their social prerogatives and inculcated their traditions." In the place of state churches, Americans relied on "voluntary means of exerting social influence that did not require a formal establishment."

A voluntarist order was not, to nineteenth century Americans, a de-institutionalized or toothless religious or political order. Benjamin Morris (1810–1867) could claim with some truth in 1864 that the United States was "a Christian nation, first in name, and secondly because of the many and mighty elements of a pure Christianity which have given it character and shaped its destiny from the beginning. It is pre-eminently the land of the Bible, of the Christian Church, and of the Christian Sabbath."[8] Like the Methodist Bangs, Presbyterian Morris declared that Christianity was an aspect of a free society. America was "the land

---

6. Emily Conroy-Krutz, *Christian Imperialism: Converting the World in the Early American Republic* (Ithaca: Cornell University Press, 2015), 1.

7. Noll, *America's God*, 189–90.

8. Benjamin F. Morris, *Christian Life and Character of the Civil Institutions of the United States* (Philadelphia: George W. Childs, 1864), 11.

of great and extensive and oft-repeated revivals of a spiritual religion" precisely because it was simultaneously "the land of a free conscience and of free speech,—the land of noble charities and of manifold and earnest efforts for the elevation and welfare of the human race." And like Bangs, Morris submitted that a free disestablishmentarian regime lay on a foundation of society-wide Christian piety. "The chief security and glory of the United States of America," he exulted, "has been, is now, and will be forever, the prevalence and domination of the Christian Faith." If the Christian-influenced American republic had not "realized all the possible blessings of a free government, the reason lies less in the genius of the economy than in the acknowledged imperfections of human nature itself."

The nature of disestablishment and the sociology of revivals in the nineteenth century led historians of American Christianity to focus on a perceived lack of institutionalism or churchliness among American Protestants. In *Skepticism and American Faith*, Christopher Grasso rightly complained that "when discussing the importance of Christianity to American society, most commentators focused less on the term 'religion' than on 'faith.'" [9] The reason, Grasso proposed, was "perhaps because champions of a Christian America preferred to speak of 'faith' rather than 'religion' because the latter suggested instituted modes of worship and other practices—precisely those things that the First Amendment seemed to say the government could not establish." Protestants relied on social action to effect morality and piety, but they did not rely *only* on social change.

Protestants' embrace of social influence to perpetuate their faith and their conceptions of a Christian moral order

---

9. Christopher Grasso, *Skepticism and American Faith: From the Revolution to the Civil War* (Oxford: Oxford University Press, 2018), 76

did not preclude them from using the state as an appropriate vehicle for moral and social reform and a more virtuous Protestant social and civil order. Mark David Hall argues persuasively that Protestant religion had an undeniably social and political character in the Early National United States. "The first priority for most evangelicals was sharing their faith, but a close second was reforming society. Among their chief concerns were the abolition of slavery and protecting the rights of Native Americans."[10] Religion in the Early Republic elevated women into the political sphere in ways they had not participated in the eighteenth century: "For the first time, numerous women—notably evangelical women—became involved in politics." While some historians explain evangelical women's "activism as an attempt to gain power or control others…these nineteenth-century believers were motivated by their Christian convictions to seek freedom and justice for enslaved Africans and oppressed Native Americans."

While religious Americans led the way in the efforts to perpetuate the Protestant order, those Americans who did not identify with any particularly religious tradition (and those who could be classed with freethinkers of the era) understood the essentially Protestant nature of the American order. "Church people and the unchurched alike," wrote religious historian Martin E. Marty, "thought of the new republic as a Protestant domain. Geographies, spellers, and readers from 1804, 1806, 1817, 1835, and 1846 included charts delineating the religions of the nations of the world. The United States was always listed as Protestant."[11] There

---

10. Mark David Hall, *Proclaim Liberty Throughout All the Land: How Christianity Has Advanced Freedom and Equality for All Americans* (Nashville: Fidelis, 2023), 10–11.

11. Martin E. Marty, *Righteous Empire: The Protestant Experience in*

was never an official reason given for the listing, Marty noted, and in fact in the Early Republic there was never a majority of the population who held membership in churches. Civil officials were not supposed to favor any sect over another politically, and there were, Marty rightly states, significant numbers of non-Protestant immigrants arriving in the United States by 1846. "But by observation and instinct Americans had come to call their territory Protestant."

Early Republic Americans did not debate the Protestant nature of their moral and religious order, nor did they contest the result of the constitutional settlement on religion to a considerable degree publicly. The variety of Protestant sects and the presence of Roman Catholics meant that the preclusion of a federal state church remained widely popular in Early National religious discourse. Ellis M. West notes in *The Free Exercise of Religion* that by 1790, "although there was not complete agreement on the free exercise of religion, the great majority of those who championed it did agree on its basic, general meaning." [12]

The Constitution's actual intent with regard to disestablishment was somewhat more controversial. Merely looking at the text of the Constitution, West rightly notes, does not provide an accurate representation of the meaning of disestablishment or the practice of ideas like the free exercise of religion. "How Americans understood the religion clause per se is relatively unimportant," argues West. "Rather what is truly important is how they understood the principle that those clauses, like similar state laws, were

America (New York: Harper & Row, 1977), 15–16.

12. Ellis M. West, *The Free Exercise of Religion in America: Its Original Constitutional Meaning* (New York: Palgrave MacMillan, 2019), 23–24.

intended to uphold—the free exercise of religion."[13] West proposes that the federal Constitution meant to remove the ability (and intent) to legislate on any religious controversy or question from the federal government. This is accurate, inasmuch as most Americans in the late eighteenth and early nineteenth century did not see the federal Congress as having the right to legislate on much at all compared to the prerogatives of the several states. Historians have likewise noted that the states generally followed Virginia in disestablishing churches, a process that ended finally in 1833 with Massachusetts. What this fails to account for was the aggressive ways in which state legislatures and even the federal Congress at times nonetheless defended institutional Christianity and even strengthened it through positive law. Political democratization and liberalism in the nineteenth century, instead of bringing about the removal of Christianity from the public square, strengthened it.

Historians of disestablishment concede that federal constitutional disestablishment did not usher in practical disestablishment as it became widely understood in the American republic. Steven K. Green argues that members of the Constitutional Convention most enthusiastic about disestablishment understood that their policies in Virginia had not actually accomplished their final aim of stripping religion of political power. In fact, Green rightly posits, the Constitutional Convention in 1787 did not remove religion from civic and state institutions. Churches might have lost property and power, but they did not lose their place as social institutions charged with the upkeep of public morals and republican virtue. The new republic was, in spite of the efforts of Jefferson and Madison, "popularly described as a 'Christian nation,' which was represented through re-

---

13. West, *The Free Exercise of Religion in America*, 24.

vivals and reform associations, blasphemy and sabbath laws, religious oath requirements, and state maintenance of a Protestant-oriented public school system."[14] Historians also acknowledged the existence of *de facto* Protestant empire "where Protestant/Evangelical beliefs and values dominated the nation's culture and institutions." The proliferation of revivalist sects during the Second Great Awakening, the rise of the Latter Day Saint movement, and immigration of large numbers of Irish Roman Catholics during the antebellum years certainly kept religion from being uniform across the United States, but institutionally, the United States remained convincingly Protestant. It was, Green maintains, "only through the experiences of the nineteenth century that earlier notions of church-state separation found their awkward application," which led eventually "to a second disestablishment, this time in the nation's civic institutions—primarily in education and law."[15] Green rightly notes that it was the second disestablishment of the Gilded Age and the Progressive Era that "facilitated" the secular disestablishmentarian of the twentieth and twenty-first century, not the disestablishment of the Constitutional Convention of 1787.

Historians and sociologists in the latter part of the twentieth century missed the essential retention of Christianity in the civil, social, and political spheres of the new American nation because they spent significant amounts of time parsing out the difference between the relationship with Christianity and the relationship with the church. Sectarian commentators and some secularists routinely rejected

14. Steven K. Green, *The Second Disestablishment: Church and State in Nineteenth-Century America* (New York: Oxford University Press, 2010), 9.

15. Green, *The Second Disestablishment*, 8.

the idea that Christianity existed outside the church, as if individuals, places, cultures, and societies could not be Christian. Church historians of the midcentury—influenced either by liberalism or by an overreliance on historic taxonomies from the Fundamentalist-Modernist Controversies of the 1920s—created dichotomies and rhetorical separations and assertions that were either ahistorical or unintentionally contrived. Church historians like Sidney Mead unhelpfully conflated any institutional Christianity with state churches and "Christendom," ignoring the fact that the church is not the only institution historically conceived of as Christian. He argued in 1977 that in the eighteenth century Christians committed to the ideal of persuasion were more representative of Christianity in the United States "than were the orthodox defenders of Christendom's Established churches, and those who to make Christendom's species of institutionalized religiosity part of the common law of the land."[16]

Mead's point would be helpful if a sizable number of Americans had believed that they needed to perpetuate so-called Christendom or legislate a state church in order to maintain institutional Christianity, but they did not. Christian proclamations from presidents and governors, the common law's historic Christian influences, colleges and universities, and church interactions with civic and state actors were, to the minds of early republic religious and political actors, more than enough to sustain Christian institutions consistent with the disestablishmentarian political regime.

The idea that the United States Constitution allowed the federal and state governments to sustain religion, and even institutional religion, may sound foreign to some Prot-

---

16. Sidney E. Mead, *The Old Religion in the Brave New World: Reflections on the Relation between Christendom and the Republic* (Berkeley: University of California Press, 1977), 8.

estant readers at the beginning of the twenty-first century. Seventy years of jurisprudence from the Supreme Court and more recent battles over questions of "theocracy" or so-called Christian Nationalism have convinced a significant number of American evangelicals that any state involvement with Christianity is both un-American or an invasion of supposedly pure religious practice. In conservative Calvinist circles this has been particularly pronounced, with breathless denunciations of theocracy or liberalism being thrown about by partisans of a secularist spirituality of the church and devotees of robust public Christianity respectively. The United States' religious order was from the beginning neither theocratic nor secular. The notion that disestablishment created a secular order is a distinctly mid-twentieth century creation. In the 1947 case *Everson v Board of Education*, the court argued that "Neither a state nor the Federal Government can set up a church. Neither can pass laws which aid one religion, aid all religions, or prefer one religion over another." States and the federal government could not levy any money whatsoever "to support any religious activities or institutions, whatever they may be called, or whatever form they may adopt to teach or practice religion." States and the federal government could not "openly or secretly, participate in the affairs of any religious organizations or groups and vice versa." "In the words of Jefferson," said the Supreme Court, "the clause against establishment of religion by law was intended to erect 'a wall of separation between Church and State.'"[17]

---

17. *Everson v the Board of Education of the Township of Ewing et al*, 330 U.S. 1 (1947). See also Michael A. Paulsen, "Religion, Equality, and the Constitution: An Equal Protection Approach to Establishment Clause Adjudication," *Notre Dame Law Review* 61 (1986): 311–17.

Popular as the idea of separation of church and state might be among secularists, neoliberal evangelicals, and some sectarian Christian groups, it was not the vision of the writers of the Constitution, nor was it a reason they supported federal disestablishment. Daniel Dreisbach rightly notes that construing the First Amendment's religious provisions as a wall of separation "would have come as a surprise to the members of the first federal congress who framed the amendment." [18] The first Congress "appropriated funds from the public treasury to pay for Congressional chaplains, enacted legislation pertaining to oaths, issued religious proclamations, and reauthorized the Northwest Ordinance." The Northwest Ordinance, an early draft of which was written largely by none other than Thomas Jefferson, declared religion "necessary to good government and the happiness of mankind." These declarations, Dreisbach argued, are not reconcilable with *Everson*'s innovations.

Even in the nineteenth century United States, with widespread acceptance of the fact of disestablishment, ambiguity existed over what disestablishment meant in practice. Edward Norris Kirk (1802–1874), a Congregationalist and Presbyterian minister trained at Princeton Seminary under Archibald Alexander, envisioned religion and particularly Protestant churches as the moral catechizer for republican society. Kirk was a proponent of disestablishment, but he did not see a disestablished church as a closed institution. The church's moral influence necessarily tied it to the state and to society. In 1848 he argued that the institutions that sustained "modern society and civilization" were

18. Daniel L. Dreisbach, "The Meaning of Church and State: Competing Views," in *The Oxford Handbook of Church and State in the United States*, ed. Derek H. Davis (New York: Oxford University Press, 2010), 216.

family, state, school (or education), and the church.[19] All, Kirk declared, were gifts "of our beneficent Creator; and are all sanctioned by his authority." It was "to men, however, who represented in their persons, not the Family, nor the Academy , nor the Commonwealth, but the Church , that our Lord announced, 'Ye are the salt of the earth.'" Christ designed the church's influence to show society "that as salt is endowed with the property of preserving animal and vegetable esculents from decay, so THE CHURCH IS THE CHIEF CONSERVATIVE POWER IN THE MORAL WORLD." That moral influence, according to Kirk, preserved "man and society from that degeneracy to which they are ever tending."

Differences of opinion regarding the nature of the constitutional settlement on religion and the federal state were ostensibly settled through the First Amendment's *de facto* establishment of a non-sectarian and religiously neutral federal government, but to Kirk that did not obviously preclude state establishments or a religious federal politics. His ambivalence about the constitutional settlement indicated that it was neither universally celebrated nor, more importantly, even understood as late as 1850: "The relations of the civil to the religious institutions of our country are by no means fully and clearly determined. Twice, this question has been practically solved."[20] New England's Pilgrim fathers, he said, "made the civil and ecclesiastical states identical." The New England theocracy "produced some very evil consequences," which Kirk believed led to the "Revolutionary fathers" choosing "an opposite course" that made religion and the

------

19. Edward Norris Kirk, *The Church Essential to the Republic. A Sermon* (New York: American Home Missionary Society, 1848), 3.

20. Kirk, *The Church Essential to the Republic*, 5.

state "two distinct and independent empires; to occupy the same territory, and control in part the same persons; but to know almost nothing of each other's existence."

The contemporary constitutional arrangement, for all its benefit, according to Kirk still had "its share of human imperfection," especially regarding the relationship between education, religion, and republican society at large: "It has not settled, for example, on clearly defined principles, what position the school shall occupy, relatively to the Church and the State." Norris worried that "every discussion about introducing the Bible, and even history in schools, has betrayed the imperfectness of our theories." Unlike more jingoistic Protestants of the era, Kirk did not dismiss the concerns of Roman Catholics as they navigated the Protestant civil and educational order's usage of Protestants hermeneutics and Whiggish history in public schools, noting that "The Romanist naturally fears both these sources of knowledge." Kirk argued that Catholic concerns were not "logically irrefutable, as the matter now stands," when they objected "to introducing the Bible and history into a school which he assists in sustaining, and to which he sends his children." Religious Americans, he noted, were nonetheless "not prepared to make common education entirely secular." Therein lay the conundrum of the constitutional settlement. "To make instruction religious, it must assume some shape, be founded upon some doctrine; it must use a Bible, King James, or the Douay version; a worship, liturgical or spontaneous."

Kirk's questions about the place of religion in education illustrated the degree to which the United States' disestablishmentarian regime remained essentially conservative socially. The domestic order sustained by the American republic upheld what were perceived as traditional notions of gender and family. Political liberties that Early Republic

Americans—both men and women—associated with re-publicanism and democracy upheld the Christian family and social order; Christianity, democracy, and family, exist-ed in a mutually affirming symbiosis. Social reformer and women's rights activist Catharine E. Beecher's 1846 work on domestic economy for women proposed that women should receive the Declaration of Independence's procla-mation—that all men were created equal, and that all were entitled to life liberty and the pursuit of happiness—as "only another mode of expressing the fundamental princi-ple which the Great Ruler of the Universe has established, as the law of His eternal government. 'Thou shalt love thy neighbor as thyself;' and 'Whatsoever ye would that men should do to you, do ye even so to them.'"[21] These scriptural forms, Beecher wrote, were those which God, the "Supreme Lawgiver" required "that each individual of our race shall regard the happiness of others, as of the same value as his own; and which forbid any institution, in private or civil life, which secures advantages to one class, by sacrificing the interests of another."[22] Democracy, to Beecher, entailed mu-tual forbearance and social solidarity, not sociological lev-eling. "The principles of democracy," Beecher flatly stated, "are identical with the principles of Christianity."[23]

This supposed Christian and democratic order main-tained traditional social hierarchies even as it elevated the place of women. Republican ideology in the late eighteenth

---

21. Jeanne Boydston, *The Limits of Sisterhood: The Beecher Sisters on Women's Rights and Woman's Sphere* (Chapel Hill: University of North Carolina, 1993), 130.

22. Catharine E. Beecher, *A Treatise on Domestic Economy: For the Use of Young Ladies at Home, and at School* (Boston: Thomas H. Webb, 1843), 25.

23. Boydston, *The Limits of Sisterhood*, 130.

and early nineteenth centuries encouraged the presence of the republican motherhood, which posited that women had their own duties regarding political catechesis for adolescents. The American republic, argues Mary Beth Norton, stressed "the household as the source of virtue and stability in government," which necessarily turned focus on women as political actors in innovative ways. [24] Before the American Revolution women were not seen as political actors. By the turn of the nineteenth century American political writers "proclaimed the importance of American's female citizens" to such a degree it seemed "as though republican theorists believed that the fate of the republic rested squarely, perhaps solely, upon the shoulders of its womenfolk."

Nineteenth century women understandably saw their own efforts as transcendentally Christian and democratic, political and hierarchical, and fundamentally American. Beecher herself did not follow the traditional route of marriage and childbearing, yet firmly declared that it was "needful that certain relations be sustained, which involve the duties of subordination."[25] In the relationship between magistrate and subject, she noted, one was "the superior, and the other the inferior." The same principle applied to "relations of husband and wife, parent and child, teacher and pupil, employer and employed, each involving the relative duties of subordination." Superiors, "in certain particulars," were to "direct, and the inferior is to yield obedience." "Society could never go forward harmoniously," Beecher warned, "nor could any craft or profession be successfully pursued, unless these superior and subordinate relations be

---

24. Mary Beth Norton, *Liberty's Daughters: The Revolutionary Experience of American Women, 1750–1800* (Ithaca: Cornell University Press, 1980), 243.

25. Beecher, *A Treatise on Domestic Economy*, 26.

instituted and sustained." Beecher did not see social hierarchies as stifling. In democratic states, each individual was "allowed to choose for himself, who shall take the position of his superior. No woman is forced to obey any husband but the one she chooses for herself; nor is she obliged to take a husband, if she prefers to remain single." Domestic workers and artisans, "after passing from parental control, can choose the employer to whom he is to accord obedience, or, if he prefers to relinquish certain advantages, he can remain without taking a subordinate place to any employer." Under the United States' Christian democratic Constitution subjects had "equal power with every other, to decide who shall be his superior as a ruler." Even weak, poor, and illiterate members of American society had "the same opportunity to determine this question, as the richest, the most learned, and the most exalted."[26] Americans from reformers like Beecher to conservatives in the era believed that democratic and disestablishmentarian political order did not level or revolutionize society's hierarchies; constitutional democracy and free churches instead maintained, perpetuated, and strengthened familial and social hierarchy.

Disestablishmentarian commitments regarding church and state did not revolutionize family or other institutions that upheld life in the Early American Republic, nor did the United States enter the family of nations perceived by knowledgeable commentators as a sanctuary for secularism, social democracy, or social egalitarianism. European conservatives and liberals—some of whom remained committed to historic religious establishments and some of whom wanted to remove state support for a specific church or churches in favor of generalized government support for religion—reevaluated state churches and religious establishments in the

---

26. Beecher, *A Treatise on Domestic Economy*, 25-26.

era that followed the end of the Napoleonic Wars in 1815. European Protestants in the nineteenth century stopped short of the constitutionally mandatory disestablishment but they shared concerns that state churches could potentially be used as props for resurgent absolutism.[27]

Even establishmentarians like Swiss theologian Frédéric de Rougemont (1808–1876) could offer a qualified endorsement of disestablishment in the United States on the grounds that a federal state church would be an unnecessarily centralized institution. "If a nation, contrary to the normal run of things," was made up "of a number of small societies or colonies each with its own language, character, and church" and if "as a nation, it has no specific religion, then the state—which represents it—cannot make an alliance with any particular church" and could "only grant a place in its legal and political institutions to religious principles on which all the churches within its boundaries are in agreement, such as Sunday observance and the oath."[28] It was under the theory of the federal state not being adequate to represent smaller societies throughout the Union, Rougemont said, that "we would endorse the separation of church and state in the United States of America, while defending the alliance of church and state in Europe." Rougemont did not see the United States constitutional order as creating a society for religious individualists either. Individualists in the United States and elsewhere, argued Rougemont, sacralized "the exceptional situation of an ex-

---

27. Andrew C. Gould, *Origins of Liberal Dominance: State, Church, and Party in Nineteenth-Century Europe* (Ann Arbor: University of Michigan Press, 1999), 1–2.

28. Frédéric de Rougemont, *The Individualists in Church and State* (1844; repr., Alten, The Netherlands: Wordbridge Publishing, 2018), Kindle.

tremely religiously fragmented society." Individualists, declared Rougemont, took religious anarchy as their "starting point." "For them it becomes the rule. And from it they deduce the doctrine of the absolute separation of church and state." Individualists denied "even the formal possibility of an accord between the two; so that any union, or alliance, is heresy in theory and adultery in fact." Rougemont's denunciations of disestablishment, therefore, were intended to "confront this dogma of the absolute separation of church and state—of the temporal and the spiritual—rather than the state of affairs in the United States, which is justified by their religious anarchy."

The variety of Protestant churches that appeared to establishmentarians as a sort of religious cacophony nonetheless exercised a powerful and relatively united influence on society in the United States. The affectual institutional power of Christianity in the American republic shocked French sociologist and later parliamentarian and cabinet member Alexis de Tocqueville when he arrived in the United States in 1831. In his opus *The Conservative Mind*, Russell Kirk noted that for Tocqueville, a democratic people simplified religion but it nonetheless remained in society "as an abiding force, helping to counteract that materialism which leads to democratic despotism." [29] Disestablishment did not remove religion from the civil society or political life. Roman Catholic priests in the United States informed the French nobleman that precluding state churches from the federal political order established them in what Kirk helpfully paraphrased as a peaceful dominion for religion.

The Early Republic United States' religious order might have been a disestablished dominion but it was a

---

29. Russell Kirk, *The Conservative Mind: From Burke to Eliot* (Washington DC: Gateway Editions, 2016), 216.

dominion nonetheless, with institutional power that was not easily movable and that kept irreligious radicals both in churches and in politics bound to conservative understandings of morality in society. The influence of religion in the United States was not, averred Tocqueville, confined merely to "manners."[30] Instead religion's influence extended to "the intelligence of the people." Actual religious devotion and piety, Tocqueville argued, was not foundational to the maintenance of religion in society. He observed that, in the United States, some professed the doctrines of Christianity "from a sincere belief in them," while others did so "because they are afraid to be suspected of unbelief." Christianity, therefore, reigns without any obstacle, by universal consent." The consequence of the American settlement, argued Tocqueville, was "that every principle of the moral world is fixed and determinate, although the political world is abandoned to the debates and the experiments of men." American minds were "never left to wander across a boundless field." Whatever the intellectual pretensions of certain Americans might be, those pretensions were "checked from time to time by barriers which it cannot surmount." Religion's effect on law and society in the United States was such that even revolutionaries were "obliged to profess an ostensible respect for Christian morality and equity, which does not easily permit them to violate the laws that oppose their designs."[31] No American, Tocqueville declared, "has dared to advance the maxim, that everything is permissible with a view to the interests of society; an impious adage, which seems to have

---

30. Alexis de Tocqueville, *Democracy in America* (London: Longman, Green, Longman and Roberts, 1862), 1:361–62.

31. Tocqueville, *Democracy in America*, 1:361-62.

been invented in an age of freedom to shelter all the tyrants of future ages."[32]

Tocqueville's famed analysis of American religion in *Democracy in America* provided a helpful depiction of religious liberty's expression in the United States. Even as he traveled throughout North America, however, Protestant divines articulated a vision of religious freedom that expressed the principle not in language of democracy or liberalism, but as freedom of choice *within* a broadly Protestant order that tolerated religious minorities. On July 4, 1832, the minister of Plymouth, Massachusetts's Third Congregational Church, Frederick Freeman (1799–1883), told worshipers in a neighboring town that religious freedom consisted of "the unmolested right of a spirit of free inquiry," freedom of choice in religious views, free expression of chosen religious views, freedom to choose mode of worship, place of worship, and religious teacher, the right to defend preexisting religious views by argument, and the prerogative to expand religion via moral suasion.[33] Most telling was the minister's declaration that true religious liberty did not include "raves and talks of 'Church and State,' while the idea of such union" was only in the mind of those trying to tear down certain religious groups.[34] Religious sectarians and irreligious radicals both rejected true religious liberty in favor of intellectual and spiritual slavery. Sectarians and radicals used sensationalized fears of civil disenfranchisement, "invectives, bitter sarcasms, uncivil treatment, frowns, un-

---

32. Tocqueville, *Democracy in America*, 1:362.

33. Frederick Freeman, *Religious Liberty: A Discourse Delivered at the Congregational Church at Hanson on the Fourth of July, 1832* (Plymouth: Benjamin Drew Jr., 1832), 2.

34. Freeman, *Religious Liberty*, 21.

neighborly and unfriendly coldness and distance," which replicated the chains and dungeons and torture of medieval religious persecutions.[35] There were, Freeman lamented, "ways of tyrannizing over one's religious liberty, beside the fear of the sword, the rack and the faggot. And those ways, I fear, are constantly resorted to in too many instances where there is a loud cry for liberty."[36]

The disestablishmentarian order never coerced Early Republic Protestants to perceive of religious liberty as an absolute or even egalitarian principle, nor was removing or denigrating religion included in the perceived orthopraxy of disestablishment. In an 1828 fast day service William Cogswell (1783–1850), a Massachusetts Congregationalist cleric, told his congregation in Dedham that citizens had a right to regulate their involvement with religion, but stopped short of acceding to a right to irreligiosity or amoral citizenship. Cogswell felt "bound to condemn 'evil surmisings'" but he argued that the state could not "compel any man to believe or act on this subject as we do. Equal rights of conscience are the natural and legitimate inheritance of all." He granted "the liberty to others, which we claim to ourselves, believing that all are alike responsible, and must stand or fall to their own Master, who is Christ, and to no earthly tribunal." Even those who exercised a right to conscience nonetheless, he argued, should "exercise themselves to have always a conscience void of offence, toward God, and toward man." Cogswell believed that religious liberty still meant that "important principle" of recognizing the conscience's duty to God "should ever be maintained." He declared that "no person should be disfranchised for his

---

35. Freeman, *Religious Liberty*, 23.

36. Freeman, *Religious Liberty*, 24.

belief and conduct in things religious, unless he so use his liberty, as to impair the liberty of others, or corrupt the public morals." Cogswell's articulation of religious liberty had a preexisting and non-negotiable social and moral foundation predicated on a Protestant civil and intellectual order.[37]

Cogswell's presumption on the endurance of Protestant Christianity was not limited to ministers, nor was it a view that did not have currency with state actors, governors, judges, legislatures, presidents, and state colleges all maintained Christianity in various institutional capacities. Tocqueville recalled that while he was in America, "a witness, who happened to be called at the Assizes of the county of Chester, (State of New York,) declared that he did not believe in the existence of God, or in the immortality of the soul."[38] The presiding judge "refused to admit his presence, on the ground that the witness had destroyed beforehand all the confidence of the Court in what he was about to say. The newspapers related the fact without any further comment."

The maintenance of a historically Protestant order did not represent a programmatic attempt to create a unitary Christian nation wedded to politicizing Christianity. At the beginning of the Union's constitutional life in 1788 few Americans thought they lived in anything less than Protestant-influenced society wherein religion remained institutionally entrenched. The Protestant foundation of the United States was undeniable, but Americans understood that Protestantism guaranteed broad religious liberty. The federal union was never meant to create a secular state or

---

37. William Cogswell, *Religious Liberty: A Sermon, Preached on the Day of the Annual Fast in Massachusetts, April 3, 1828* (Boston: Pierce and Williams, 1828), 6.

38. Tocqueville, *Democracy in America*, 1:362.

states, but it also was not mean to create a specific type of religious citizenry. In 1836, John Hughes (1797–1864), Roman Catholic soon-to-be-Archbishop of New York, cheerfully admitted that aspects of Protestantism created a civil milieu which allowed Roman Catholics increasingly expansive rights even as he debated a Presbyterian minister on whether Roman Catholicism or Presbyterianism was more inimical to civil and religious liberty.[39]

Religious historians and political scientists rightly push back against the notion of a de-churched, de-Christianized, and anti-religious advent for the United States. Yet the largely Protestant Founders rejected religious tests to sustain a specific type of religiosity. This rejection was not to actualize secularism, but to establish a broad-based religious order that included Jews, Catholics, Muslims, and others. Their successive inclusion nonetheless rested on the Anglo-Protestant foundation of civil liberty. Tocqueville stated flatly that "Americans combine the notions of Christianity and of liberty so intimately in their minds, that it is impossible to make them conceive the one without the other."[40] The nineteenth-century United States' religious order would never be anything less than Protestant, but it would understandably also eventually be more than Protestant.

---

39. John Hughes and John Breckenridge, *A Discussion of the Question, Is the Roman Catholic Religion, in Any or in All the Principles of Its Doctrines, Inimical to Civil or Religious Liberty? And of the Question, Is the Presbyterian Religion, in Any or in All the Principles of Its Doctrines, Inimical to Civil or Religious Liberty?* (Baltimore: John Murphy, 1836).

40. Tocqueville, *Democracy in America*, 1:363.

CHAPTER II

JEFFERSON

At the beginning of the nineteenth century, Thomas Jefferson's status as the greatest living American seemed assured. He had authored the Declaration of Independence at thirty-three years old and over the next two decades became a celebrated diplomat, intellectual, and statesman. Jefferson's legacy as a religious thinker has generally hinged on his authorship of the Virginia statute on religious freedom and his commitment to disestablishment in his home commonwealth. Baptists and later generations of evangelical Protestants saw Jefferson as the key political ally in disestablishing religion and offering religious liberty to their co-religionists. Thomas S. Kidd and Barry Hankins called Jefferson and Madison the chief allies of Baptists in fulfilling the latter's desires for what they perceived as true religious liberty. Jefferson's role "in collaboration with the Bible-believing Baptists was spiritually ironic." [1] Kidd and

---

1. Thomas S. Kidd and Barry Hankins, *Baptists in America: A History* (New York: Oxford University Press, 2015), 59.

Hankins posited that Jefferson in fact "remained a religious skeptic throughout his life."

Disestablishment represented only one aspect of Jefferson's thought however, and he was far from passive in his dislike of institutional Christianity. The Jeffersonian "wall of separation," posited his 1802 letter to the Danbury Baptist Association, has been praised by evangelicals in the twentieth and twenty-first centuries. Russell Moore in his book *Onward*, for instance, argued that Christians could live happily with separation so long as the state did not weigh in on religious matters: "A state that sees some aspect of Christian witness as bigoted and dangerous will not long stay on the other side of that wall."[2] But what Moore and other evangelicals failed to note is that Jefferson himself saw much of traditional Christianity, especially religious institutions, as bigoted and dangerous, and he saw separation as a way of keeping churchly influence from broader society. Jefferson's legacy was more about separating religion from the civil sphere than it was about merely removing the privileged position of state churches. The third president was largely quiet about his skepticism in public—all that we know about it comes from a few lapses in *Notes on the State of Virginia* and private correspondence, some of it not even sent. Yet his private views are evident enough in his public policy, and his supposed rights of conscience ran only one way: toward de-churching society. While the Virginian might not have hated "religion," he loathed churchly institutions and Protestant clerics. This stemmed not only from his pronounced anti-clericalism, but from a belief that aspects of the Christian Bible were antagonistic toward the natural law regime he hoped to perpetuate in the

---

2. Russell D. Moore, *Onward: Engaging the Culture Without Losing the Culture* (Nashville: B&H, 2015), 23.

new American republic. Federalist divines—so often seen as reactionaries—and even some conservative Republican devotees of Jefferson in fact had good reason to think that Jefferson's ideas might unhinge and unmoor the historic Protestant social order they understood themselves to have inherited and believed they needed to maintain. Broad acceptance of disestablishment as an accomplished political fact did not mean that Jeffersonian separation doctrines were popular or even the norm in the Early National United States.

The political success of disestablishment and the numerical growth of its most obvious beneficiaries—Baptists and Methodists—obscured to later historians and clerics the continuing commitment of Anglicans, Congregationalists, and some Presbyterians to the close relationship between church and state that religious Americans believed could endure even in a disestablished religious order. George Washington, an Anglican vestrymen, broadly affirmed disestablishment but, as Michael Novak and Jane Novak have noted, broke with Jefferson and Madison on the idea that "disestablishment was a necessary consequence of religious liberty."[3] The first president "held both in principle and in practice...that government ought to endorse religious seriousness in general, since a long-lived republic" depended on a virtuous citizenry. Washington also saw government rightly accommodating itself to "to the claims of conscience in various religious bodies, in a manner consistent with the common good and public order."[4] It is common to note that Washington did not take

3. Michael Novak and Jane Novak, *Washington's God: Religion, Liberty, and the Father of Our Country* (New York: Basic Books, 2006), 112.

4. Novak and Novak, *Washington's God*, 113.

communion, and his relationship with religion has been litigated too many times to count. But on the question of religion and the state, he affirmed the long-time understanding among Protestants and Anglicans that church and state both played a role in upholding civil society, and that they could cooperate in doing so. The extreme disestablishmentarianism of Jefferson and Madison—churches weren't able to incorporate again in Virginia until the beginning of the twenty-first century—"did not exhaust the range of the Founders' thinking about matters of church and state, and their views were far more narrow than Washington's." Washington's identification with the nascent Federalist Party during his presidency stemmed from the conservative beliefs regarding church and state that he shared with the party. While they did not see state churches as a necessity to ensure a virtuous social order and promote virtue, they did see the public presence of religion, and particularly Christianity, as non-negotiable. Historian Patrick Allitt has noted that "while the First Amendment to the Constitution declared that Congress should pass no laws relating to an established religion...it said nothing about the states, several of which retained established churches for several decades after the Revolution."[5] States like Connecticut and Massachusetts into the nineteenth century "followed the European erastian tradition, according to which the church was a branch of the state and subsidized by the state, unifying it and embodying its religious and moral will."[6] Jeffersonian separation appealed to evangelical groups without long traditions as the natural alternative to New England

---

5. Patrick Allitt, *The Conservatives: Ideas and Personalities throughout American History* (New Haven: Yale University Press, 2009), 15.

6. Allitt, *The Conservatives*, 16.

Erastianism, but this created a historical binary where there were in fact other ways in which public Christianity was upheld than state-supported churches.

Anglican vestrymen like Washington and others in the federal Congress and state legislatures implemented the constitutionally disestablished religious milieu but without Virginia's particularly aggressive disposition to de-church their political and social realms. The Old Dominion's *en masse* secularization program was an anomaly, and states allowed a wide variety of privileges for Episcopal churches and other bodies to remain in place. Even the retention of property served as a vehicle for Episcopalians in New York, for example, to exercise a "disproportionate influence" politically and socially well into the nineteenth century because of their wealth.[7] As late as the 1850s Episcopal rectors believed that the United States government and certain states had overstepped the bounds of prudence and a rightly ordered society by stripping established churches of their historic civic and social functions and rights beyond that of state financial support. After 1786, the Commonwealth of Virginia requisitioned church lands, for example, without compensation. John Norton, a Kentucky rector and biographer of bishop William White (1748–1836), believed that a clique of godless politicians had set out to use disestablishment to harm Anglicans. "The Episcopal Church," he lamented, "had scarcely begun to recover from the effects of past misfortunes" when Jefferson and Madison set

---

7. Kyle T. Bulthuis, "Religious Disestablishment in the State of New York," in *Disestablishment and Religious Dissent: Church State Relations in the New American States 1776-1833*, ed. Carl H. Esbeck and Jonathan J. Den Hartog (Columbia: University of Missouri Press, 2019), 134.

their dissenters on Episcopal churchmanship.[8] Anglicans, Norton noted, could "point to Washington, and Jay, and Morris, and Madison, and Marshall, among her members, as evidence that the Episcopal government harmonized most perfectly with the free institutions of the land," but that was not enough for Virginia dissenters and their Jeffersonian republican leaders. "The old leaven of opposition," Norton groaned, remained entrenched in Virginia. "The children of those who had broken down the 'carved work' of the sanctuary, 'with axes and hammers,'" also seized with "unprincipled greediness," on Episcopal glebes "and other temporal possessions." Many of those who dispossessed the church, Norton warned, "had grown up in the faith" but had been "warped by the" Jeffersonian and extreme Republican "prejudices, of their fathers."

Jefferson's personal war against churchly authority and the proposition that religious institutions could bind consciences—which he viewed as innately tyrannical—led him to attack the idea of divine inspiration. He famously wrote *The Life and Morals of Jesus of Nazareth*, popularly called the Jefferson Bible, and also admonished friends and family concerning the necessity of reading the Bible skeptically. "Those facts in the Bible which contradict the laws of nature, must be examined with more care, and under a variety of faces."[9] Readers needed to "recur to the pretensions of the writer to inspiration from god" and "examine upon what evidences his pretensions are found, and whether that evidence is so strong as that its falsehood would be more probable than a change in the laws of nature in the case he

---

8. John N. Norton, *The Life of the Rt. Rev. William White, D. D., Bishop of Pennsylvania* (New York: Church Book Society, 1856), 44.

9. Peter Manseau, *The Jefferson Bible: A Biography* (Princeton: Oxford University Press, 2020), 27.

relates." Jefferson proposed that the Bible should read like the histories of Livy or Tacitus. While the proposition of reading sacred texts historically did not entail a rejection of Christian metaphysics or traditional Protestant understandings of the ties between explicitly Christian morality and the maintenance of the civil and social orders, it did lead him to see the maintenance of orthodox Christianity as *adiaphora*. If Jesus wasn't God, he told his nephew, it was hardly something that should bother anyone. There were, he said, plenty of other enticements to virtue.[10]

The question of virtue in society motivated Early Republic clerics and politicians to see Jefferson's expression of the church and state settlement as atheistic and incompatible with traditional Protestant understandings of a rightly ordered society. Federalist newspapers, politicians, and divines denounced Jefferson as an infidel and anti-Christian throughout the 1790s, and the attacks increased as Jefferson's election became more likely in 1800. Evidence that Jefferson's religious views were public knowledge and not at all hidden was found in the breathless editorials of Federalist newspapers.[11] After relaying Jefferson's sentiments on religion in *Notes on the State of Virginia, The American Aurora* warned that Jefferson was an avowed enemy of "all religious establishments." [12] Given this information, the *Aurora* de-

---

10. Manseau, *The Jefferson Bible: A Biography*, 28–30.

11. Noble Cunningham, *The Jeffersonian Republicans: The Formation of Party Organization, 1789–1801* (Chapel Hill: University of North Carolina Press, 1957), 153–54, 160.

12. Richard Rosenfeld, *American Aurora, A Democratic Republican Returns: The Suppressed History of Our Nation's Beginnings and the Heroic Newspaper that Tried to Report It* (New York: St Martin's Griffin, 1997), 782.

manded to know who among its readers "will now give his vote for this audacious howling atheist."

The threat to society from atheism served as a chief theme in sermons for Timothy Dwight IV (1752–1817).[13] He served as a Congregationalist minister and then president of Yale College for twenty-two years, until his death in 1817, at which point his legacy seemed complete. Born into one of Massachusetts's and New England's leading families, Dwight's vocation as a Congregationalist minister followed family tradition. In 1777 Dwight joined the Continental Army as a chaplain and proved to be popular, with soldiers and his superiors commending him in their reports. After the war, he married the daughter of one of New York's most prominent bankers. Although joined to his home region's elites through family ties and marriage, Dwight's conservatism meant that he did not see the new-fangled ideas of the late eighteenth century as beneficial for society or virtuous. He deplored the growth of religious skepticism, and he warned his students about it regularly. Dwight's 1785 epic poem *The Conquest of Canaan* cast the North American republic in the role of the people of Israel conquering a pagan continent and subduing pagan peoples. In Dwight's framing, the American republic, like Israel, could not ignore the divinity without consequences.[14]

---

13. For studies of Dwight, see Peter K. Kafer, "The Making of Timothy Dwight: A Connecticut Morality Tale," *William and Mary Quarterly* 47, no. 2 (1990): 189–209; Robert J. Imholt, "Timothy Dwight, Federalist Pope of Connecticut," *New England Quarterly* 73, no. 3 (2000): 386–411; Gregory Clark, "Timothy Dwight's Moral Rhetoric at Yale College, 1795–1817," *Rhetorica: A Journal of the History of Rhetoric* 5, no. 2 (1987): 149–61.

14. Timothy Dwight IV, *The Conquest of Canaan: A Poem, in Eleven Books* (Hartford: Elisha Babcock, 1785), 2.

Atheism represented not merely a spiritual threat to the American republic, according to Dwight. It also threatened the social and cultural life of the new American Union as well. In good Puritan fashion, Dwight believed that the story of human history was a battle between good and evil. Humans might be on the side of good—God; Jehovah; Yahweh; the Abrahamic deity and his subordinates—or they could ally with the forces of evil. God sometimes picked particular peoples to accomplish his will, and Dwight believed that Puritan New Englanders were in fact God's chosen people. Ernest Lee Tuveson noted that for Dwight, the experience of the first divinely chosen people—the ancient Hebrews—necessarily became the model for Israel's successors.[15] *The Conquest of Canaan* relied on biblical motifs, but their purpose was not sentimental or even merely spiritual. They were a blueprint for cultural, political, and social action in the newly independent United States. Dwight, noted Tuveson, "interspersed a number of parallels between biblical figures and their counterparts, American soldiers who fell in defense of liberty." God had "given the land—a continent—to the new republic as he did the promised land to the Israelites of old." Early National New Englanders affirmed Dwight's poetic assertion that God had given them "the fair empire of the promis'd land," where they had been ordained by heaven to "hold the sacred sway." The Puritan commonwealth given by God, and now part of the United States, was not to be a languid one. God demanded, in Dwight's word, the "voice" of the

---

15. Ernest Lee Tuveson, *Redeemer Nation: The Idea of America's Millennial Role* (Chicago: University of Chicago Press, 1968), 106

chosen people, and his expectations animated laypeople to bring about God's kingdom in their new republic.[16]

Dwight argued that an atheistic society could not functionally achieve either spiritual or temporal benefits for itself. He argued in one sermon that "the consequences of these doctrines, or of Atheism generally, are in the text declared in these words, *They are corrupt; they have done abominable works: there is none that doeth good.*"[17] Dwight fundamentally believed that "Atheists are corrupt; they do abominable works: there is none of them that doeth good." The character of Atheists, "seen by the Psalmist, and declared by the Spirit of God, three thousand years ago, has not changed for the better, at any period, down to the present day." Atheists, warned Dwight had always been corrupt. "They have ever done abominable works; there has never been among them a single good or virtuous man." As far as Dwight was concerned, skepticism over the existence of God undermined New England's self-conception as God's chosen people, and the fundamental cultural, social, and political structures in human history. Humans necessarily needed a divine order and purpose. Subordinating themselves to the perceived demands of the Christian God allowed humanity to achieve humanity's natural ends, which Calvinist New Englanders found in the Westminster Catechism: to glorify God and enjoy him forever. Toleration of atheism obliterated this mission for Early National New Englanders.

In Early National New England, the charge of atheism not only called into question a man's moral or social stand-

---

16. Dwight, *The Conquest of Canaan*, 1.

17. Timothy Dwight IV, *Theology: Explained and Defended in a Series of Sermons* (New York: Harper & Brothers, 1846), 1:100.

ing. It implied a measure of seditious behavior as well. *De facto* religious politics dominated New England after the promulgation of the United States Constitution in 1788, and State churches remained untouched by the disestablishmentarian trends emanating from Virginia. Connecticut ministers, for instance, touted the essential tie between church and state during the early years of the new American republic. The chief minister of Hartford's First Congregational church told his parishioners that civil and ecclesiastical institutions were not independent of each other. Elizur Goodrich (1761–1849), a divine from Durham, noted to congregants that the magistracy and ministry had different but not opposite ends: "They mutually assist each other, and ultimately center in the same point. The one has for its object the promotion of religion and the cause of Christ; the other aims immediately at the peace and order of mankind." [18] The perceived essential ties between promoting religion, the cause of Christ, and the peace and order of mankind did not escape the Federalist-dominated state legislature of Connecticut. Federalists' strength in New England and their affiliation with state-sponsored religion against Jefferson's disestablishmentarians meant that constituencies for disestablishmentarian politics in New England, and Connecticut and Massachusetts especially, were poorly organized and weaker than they were in the Mid-Atlantic and southern states. Connecticut and Yale College saw little reason to change the centuries-old religious settlement. The number of religious dissenters— particularly Baptists—grew in the final decade of the eighteenth century and the opening decade of the nineteenth, but Robert Imholt rightly observes that "belief that Prot-

18. Robert J. Imholt, "Connecticut: Land of Steady Habits," in Esbeck and Den Hartog, *Disestablishment and Religious Dissent*, 328.

estant Christianity underlay Connecticut law, politics, and society remained strong."

By necessity, state churches relied on politics for their maintenance. In the Early Republic, the Federalist Party's conservatism on church and state meant that almost by necessity, establishmentarians were politically partisan. Establishmentarian Congregationalists like Dwight publicly and vocally supported the Federalist Party and publicly denounced Jefferson's Republicans. Jefferson himself increasingly appeared as a dangerous radical to Federalists and in particular New Englanders. In 1797, Philip Mazzei (1730–1815), a Florentine merchant and doctor who lived in Virginia in the 1780s, gave pieces of his correspondence with Jefferson to a Parisian newspaper. The letters confirmed the suspicions of New Englanders like Dwight who believed that Jefferson was an irreligious skeptic who had been radicalized by godless French philosophers during his time as the American minister in France. In the letter Jefferson called the Federalist administration of George Washington and the Federalist-controlled Congress and courts "Anglican, monarchical, and aristocratic."[19] Federalists, said Jefferson, preferred the calm of despotism to what he called the "boisterous sea of liberty."[20] Jefferson routinely associated anti-democratic and religious politics with despotism, and in many ways saw churchly or institutional religion as the first cause of tyranny. Brooke Allen argues in *Moral Minority: Our Skeptical Founding Fathers* that Jefferson saw Christian ministers as his chief enemy, especially

---

19. John Ferling, *Adams vs. Jefferson: The Tumultuous Election of 1800* (Oxford: Oxford University Press, 2004), 76.

20. Thomas Jefferson, Thomas Jefferson to Lafayette, 26 December 1820, *Founders Online*, https://founders.archives.gov/documents/Jefferson/03-16-02-0400.

as the election of 1800 approached. When Jefferson "swore upon the altar of God eternal hostility to every form of tyranny over the mind of man," he was, according to Allen, striking out against the tyranny not of "political tyrants but of religious ones, not of kings but of ambitious clergymen jockeying for power."[21]

Jefferson's skepticism had a distinctively anti-churchly tone. Protestant ministers interested in politics, and especially those interested in Federalist politics, he called "'the genus irritabile vatum,' who are all in arms against me."[22] And so they were. Timothy Dwight told a Connecticut senator that unless politicians and ministers worked together to stop Jefferson's election, they would "lose the only and certainly best, opportunity of securing public safety. The introduction of Mr. Jefferson will ruin the republic."[23] A New York Presbyterian opined that that the election of Jefferson represented the "deliberate surrender of the cause of Jesus Christ" in the United States." The ministers' fears were not, however, the dreads of partisan hacks fearful of losing power. They saw Christianity as underpinning the societal order and providing purpose for human existence. Christianity's place in culture and society meant it needed a place in law and politics as well. Jedediah Morse (1761–1826), the father of Samuel Morse of Morse code fame, preached a sermon in 1799 noting that it was to "the kindly influence of Christianity" that Americans owed

21. Brooke Allen, *Moral Minority: Our Skeptical Founding Fathers* (Chicago: Ivan R. Dee, 2009), 73.

22. "Race of angry soothsayers." Thomas Jefferson to Benjamin Rush, Monticello, 23 September 1800, *Founders Online*, https://founders.archives.gov/documents/Jefferson/01-32-02-0102.

23. Eric C. Smith, *John Leland: A Jeffersonian Baptist in Early America* (New York: Oxford University Press, 2022), 164.

"that degree of civil freedom, and political and social happiness" which the United States enjoyed as the new century dawned.[24] Morse, who spent much of his career defending orthodox Congregationalist Calvinism from the rising tide of Unitarianism in New England, warned that "all efforts to destroy the Foundation of our holy religion, ultimately tend to the subversion also of our political freedom and happiness." Whenever and wherever "pillars of Christianity shall be overthrown, our present republican form of government, and all the blessings which flow from them, must fall with them."

Undeterred by clerical opponents, Jefferson claimed to Benjamin Rush (1746–1813), one of his fellow Founding Fathers, that he hoped his views on religion would please "the rational Christian or Deist; & would reconcile many to a character they have too hastily rejected."[25] Rational Christianity he left undefined, but associating it with deism meant that hard metaphysical commitments to the Christian creeds over and against the ideas of the Enlightenment would preclude someone from being truly rational. The excesses of the French Revolution, he groaned, had stalled the progress of humanity away from medieval superstitions and "had given to the clergy a very favorite hope of obtaining an establishment of a particular form of Christianity thro' the US." Jefferson's complaint that partisan clergy were the only devotees of historic Christianity's place in the cultural, social, and political life of the American republic was over-

---

24. Jedediah Morse, "The Present Dangers and Consequent Duties of the Citizens" in *The Fear of Conspiracy: Images of Un-American Subversion from the Revolution to the Present*, ed. David Brion Davis (Ithaca: Cornell University Press, 1971), 46.

25. Thomas Jefferson to Benjamin Rush, Monticello, 23 September 1800.

stated. Patrick Henry (1736–1799), Jefferson's predecessor as governor of Virginia and a committed proponent of Jefferson's own ideological commitments, nonetheless balked at Jefferson's deism, which Henry saw as synonymous with irreligiosity. Henry had during the 1780s praised the writings of Thomas Paine, but by 1796 the former had become so horrified by the anti-religious violence of the French Revolution and Paine's intellectual role in sowing the seeds of the Terror that he broke irrevocably with Paine, Jefferson, and even the Republican Party. Thomas S. Kidd noted that by the end of Henry's political life, the Virginian believed that "Paine's writings and Jefferson's well-known skepticism" challenged the United States' "spiritual foundations."[26] Henry saw that Americans "could no longer take their religious heritage for granted." He "feared that without fidelity to long-established religious precepts, the United States would spin apart in an atheistic whirlwind, just like Revolutionary France."

Fears that Jefferson might inaugurate an anti-religious order that unmoored republican society's moral and religious foundations were not merely a Federalist fever dream. They were shared by Virginians like Henry who shared some of Jefferson's deepest Republican commitments as well. Jefferson had told Benjamin Rush that "the Episcopalians & Congregationalists" were especially troublesome for their lingering establishmentarian beliefs on church and state in 1800, but during and after his presidency he included Presbyterians—none of whom in Virginia supported the erection of state churches—in his list of problematic and

---

26. Thomas S. Kidd, *Patrick Henry: First Among Patriots* (New York: Basic Books, 2011), 234.

invasive religious groups.[27] Jefferson's claims that his dises-tablishmentarianism rested on an absolute commitment to the rights of conscience seem less convincing when coupled with his obvious dislike for organized Christianity.

The extent to which Jefferson disliked churchly or creedal Christianity was already well-known in 1800, albe-it largely by means of rumor—as noted, although relative-ly candid in private, Jefferson reined in his skepticism in public. After his presidency Jefferson wrote more candidly about his own beliefs, but even his actions during his polit-ical career indicate a relatively enduring dislike of doctrines such as the Trinity. Jefferson's deism—which appeared to have solidified into Unitarianism as he grew older—reject-ed the Trinity vehemently. He viewed the doctrine as the source of religious intolerance. The belief that God was one person and that Christ was not divine had been, he argued, the belief of the primitive Christian Church. The "unity of the supreme being" was not, he raged, "ousted from the Christian creed by the force of reason, but by the sword of civil government wielded at the will of the fanatic Athanasius."[28] Jefferson called the Athanasian Creed a "ho-cus-pocus phantasm of a god like another Cerberus, with one body and three heads" which "had its birth and growth in the blood of thousands and thousands of martyrs." The strongest proof of what Jefferson called the "the solidity of the primitive faith" was its restoration "as soon as a nation arises which vindicates to itself the freedom of religious

27. Thomas Jefferson to Benjamin Rush, Monticello, 23 September 1800.

28. Thomas Jefferson to James Smith, Monticello, 8 December 1822, in *The Papers of Thomas Jefferson, Retirement Series*, vol. 19, *16 September 1822-30 June 1823*, ed. Daniel P. Jordan (Princeton: Princeton Univer-sity Press, 2022), 214.

opinion, and its eternal divorce from the civil authority." For Jefferson, the American religious settlement was not simply a soil in which Unitarianism was permitted to grow, but itself the fruit that proved the truth of Unitarianism. Disestablishment's naturally corollary was the growth of Unitarianism and a rejection of the Christian Trinity. This was hardly a view shared by his enthusiastic Baptist and Presbyterian supporters, but they eventually learned that the third president held it deeply, much to their surprise and chagrin—particularly when Jefferson began picking potential faculty members for the University of Virginia.

Evangelicals should not have been too surprised at Jefferson's views on religion. As early as the mid-1780s, in his *Notes on the State of Virginia*, he famously argued that "it does me no injury for my neighbor to say there are twenty gods, or no God. It neither picks my pocket nor breaks my leg."[29] Jefferson's deism and deism in general was not libertarian, operating in harmony with historic Christianity or other traditional religions. It was programmatically committed to replacing historic Protestantism in American society. Elihu Palmer (1764–1806), a Jefferson devotee, authored *Principles of Nature; or, a Development of the Moral Causes of Happiness and Misery among the Human Species*, in which he argued that deism represented the final development in human intellectual, religious, and political freedom. Palmer argued that Luther, Calvin, and the other magisterial Reformers "were at least as superstitious, fanatical, and narrow-minded as the Catholic church from which they separated." Religious groups committed to rationality and reason threw off the old superstitions. Christopher Grasso notes that Palmer saw the destruction of Protestant-

29. Thomas Jefferson, *Notes on the State of Virginia* (Boston: Lilly and Wait, 1832), 166.

ism as a metaphysical necessity: "Arminians cast off Calvinism and restored the importance of human agency; Arians and Socinians moved toward a more realistic understanding of Jesus; and universalists abandoned limited atonement and endless punishment."[30] Rejecting Protestant religiosity and the historic political and social commitments built on Protestantism was not incidental to deism; it was part of a broader project to remake society. Deists hoped to "spread enlightened philosophy through print," encourage "people to use their reason," urge skepticism "about the claims of revealed religion," and place "faith, politics, and knowledge on natural, rational foundations."[31] They wedded this to distinctly political aims. Deists and their allies fought "for republican liberty and equality, at the ballot box or with a sword if necessary."

Deist Reformers "like Palmer and his friend Thomas Paine tried to combine a skeptical critique of revealed religion (especially Christianity) with a program for a simplified, liberated religion of reason and nature."[32] Paine's ubiquity within radical causes during the Federalist years of the 1790s, and Jefferson's association with Paine, showed religious Americans, and not just Federalists, that Jefferson did in fact represent a threat to religion in the new American republic. While Federalists might have overstated the degree to which Jefferson could make immediate changes to the American order, they were not wrong to perceive in Jefferson a greater enemy to churchly religion than Jefferson's partisans admitted him to be. Nor were the Federalists a niche group of New England reactionaries. William Linn

---

30. Grasso, *Skepticism and American Faith*, 98.

31. Grasso, *Skepticism and American Faith*, 99.

32. Grasso, *Skepticism and American Faith*, 99.

(1752–1808), a Calvinist minister from Northern Ireland who served as the House of Representatives Chaplain, sneered and pantomimed Jefferson. "Let my neighbor once persuade himself there is not God and he will soon pick my pocket, and break not only my leg but my neck."[33]

The election of Thomas Jefferson in 1800 renewed attention to the question of church and state relations in the Early Republic. Jefferson's 1802 letter to the Danbury Baptist Association gave the American republic's political lexicon the phrase "separation of church and state," but that term was not analogous to the constitutional settlement on disestablishment, which was more narrowly limited to precluding a federally sponsored national religious establishment—an equivalent of the Church of England, for instance. A year after Jefferson's correspondence with the Connecticut Baptists, a pamphlet appeared, curiously entitled *Two Sons of Oil*. The book-length essay's name came from two oil-anointed offices inferred from the biblical book of Zechariah: civil minister and religious minister. The author, Samuel B. Wylie (1773–1852), was a Reformed Presbyterian—popularly termed "Covenanters," from their theocratic Scottish predecessors—minister and professor at the University of Pennsylvania. He opened a debate on the "Constitution's compatibility with Christianity and the proper bounds of religious uniformity in the newly founded republic."[34] More importantly, the presence of divines like Wylie in prominent churches and universities—he pastored

---

33. William Linn, *Serious Considerations on the Election of a President: Addressed to the Citizens of the United States* (New York: John Furman, 1800), 19.

34. Steven Wedgeworth, "'The Two Sons of Oil' and the Limits of American Religious Dissent," *Journal of Law and Religion* 27, no. 1 (2011), 141.

a church in Philadelphia for half a century, and taught and then served as Provost at the University of Pennsylvania for two decades—challenged "certain 'Christian' understandings of early America and the Constitution." Wylie's public debate with William Findley (c.1741–1821), himself a descendant of Scottish Covenanters, also posed problems "for attempts at a coherent theory of secularity, natural law, and the common good in our own day."

Wylie could be both a convinced "theocrat" as well as a convinced believer in disestablishment. While he never countenanced sedition or even a change to the republic's fundamental laws broadly, Wylie argued that he (and any Covenanter) could not support the United States because, among other things, the federal constitution did not explicitly recognize the existence of God, and because the United States sanctioned slavery.[35]

Beginning with the 1800 presidential campaign, religious observers and writers worried about the rise of public irreligiosity associated with the personal and political beliefs of Thomas Jefferson. Linn went so far as to warn Christians against voting for Jefferson, a warning "founded singly upon his disbelief of the Holy Scriptures; or, in other words, his rejection of the Christian Religion and open profession of Deism."[36] Theodore Dwight (1764–1846), the brother of Yale president Timothy Dwight IV, saw a dark post-Jefferson regime "governed by blockheads and knaves," where "ties of marriage with all its felicities" were "severed and destroyed," and where "your wives and daughters are thrown into the stews; our children are cast into

---

35. Wedgeworth, "'Two Sons of Oil,'" 147–48.

36. Linn, *Serious Considerations*, 12.

the world from the breast and forgotten."[37] In a United States ruled by Jefferson's Republicans, "filial piety is extinguished, and our surnames, the only mark of distinction among families, are abolished. Can the imagination paint anything more dreadful on this side of hell?"

Although Linn and Dwight did not share Wylie's Covenanter political theology, they shared a belief that Jefferson's rhetoric and politics represented a departure from the religious politics of his two Federalist predecessors. Historiographic assumptions regarding a secular founding understandably focus on Jefferson, but neither the Constitution, nor prominent clerics and intellectuals at the beginning of the nineteenth century assumed a state-enforced secular republic. In fact, they assumed that the United States' republican social and civil framework, along with the states' institutional frameworks, relied on public Christianity. Washington was comfortable with religion in political life, and even Madison, the most convinced of disestablishmentarians, worked to create federal chaplaincies for the Senate, House, and other federal institutions.

Scholars devoted to the idea of a secular founding argue, like Steven K. Green in *Inventing a Christian America*, that a Christianized American republic was a creation of religious activists. "The myth of America's religious origins arose incrementally, not as a comprehensive account, over a forty-year period, roughly from 1800 to 1840"—so says Green.[38] Green does not deny the presence of Christian

---

37. Theodore Dwight, *An Oration, Delivered at New-Haven on the 7th of July, A.D. 1801: Before the Society of Cincinnati, for the State of Connecticut Assembled to Celebrate the Anniversary of American Independence* (Hartford: Hudson and Goodwin, 1801), 29.

38. Steven K. Green, *Inventing a Christian America: The Myth of the Religious Founding* (Oxford: Oxford University Press, 2015), 201.

influence in the Founding Era altogether, but he wrongly relegates Christian influence to a fringe minority: "A handful of people during the founding period, orthodox clergy in particular...never abandoned their belief in an active superintending providence or their willingness to think in biblical types." That Wylie's work elicited a response from a sitting congressman, and that it went through several editions, indicated that his message appealed to more than a mere political or social fringe, and his status as a professor at an elite university meant that his intellectual credentials were secure.

Wylie's, Dwight's, and Linn's responses to Jefferson's accession create a problem for Green's secular thesis, however. Wylie and his brethren were not trying to contrive a story of a Christian America. Instead, they were trying to *preserve* one, fighting a rear-guard action against the beginnings of a new regime wherein the United States' religious roots were reimagined as playing a negligible role in its creation. 1800 more properly saw the invention of a secular America, not a Christian one. There was no need to invent an explicitly Christian founding, largely because the Christian socio-civil foundation of the republic was already largely assumed. Claims that Virginia's disestablishment and that state's particular brand of irreligious and even secular politics informed the Constitutional era have been, as Mark David Hall rightly notes, massively overstated.[39]

The Covenanter theology that underpinned Wylie's arguments was never supported by a majority of American statesmen in the Founding Era or Early Republic, nor did even a sizable plurality of American citizens worship in

---

39. Mark David Hall, *Did America Have a Christian Founding?: Separating Modern Myth from Historical Truth* (Nashville: Thomas Nelson, 2019), 66.

Presbyterian or Reformed churches. Nonetheless, the perception that Jefferson was enforcing secularism on a Christian socio-civil milieu created the circumstances whereby political theology was rightly understood not as a reactionary response to the Republican administration but as an intellectual and political pursuit that had long defined Colonial North America and the Early National United States. The incompatibility of Covenanter theocracy, specifically, with the *longue duree* of colonial and subsequently Constitutional practice in the United States did not mean accepting the invention of a secular Founding.

Most Protestants in the first decade of the nineteenth century did not affirm the idiosyncratic church and state doctrines of the Covenanters, but neither did they believe that disestablishment removed the church from the social or civil order. Likewise, Early Republic Protestants assumed that the church was a merely spiritual institution that was not affected by social and political changes. Presbyterian minister and King's College—now Columbia University—professor John McKnight (1754–1823), like most Presbyterians in the United States at the beginning of the nineteenth century, celebrated disestablishment as a definitive corrective of an unnatural misalliance that began with Constantine. Constantinian establishmentarianism was a "heterogeneous and incestuous connection between the kingdoms of this world, and the kingdom of Christ; which, from the reign of Constantine, down to the present day," had been "the source of incalculable mischief, both to the interests of true religion, and the civil and religious rights of man."[40] Disestablishment renounced that connection. Church and state in the new American order each

40. John McKnight, *A View of the Present State of the Political and Religious World* (New York: Isaac Collins and Son, 1802), 9.

rested "on their own proper foundation," and exercised, "respectively, their particular and appropriate rights and prerogatives."

In McKnight's reckoning, disestablishment benefitted church and state because it made their respective duties and limits clear. Disestablishment did not, however, disconnect them in their mutual goal to preserving human liberty and ordering human life. Governments, after all, cannot be separated from the societies they govern. There was, McKnight argued, a "close and intimate connection subsisting between" civil society and the church.[41] That connection between them rendered a right understanding of their association necessary for the protection for the liberty of both. "Civil and religious liberty, though distinct, in themselves, will generally be enjoyed or lost together. The same enlarged views, and the same liberal sentiments" that tended "to secure the one, will equally tend to the promotion and establishment of the other." The same spirit "of domination and lust of power, which aims at enslaving the bodies, will equally aim at enslaving the minds and consciences of men." Communities religious and civil, "or bodies politic, will always be prosperous and happy, in proportion to the religion and virtue which they possess."

Although disestablishment removed churches from the state's sphere of control, it did not disconnect churches from society or the state entirely. Churches were affected by the same forces that influenced broader society. Disestablishment of church from the institutional civil government did not entail disconnection from the influences that affected both. The push for a more complete separation came from Jeffersonian Deists and Baptists. John Leland (1754–1841), a prominent New England Baptist and Jef-

---

41. McKnight, *A View of the Present State*, 6.

fersonian partisan, saw Jefferson as a hero for finally finishing off Protestantism's—and Christianity's—original sin of Constantinian accommodation: "That the Christian world has been in a gross error, from the days of Constantine to the present time, admits of no doubt," claimed Leland.[42] "From that period down, the Christian religion has been an institute of state policy, regulated by the laws of men, and supported by the sword of the magistrate." Protestantism, whatever its benefits, had not addressed the great sin of historical Christianity: religious establishments. "Whether in a papal or protestant mode, the principle has done incalculable mischief, and drenched the earth in blood," said Leland. Leland foreshadowed the utopian claims of the nineteenth century by asserting that America would escape history and inaugurate a new era of not only political, but also Christian history. "In the United States," Leland exclaimed, "the felonious principle has been apprehended, tried, condemned and executed." Baptist Roger Williams (c.1603–1683) and Quaker William Penn (1644–1718) "first attacked the villain, and Thomas Jefferson did more than any one man to bring him to the stake." Leland warned that "some few roots of this principle are yet in the soil of Massachusetts, interwoven in the constitution and laws of the state; but the spirit of the people triumphs over those evil roots." Leland placed his hopes for a disestablishmentarian order in populist democracy. There were, he noted, "but few places in the state where the people would succumb to a *legal* distraint for *religious* uses."

Baptists needed disestablishment to mean more than merely disestablishing the Anglican Church. They needed to defang the socio-religious order that regarded their emo-

---

42. John Leland, *The Writings of the Late Elder John Leland*, ed. L. F. Greene (New York: G. W. Wood, 1845), 553.

tionally-charged worship as unusual at best and heretical at worst. Leland recorded happenings at Baptist tent revivals along the James River in the summer of 1785. "At Associations, and great meetings," he saw souls awakened, in his words, "who afterwards give clear, rational accounts of a divine change of heart."[43] Certain exercises—typically physical convulsions often resulting in the new convert falling to the ground and writhing uncontrollably—"were not confined to the newly convicted, and newly converted, but persons who have been professors a number of years." These converts and enthused believers "at such lively meetings, not only jump up, strike their hands together, and shout aloud, but will embrace one another, and fall to the floor." Leland had "never known the rules of decency broken so far as for persons of different sexes, thus to embrace and fall at meetings." He admitted that these apparently spiritual confirmations of revivalist preaching were not "seen in all parts of the state, at times when God is working on the minds of the people." Instead, "under the preaching of the same man, in different neighborhoods and counties, the same work, in substance, has different exterior effects." Baptist flirtation with revivalism often drew the ire of public authorities. What Baptists defended as religious freedom, states prosecuted as public disorder. This did not stem from states' commitments to lingering Anglican political theology. Even in disestablished Virginia, a majority of people in the Commonwealth viewed Baptists and Methodists with suspicion. Christine Leigh Heyrman observed in her book *Southern Cross: The Beginnings of the Bible Belt* that "obnoxious as Baptists and Methodists were to many members of the Anglican gentry, many white southerners of lesser means liked these religious upstarts no better.

---

43. Leland, *Writings of the Late Elder John Leland*, 115.

White middling farmers might not have wanted to maintain the church of England institutionally, but that did not
mean they embraced a socio-religious order committed to
en masse religious freedom."[44] It was not, Heyrman argued,
"only members of the gentry or Anglican clergymen who
violently opposed early evangelicals." When a Baptist minister was arrested in the 1770s, locals gathered in significant
numbers to harangue him. When Baptists tried to preach
in jail cells, townspeople disrupted that too.

A wholesale remaking of society, and not merely disestablishment, was the goal of Early Republic Baptists.
Leland's Jeffersonianism and disestablishmentarian intellectual framework, Mark Noll notes, "clearly distinguished
between political and religious spheres of life."[45] The Baptist
minister "was a determined foe of all hierarchies—social,
commercial, medical, and legal, as well as clerical—and of
every effort to coerce the conscience." Leland campaigned
against the Christian and Protestant past and urged that individuals, according to Nathan O. Hatch, "free themselves
of natural authorities: church, state, college, seminary, even
family."[46] Hatch rightly noted that Leland "carried the
ideological leverage of evangelical urgency and Jeffersonian
promise." Most importantly for the relationship of religion
to society broadly, Leland "proclaimed a divine economy
that was atomistic and competitive rather than wholistic
and hierarchical." Leland combined religion and politics
even as he ostensibly tried to separate them. He proselytized

---

44. Christine Leigh Heyrman, *Southern Cross: The Beginnings of the
Bible Belt* (New York: Alfred A. Knopf, 1997).

45. Noll, *America's God*, 152.

46. Nathan O. Hatch, *The Democratization of American Christianity*
(New Haven: Yale University Press, 1989), 101.

citizens with a kind of "liberal individualism" which "could be easily embraced at the grass roots." Ordinary Americans "gladly championed the promise of personal autonomy as a message they could understand and a cause to which they could subscribe—in God's name no less."

The election of 1800 definitively turned the *telos* of federal politics against traditional Protestant conceptions of church and state. And yet that did not mean a majority of Americans supported the Jeffersonian conception of church and state. New England Federalists remained intransigent. So too were intellectuals in Early National colleges and churches. The court system of the United States, filled with southern and northern Federalists appointed by Washington and Adams, also pushed against the rising tide of religious de-institutionalization. Throughout the first half of the nineteenth century, intellectual, religious, and judicial elites remained committed to older Protestant understandings of church and state whereby two separate institutions worked hand in hand to maintain the civil and social orders. The bulwark they created proved surprisingly resilient. Jeffersonian separationism was not *de facto* disposition of society in the Early Republic. As late as 1839, John L. O'Sullivan (1813–1895), a Democratic editor, argued that Americans who continued to "venerate the rubbish, the prejudices, the superstitions of other times and other lands, the theocracy of priests, the divine right of kings, the aristocracy of blood, the metaphysics of colleges, the irrational stuff of law libraries" would eventually be overawed by "the mighty impulse of the age;" and "carried onward by the increasing tide of progress."[47] Forces of tradition like the old socio-civil conceptions of the Reformation would

47. John L. O'Sullivan, "The Great Nation of Futurity," *United States Magazine and Democratic Review* 6, no. 23 (1839): 426–30.

not, he hoped, withstand "the glorious movement of the masses." Like John Leland, O'Sullivan hoped to eventually to sweep away the hierarchies and institutions of old. But "the retrograde tendencies of our laws, our judicature, our colleges, our literature" stood in the way. From the election of Jefferson onward, historic Protestant legal frameworks in state laws, judges, colleges and universities, and the burgeoning American literati all upheld Protestantism's fundamental place in American culture, politics, and society, whether Jefferson liked it or not.

CHAPTER III

LEGISLATION

Politicians, clerics, and religious commentators in the nineteenth century understood that the federal Constitution did not defang institutionalized Christianity in the respective state constitutions. Philip Schaff argued in his *Church and State in the United States* that the federal Constitution "did not abolish the union of church and state where it previously existed, nor does it forbid any of the States to establish a religion or to favor a particular church."[1] The United States Constitution left the states "free to deal with religion as they please, provided only they do not deprive any American citizen of his right to worship God according to his conscience." The Constitution, Schaff noted, did not say "'no State shall make a law respecting an establishment of religion'; nor: 'Neither Congress nor any State,' etc., but simply: 'Congress shall make no law, etc.'" Individual states retained "every power, jurisdiction, and right which they

---

1. Philip Schaff, *Church and State in the United States: Or, The American Idea of Religious Liberty and its Practical Effects* (New York: Charles Scribner's Sons, 1888), 245.

had before, except those only which they delegated to the Congress of the United States or the departments of the Federal Government." Schaff believed that some state provisions regarding religion had been left to the states because of the Ninth and Tenth Amendments. That argument wasn't novel, and Schaff quoted Early Republic Supreme Court Justice Story to support the assertion. Story wrote that the "whole power over the subject of religion is left exclusively to the State governments, to be acted upon according to their sense of justice and the State constitutions."

Schaff identified the culmination of a trend that began in 1800, but the trend was never as total or complete as Schaff and some American commentators thought. American states still retained the legal right to pass acts dealing with public religion throughout the nineteenth century. There was nothing in the United States Constitution that prohibited a state like Virginia or Pennsylvania from potentially banning Roman Catholicism. Wide latitude on retained establishmentarian structures, combined with evangelical revivals, meant that religion and politics were deeply tied after 1800. Geoffrey Stone rightly states that from the turn of the nineteenth century to the 1840s, evangelical Protestants "converged on American politics *en masse*."[2] Evangelical divines and their political allies "politicked for Sunday closing laws, blasphemy prosecutions, temperance legislation, and a host of other morals-based laws." "The interlocking network of churches" in collusion with state legislative actors, Stone writes, became known as the "Benevolent Empire" and had as its goal the creation of "a functional equivalent of an established church." Stone continues: "The

---

2. Geoffrey R. Stone, *Sex and the Constitution: Sex, Religion, and Law from America's Origins to the Twenty-First Century* (New York: Liverlight, 2017), 137.

central premise of the evangelical political movement was that morality is necessary for republican government and Christianity is necessary for morality." Because evangelical Protestants, Stone proposes, came dangerously close to believing that only Christians could be good citizens, they believed they had to work to create a more Christian society.

Stone rightly identifies the rise of the Benevolent Empire, but he is wrong to attribute it merely to the presence of evangelicals involved in social and political reforms. A generally Protestant political order existed within the states well before the rise of evangelical reform movements in the nineteenth century. Evangelical reformers did not create a legal milieu wherein their social and political commitments could be successful. They used already established political orders that retained institutional commitments to (generally Protestant) Christianity. Evangelicals of the nineteenth century did not have *as a goal* the creation of the functional equivalent of state church. They believed state legislatures maintained institutional commitments to Christianity that meant Protestantism *already* functioned as a *de facto* state religion. In more ways than one the evangelical Protestant political project was an attempt to retain a traditional order over against the religious and social changes that occurred *en masse* in the United States in the first half of the nineteenth century.

Prominent Protestant thinkers supported the disestablished religious order, but even religious liberty enthusiasts did not believe that the Constitution created a legal framework for a secular order. In 1844, well-known missionary, Presbyterian divine, and occasional tutor at the College of New Jersey Robert Baird (1798–1863) published his history of American Christianity, *Religion in America*. Mark Noll called Baird's work "an important account of basic Evangelical convictions."[3] Baird's book became what Noll called "the most comprehensive history published to that date of religion in America." Noll noted Baird's prioritization and promotion of voluntarist principles and voluntary organizations, which formed important foundations for evangelical religiosity in the antebellum United States. Baird's disestablishmentarian credentials were such that he suggested that true evangelical churches were committed to ensuring that the civil magistrate did not interfere with the doctrine, discipline, and government of the church.

Baird's disestablishmentarianism and voluntarism never precluded his belief that the United States' Constitution provided for a substantive institutional and legal commitment to Christianity in the American republic. He disagreed with those who argued that because "no mention of the Supreme Being, or of the Christian religion, is to be found in the Constitution of the United States," that the United States' fundamental law was either "infidel" or "atheistical."[4] Neither opinion, wrote Baird, "is correct." The generation of American statesmen who wrote the Constitution "were believers in Christianity, and Washington, as all the world knows, was a Christian."[5] Prominent members of the constitutional convention claimed membership in churches and lived "in a manner consistent with their profession."

Baird's claim represented accurately the basic religious composition of the members of the Constitutional Con-

3. Noll, *America's God*, 173.

4. Robert Baird, *Religion in America: Religion in America: Or an Account of the Origin, Relation to the State, and Present Condition of the Evangelical Churches in the United States* (New York: Harper & Bros., 1844), 118.

5. Baird, *Religion in America*, 119.

vention. Fifty-two of the fifty-five members of the Constitutional Convention were affiliated with Christian churches, all but two Protestant, and Baird noted that even Deist Benjamin Franklin (1706–1790) saw religion as necessarily a part of the new constitutional order. "The framers of that Constitution seem, in fact, to have felt the necessity of leaving the subject of religion, as they left many things besides, to the governments of the several States composing the Union."[6] Religion, Baird wrote, "was a subject on which these States had legislated from the very first." In nine of the thirteen original states "Christian religion had been, and in some it still continued to be, supported by law; in all, it had been the acknowledged basis of their liberty and well-being, and its institutions had been protected by legal enactments." Because states had their own longstanding establishments, federal legislation was superfluous. "Nothing, accordingly, could be more natural in the Convention than to deem the introduction of the subject unnecessary." The Constitutional Convention thought the mention of religion unnecessary because the Founders all understood that "the Constitution was not intended for a people that had no religion." They knew, argued Baird, that the fundamental law of the American republic would be for "a people already Christian," whose existing laws and legislatures "gave ample evidence of their being favorable to religion." Not speaking on religion spoke "more loudly than if they had expressed themselves in the most solemn formulas on the existence of the Deity and the truth of Christianity." The existence of God and the truth of Christianity "were clearly assumed, being, as it were, so well-known and fully acknowledged as to need no specification in an instrument of a general nature, and designed for general objects." The Constitution,

---

6. Baird, *Religion in America*, 119.

like the Bible, Baird declares, did "not begin with an argument to prove the existence of God, but assumes the fact, as one the truth of which it needs no attempt to establish." Thomas M. Cooley (1824–1898), likewise recognized that the federal Constitution did not obliterate religious legislation and politics in the American republic as much as it left "the whole power" of religious questions "exclusively to the State governments, to be acted on according to their own sense of justice, and the state constitutions."[7]

Federalism and the retention of full-throated commitments to institutional Christianity in state laws meant that Early Republic Protestants rarely indulged radicals or rebellious inclinations among the laity or among clerics. Injunctions to follow laws formed a major part of Early National Protestant preaching. In 1834, Albert Barnes (1798–1870), the pastor of Philadelphia's First Presbyterian Church, reminded congregants that the magistrate bore the sword to keep order and also "restrain and punish wickedness as an act of duty to God. This office is God's only ordinance in this world for this purpose."[8] God, Barnes argued, took "away the sword from individuals, who, in a state of nature might execute vengeance, and has given it to the magistrate." God's purpose was that punishment should be "administered by the magistrate, and according to the laws, and not by individuals, or by mobs. And it further follows from this, that if the magistrate does not punish offences according to the laws, they are to go unpunished—except as God shall himself punish them in the administrations of

---

7. Thomas M. Cooley, *A Treatise on the Constitutional Limitations which Rest Upon the Legislative Power of the States of the American Union* (Boston: Little, Brown, 1868), 470.

8. Albert Barnes, "The Supremacy of the Laws," *American National Preacher* 12 (Aug 1838), 114.

his Providence." God "commissioned no other authority to do this but the civil powers. These are the vital principles contained in the Bible on the subject of civil government."

Protestants asserted that government—with religion as its guide—filled the essential duty of regulating morality in the American republic. The number of religious laws passed by the new states and religious provisions retained by most of the state constitutions enacted between 1776 and 1800 confirmed state governments' role as the chief arbiters of morality and religious law in the United States. Popular narratives, note Carl Esbeck and Jonathan Den Hartog, envision disestablishment and the First Amendment kicking off "a bold national experiment in religious freedom...embodied in the First Amendment." [9] In fact, the striking aspect of religious legislation at the time of the Constitutional Convention of 1787 and the Federalist administrations that followed was the extent to which states ignored almost entirely the First Amendment when they crafted state law regarding religion. Esbeck and Den Hartog state in their work on disestablishment in the states that "no state modeled its constitution after the First Amendment, or even considered the amendment when making state religion law." [10] Put simply, Early Republic legislators conceived of the First Amendment very differently than modern Americans do and did not perceived the Constitution as imposing federal will on preexisting state establishments. They did not consider the First Amendment's religious provisions binding on the states, or as excluding establishmentarian principles. Consequently states did not follow the federal lead in Article

---

9. Carl H. Esbeck and Jonathan J. Den Hartog, "Introduction" in *Disestablishment and Religious Dissent*, 8.

10. Esbeck and Den Hartog, "Introduction", 9.

VI (Clause 3) of the Constitution in prohibiting religious tests for office. "Most every state had a religious-test clause until well into the nineteenth century." The U.S. Supreme Court did not even mention the religious clauses in the First Amendment until 1845, and even then it was to only "acknowledge the truism that the First Amendment did not bind the states." Virginia's extremely aggressive disestablishment, headed by Jefferson, Madison, and their political and religious allies, was never the norm for the other states. In fact, it was the most unusual. Virginia's separation of church and state never became the norm for the Union in the nineteenth century, largely because state governments realized that while church and state might be separable, religion and politics were not. A majority of Americans, and by inference most of their elected representatives, believed "religion... was instrumental to the formation of virtue, and virtue was instrumental to the self-discipline of citizens thought necessary to sustain a republic."[11]

The Federalists that dominated the United States government and its commercial cities in between 1790 and 1800 placed a premium on maintaining religion's place in the civil order. Elite churchgoers filled the ranks of government and ensured that the interest of Protestant churches would be closely guarded by the states. This was not limited to New England. New York's conservative post-revolutionary constitution retained language privileging Protestantism and effectively barred Roman Catholics and Jews from office. In Early Republic New York, according to Edward Channing's venerable history, "liberty of conscience and worship were guaranteed to every one provided that this liberty should not be understood to justify practices that were

---

11. Esbeck and Den Hartog, "Introduction," 12.

inconsistent with the peace and safety of the State."[12] New Yorkers saw the safety of the state as relying on the maintenance of a broadly Protestant social order. New Yorkers were not trying to create a theocracy. Ministers and priests could not hold political office or serve in the state militia. Rights of conscience were preserved, but at a price. Conscientious objectors had to pay for the toleration the New York legislature granted them, whenever the legislature saw fit. Toleration in New York was not absolute, even for groups that were sometimes termed Protestant. Nor was this limited toleration a fringe or reactionary belief. John Jay (1745–1829), the first chief justice of the United States Supreme Court, "proposed to give the legislature power to deny toleration to any sect that it pleased." New York's convention voted against this proposition, so Jay subsequently "moved that no Roman Catholic should enjoy civil rights or hold any land within the State." Jay lost too on this anti-Catholic provision by a vote of 19 to 10. He and his allies "succeeded, however, in securing the adoption of a clause forbidding the naturalization of an immigrant until he had renounced subjection to 'every foreign king, prince, potentate, and state in all matters ecclesiastical as well as civil.'" Since in New York "only native-born citizens and naturalized persons could exercise the franchise or hold office under the constitution, this requirement excluded from power all foreign-born Roman Catholics, and was intended so to do."

Religious thinkers assumed that legislatures took religion into account as they carried out their deliberations, and with good reason. Religiously-affiliated colleges trained

---

12. Edward Channing, *A History of the United States* (New York: Macmillan, 1920), 3:564. See also Kyle T. Bulthuis, *Four Steeples Over the City Streets: Religion and Society in New York's Early Republic Congregations* (New York: New York University Press, 2014), 50–52.

a significant number of men who sought public office in the Early National United States. Princeton's Samuel Stanhope Smith (1751–1819) told his students in 1795 that religion tended to civilize the human mind and that religious devotion held a "powerful control over the violent passions of the most vicious of mankind."[13] All of the "wise legislators of antiquity" resorted to the influence of religion to "lay the foundations of society most securely, and to promote its civilization." State legislatures in older states like New York and the new frontier states forming west of the Appalachian Mountains both heeded Smith's call to include religion and religious legislation in the foundations of their respective political and social orders. Frontier state in the old Northwest Territory did not set up state establishments, but they nonetheless institutionalized religion within the political framework set up by the Northwest Ordinances.

Ohio's constitution formed the legal foundation for the first state carved out of the massive Northwest Territory. The 1802 language of Ohio's fundamental law hardly mirrored establishmentarian language of New England, but neither did it mirror the more extensive removal of religion from government sought by Jefferson in Virginia. Ohio's fundamental law declared that "all men have a natural and indefeasible right to worship Almighty God according to the dictates of conscience; that no human authority can, in any case whatever, control or interfere with the rights of conscience."[14] The customary guarantee of rights of conscience

---

13. Samuel Stanhope Smith, *The Lectures, Corrected and Improved, Which Have Been Delivered for a Series of Years in the College of New-Jersey; On the Subjects of Moral and Political Philosophy* (New York: Whiting and Watson, 1812), vol. 1, 227.

14. *The Constitutions of Ohio: Amendments, and Proposed Amendments,* ed. Isaac Franklin Patterson (Cleveland: Arthur H. Clark, 1912), 90.

did not hide the fact that the reference to Almighty God would have been universally understood to be the Abraham-ic divinity of the Hebrew Old Testament. This definer privileged nothing less than Judaism, Islam, and Christianity, but given the demographics of Ohio's early settlement, the state's founders saw themselves as legally favoring the religion of the civilizational order, Christianity. This did not establish a religious police state. The Constitution stated that no man could "be compelled to attend, erect or support any place of worship, or to maintain any ministry, against his consent." It also announced "that no preference shall ever be given, by law, to any religious society or mode of worship, and no religious test shall be required as a qualification to any office of trust or profit." This religious test, however, should be viewed in light of the language used to describe which god Ohioans had a fundamental right to worship. Religious freedom, it was clear, was not endless even on the relatively untamed frontier of the American republic. Nor was it, as Jefferson believed, adiaphora to healthy government and societal well-being. Ohio's constitutional convention state government followed up their declaration of conditional religious freedom with a telling "But" that rejected Jeffersonian indifference to religion's presence in the civil order. "But religion, morality and knowledge being essentially necessary to good government and the happiness of mankind, schools and the means of instruction shall forever be encouraged by legislative provision not inconsistent with the rights of conscience."

The legal binding of religion, morality and state-supported education echoed the language of the Northwest ordinance, but departed from the more open-ended language of merely protecting religion in favor of the more specific identification with the monotheistic God of the Abrahamic religions. Although Ohio sat at the northwestern edge of the Union's frontier settlement, the people of the new state maintained the stolid Protestant piety and socialization of New England. The state also included a sizable number of former Virginians. Neither group allowed Ohio to become lawless, and in one community even moderate intemperance was enough to warrant the removal of an otherwise capable schoolmaster.[15] The protection of liberty of religious conscience in Ohio did not, as Michael S. Ariens noted, "give persons license to behave as they desired." Two years after Ohio joined the Union, the Ohio legislature "banned work and play on Sunday, as well as actions that could 'interrupt, molest, or disturb, any religious society or member thereof, when meeting or met together for the purpose of worship.'"[16] The same law made it illegal for anyone over the age of fourteen to profane the respective persons of the Christian Trinity. Blasphemy remained criminal for over three decades after Ohio achieved statehood.

Early National religious laws in the Midwest exemplified the broad geographic development of political Christianization in the early nineteenth century. The process by which Protestants and state legislatures reconciled themselves to the disestablishmentarian order while working cooperatively toward moral and social reform was by no means inevitable in newer states like Ohio, and it certainly was not in locales like Virginia either. Late colonial and Early Republic Virginians, perhaps more than any other Americans, embraced the ideas of the Enlightenment. The influence of Jefferson, however, was never as total as the

---

15. David McCullough, *The Pioneers: The Heroic Story of the Settlers who Brought the American Ideal West* (New York: Simon & Schuster, 2019), 147–48.

16. Michael S. Ariens, "Church and State in Ohio, 1785–1833" in *Disestablishment and Religious Dissent*, 258.

third president or his partisans presumed. William Meade (1789–1862), an Episcopal Bishop in Virginia from 1829 to 1862, complained that "during his childhood…infidelity was then rife."[17] The state's most prestigious institution of higher learning at the beginning of the nineteenth century was a "hot-bed of French politics and religion." In the years before the War of 1812, wrote the bishop, "in every educated young man whom I met, I expected to find a sceptic, if not an avowed unbeliever." Meade and other evangelicals exercised a profoundly conservative influence on Virginia's society. They embraced American legislative presumptions precisely because they believed that a free church working in tandem with a free state would restore a more authentically Christian society in the Commonwealth.

Adhering to the legacy of the American Revolution, Virginia evangelicals believed, had purged Virginia of the aberration of Enlightenment sympathies in an otherwise historically Christian society. Charles F. Irons states that Episcopalians and Presbyterians made conscientious efforts to "get right with the revolution."[18] John Holt Rice (1777–1831), an influential Presbyterian minister and magazine editor, told the Virginia House of Delegates that the principles of the Presbyterian Church in the American republic were "decidedly republican."[19] Meade also worked to make Episcopalians more palatable to a republican and democratic society. He explained that far from being beneficiaries of

17. John Johns, *A Memoir of the Life of the Right Rev. William Meade, D.D., Bishop of the Protestant Episcopal Church in the Diocese of Virginia* (Baltimore: Innes, 1967), 178.

18. Charles F. Irons, *The Origins of Proslavery Christianity: White and Black Evangelicals in Colonial and Antebellum Virginia* (Chapel Hill: University of North Carolina Press, 2008), 112.

19. Irons, *The Origins of Proslavery Christianity*, 101.

colonial British rule, Virginia's Anglican churches had been criminally mismanaged. The American Revolution and the advent of representative government in the state had made the Episcopal Church more vibrant and had made Episcopalians more truly pious, which in turn made the Commonwealth more virtuous, morally upright, and able to enact reform through truly religious influence on the republican legislative process.[20]

Evangelicals hoped to influence the legislative process through democratic means, but they stopped short of affirming the principle of *Vox populi, vox Dei* or the right of democratic electoral majorities to govern on all aspects of civil life. Evangelicals in particular broke with democracy on the question of the state's ability to legislate regarding the Christian Sabbath. Robert Hamilton Bishop (1777–1855), Presbyterian divine and president of Ohio's Miami University, "acknowledged that public opinion even in Christian lands will support the sentiment of the profane man and the infidel in this case, rather than the sentiment of the man of piety and devotion."[21] Public opinion, however correct, or however accurately ascertained, "is only the aggregate opinion of the multitude which composes the community."[22]

Public opinion willingly acceded to and even spurred on religious legislation well before the revivals of the early nineteenth century instigated popular religion in the Second Great Awakening. Even at the beginning of the Amer-

---

20. William Meade, *A Brief Review of the Episcopal Church in Virginia: From Its First Establishment to the Present Time* (Richmond: William McFarland, 1845), 5–7.

21. Robert Hamilton Bishop, "The Man That Gathered Sticks on the Sabbath," *The National Preacher* 9 (Sept 1834), 49.

22. Bishop, "The Man That Gathered Sticks on the Sabbath," 49-50.

ican republic's constitutional life the states reemphasized religion's place in their respective legal, political, and social orders.

Vermont entered the Union in 1791 as a former semi-independent republic. Although it had never had a state church, Vermont quickly wrote key provisions of institutional and public Christianity into its fundamental law. Vermont did not simply codify the observance of the Sabbath; the state *forced* its observance, barely a decade after Virginia removed institutional Christianity from public life. The 1797 "act to enforce the due observance of the Sabbath" declared that "some portion of time ought to be set apart for relaxation from worldly labors and employments, and devoted to the social worship of Almighty God, and the attainment of religious and moral instruction."[23] Sabbath observance, stated the Vermont legislature, was "in the highest degree, promotive of the peace, happiness and prosperity of the people."[24] They mandated that "the first day of the week shall be kept and observed, by the good people of this State, as a Sabbath, holy day, or day of rest from secular labors and employments." On Sundays citizens of Vermont could not "exercise any secular labor, business, or employment, except such as necessity and acts of charity shall require."

Every New England state passed a similar law, as did most Mid-Atlantic states. In 1821 Connecticut implemented even stronger language to its constitution regarding the Sabbath. New York state passed a law prohibiting Sunday activity even as the state democratized politically. The New York legislature outlawed Sunday travel, servile labour, and

---

23. Harmon Kingsbury, *The Sabbath: A Brief History of Laws, Petitions, Remonstrances and Reports, with Facts and Arguments, Relating to the Christian Sabbath* (New York: Robert Carter, 1840), 14–15.

24. Kingsbury, *The Sabbath*, 15.

working in 1813.[25] The same law forbade "unlawful exercises and past times" on Sundays. In 1834, Maine passed a law prohibiting "travel, ordinary labor, and business" on Sundays.[26] Michigan announced that "in every community, some portion of time ought to be set apart for relaxation from worldly care and employments, and devoted to the social worship of Almighty God."[27] Sabbath legislation was therefore a tool that the state's citizenry used to attain "religious and moral instruction, which are in the highest degree promotive of the peace, happiness, and prosperity of a people."

Federal law, Louis B. Weeks rightly notes, ignored the Sabbath as a civil and political institution in the antebellum United States.[28] Nonetheless throughout the Union's borders, Northeast, West, and South, states built the Sabbath into their civil codes and social elites held up Sabbatarian practice. Historians who presumed a sort of Jeffersonian totality in the South regarding religion rarely noted that even there states enacted religious legislation. In 1792 Virginia passed a law criminalizing "any person...found laboring at his own, or any other trade or calling," or employing his "apprentices, servants, or slaves, in labor, or other business" on the Sabbath.[29] South Carolina retained its colonial Sunday laws and proclaimed that "there is nothing more acceptable to God than the true and sincere service and worship

---

25. Kingsbury, *The Sabbath*, 16.

26. Kingsbury, *The Sabbath*, 14.

27. Kingsbury, *The Sabbath*, 22.

28. Louis B. Weeks, "The Scriptures and Sabbath Observance in the South," *Journal of Presbyterian History* 59, no. 2 (1981): 267–84.

29. Kingsbury, *The Sabbath*, 18.

of him, according to his holy will."[30] The regular and holy keeping "of the Lord's day is a principal part of the true service of God, which in many places of this province is so much profaned and neglected by disorderly persons."[31] Therefore the state charged "all and every person whatsoever," with applying "themselves to the observation of the Sabbath "by exercising themselves thereon in the duties of piety and true religion, publicly and privately." Unless Early National South Carolinians had a "reasonable or lawful excuse," the state government pronounced, its citizens on "every Lord's day shall resort to their parish church, or some other parish church, or some meeting, or assembly of religious worship." Tennessee, perhaps the most anticlerical state in the Union, passed Sabbath legislation in 1803, well before the political effects of revivalism manifested themselves. The law stated that "all and every person or persons whatsoever, shall, on the Lord's day, commonly called Sunday, carefully apply themselves to the duties of religion and piety."[32] The state penalized working on Sunday as well. The territorial government of Arkansas told its "several justices of the peace, and other civil officers of this territory, in their respective districts" to "take special notice of and bring to justice, all offenders of the laws of this territory providing for keeping holy the Sabbath day."[33]

Sabbath laws were the most common expression of religious legislation in the Early Republic, but they were not the only way in which states legislated religion. By the 1830s moral reform became a mainstay of Protestant social

---

30. Kingsbury, *The Sabbath*, 18-19.

31. Kingsbury, *The Sabbath*, 19.

32. Kingsbury, *The Sabbath*, 21.

33. Kingsbury, *The Sabbath*, 20.

activity. Changing laws was a priority for most Protestant legal reformers. Temperance and potential legislation curtailing the sale and disruption of alcohol went hand in hand with the anti-slavery cause for many northern ministers and social reformers, but even in the slaveholding South temperance proved to be a *cause célèbre*. Robert Jefferson Breckinridge (1800–1871), a member of the Kentucky House of Representatives in the 1820s and later Presbyterian minister, made clear that a primary reason for supporting the temperance cause was not only to save souls, but to better order the state. "The ruinous effects of intemperance upon the well-being of states as such," he argued in 1834, "in their aggregate capacity, has made so large a figure in all the discussions of the subject, and has been so clearly made out, that it deserves separate notice."[34] Christians' general duty was "not only to obey the laws, but to promote all attempts to have the laws themselves just and wise." Agitation on political questions and the shaping of legislation remained the "constant obligation" of pious Christians who necessarily, Breckinridge declared, regarded "the peace, order, comfort, improvement and security of the state, in a point of view merely temporal, there cannot be the least question." The temporal health of society, Breckinridge proposed, was as much in the purview of the church's obligations as society's spiritual well-being.

Early Republic and Early National Protestant conceptions of the sacred/secular distinction in some ways were less a binary or a distinction than values in a single divine hierarchy. Few religious leaders in the United States denied that the government was secular, but their reception of that

---

34. Robert Jefferson Breckinridge, *The Immorality of the Traffic, Manufacture, and Use, of Ardent Spirits as a Drink; and the Duty of Christians to the Temperance Cause* (Baltimore: Sands & Neilson, 1834), 6.

term cannot be understood as implying that the political order was irreligious. Put simply, Early Republic Protestants believed that the federal government, and all state governments after 1833, were secular inasmuch as they were not, nor did they officially maintain, *de jure* state church or churches. Secularism, however, did not remove religion from the political or social orders, nor did it free the secular magistrates from their duty to acknowledge divine prerogatives and rulership.

Antebellum Episcopalian articulations of the church's duty to society, and to government, included admonition for civil government to acknowledge God's rulership over earthly powers. When New Jersey formed a constitutional convention to revise the state's charter in 1844, the state's Episcopal bishop, George Washington Doane (1799–1859), reminded churchmen that they needed to pray for society's secular rulers, subsequently advising laypeople and the secular civil magistrates to honor God in their efforts: "The people of the State of New Jersey…have authorized, by their representatives, a Convention, to frame a Constitution for the government thereof."[35] Constitution-making, Doane declared, "was the greatest of secular trusts. Upon their fidelity and wisdom, the welfare of the present, and every future, generation of our people, must essentially depend." The wisdom to form a just government, and the fidelity to maintain constitutional liberties, both "from God," according to the bishop. He quoted the Bible's declaration that "Every good gift and every perfect gift is from above, and cometh down from the Father of lights" (James 1:17). Unless the Lord built New Jersey's constitutional house, the

---

35. William Croswell Doane, "Memoir" in *The Life and Writings of George Washington Doane*, ed. William Croswell Doane (New York: D. Appleton, 1861), 339.

labors of the lawmakers, "is but lost." He continued with scriptural admonitions: "Except the Lord keep the city, the watchman waketh but in vain" (Ps. 127:1). Christians had to ensure that "prayers, intercessions, and giving of thanks, be made for all men,' but, most especially, 'for kings, and for all that are in authority" (1 Tim. 2:1–2). Prayers for rulers and the necessity of declaring God's dominion over secular and civil life was "a precept acted out in every Liturgy of every land, through every age." The American religious order had not, warned Doane, escaped God's commands despite disestablishment. It was, he counseled "not less incumbent upon us to pray for those who have in charge from us to embody, for our use, the fundamental principles of government, and lay the ground-plan of the laws by which our rulers shall be ruled."

Doane saw the Episcopal church's role toward the state as being essentially a disestablished but nonetheless official chaplain toward the state. Church and state were separated, but both were authoritative in their respective roles toward each other. He noted that Episcopal rectors served as early chaplains to the federal Congress. Episcopalians were not free from obedience to the state. They had, the bishop stated, to submit themselves to government for the Lord's sake. But submission did not mean silence or a concession that the divine government of God over secular affairs had been overturned in the United States' constitutional order.[36]

Protestants in the United States saw divine oversight of the secular order as necessary for order and virtue, and they maintained test oaths and religious qualifications in order to ensure that lawmakers held the same socio-religious commitments as the respective state electorates. Democratization, and not secularism, instigated debate over state test

---

36. Doane, *Life and Writings*, 1:339-40.

oaths and religious qualifications for office and that debate became increasingly intense as states reconfigured their constitutions in the era of mass democratization. North Carolina's relatively strident office qualifications remained law into the fourth decade of the nineteenth century. In the years preceding the Tar Heel state's 1835 constitutional convention, Judge William Gaston—the state's most prominent Roman Catholic (1778–1844)—urged the North Carolina General Assembly to take up the cause of religious minorities, most notably Roman Catholics and Jews. Although they were not Christians, Jews had been grandfathered into public office by public officials treating them as honorary Protestants because they did not constitute a public threat to the Protestant order. When Jacob Henry (c.1775–1847), a Jew, was elected to the North Carolina House of Commons no objection was made. In Henry's second term another member of the house, Hugh C. Mills, objected to Henry taking his seat because North Carolina constitutionally barred from office those who denied the "truth of the Protestant religion" and the divine inspiration of the New Testament. A committee was appointed to investigate; they did not find Henry's actions inconsistent with the state's Protestant political order, and he continued to serve.[37]

The development of religious liberty in Southern states within a broadly Christian institutional paradigm never took the form of proscribing public worship of minorities. The inclusion of Jews in civil and political life occurred with minimal controversy. Removing Protestantism from

---

37. See Seth Barrett Tillman, "A Religious Test in America? The 1809 Motion to Vacate Jacob Henry's North Carolina State Legislative Seat—A Reevaluation of the Primary Sources," *North Carolina Historical Review* 98, no. 1 (January 2021): 1–41; also John V. Orth and Paul Martin Newby, *The North Carolina State Constitution* (Oxford: Oxford University Press, 2013), 8.

North Carolina's fundamental laws proved more difficult. Even those who favored opening up the state's civil order to broader enfranchisement of Roman Catholics demanded that the North Carolina General Assembly retain some statutory acknowledgement of Christianity as the religion of the state. When William Gaston pointed out that men without any meaningful religiosity regularly affirmed the state's Protestant provisions, he did so not in the hopes of removing the state's Christian identity, but in broadening it.[38] The officially Protestant state sat known religious skeptics in its halls of power; why should it not sit Roman Catholics? Why, Gaston asked, should the state continue to mandate religiosity that men in public office did not publicly practice while it curtailed the public practice of others? Roman Catholics, Gaston declared, were not publicly denying the Protestant religion. They merely asked to be able to hold office while practicing their own.

Gaston's eloquent plea appealed to politicos in North Carolina who wanted to democratize the state and overthrow the Protestant aristocracy that ruled through one of the most conservative—oligarchical to its enemies—constitutions in the Union. Whigs, the party of North Carolina's elite, blanched at any change to the state's political order, but even moderate Whigs who wanted to include Roman Catholics more fully in civil society worried about the consequences of removing the Protestant provisions. John Motley Morehead (1796–1866), a member of the North Carolina House of Commons, claimed that the provisions defended North Carolina's historic socio-religious order and was not meant to enforce religious belief in the state. Morehead rejected being labeled illiberal or a bigot: "Because we are in

---

38. J. Herman Schauinger, *William Gaston, Carolinian* (Milwaukee: Bruce, 1949), 189–95.

favor of retaining in the Constitution something like a Test for office, we are charged with bigotry and illiberality."[39] He argued that in every constitution "qualifications are made necessary for office." Expediency and prudence, not pursuit of universal principle, guided those who supported retaining the Protestant provisions. For Morehead, the question was less the pursuit of an ideal disestablishmentarian order and more based on the desire to "place some guard against inroads on the religion of our country." He defended Protestant laws along with restriction of the franchise to white men. North Carolina earlier in 1835 had "refused to a class of freemen the right of voting, because the color of their skin happened to differ from ours."[40] The General Assembly made the decision "not because it was just, but because it was expedient. But when we prefer keeping a guard upon our religious rights in the Constitution, we are called illiberal bigots, fanatics, etc." Morehead voted in the minority to keep the Protestant provisions. Gaston won the battle, but, interestingly enough, voted to keep Jews and atheists out of office. Protestant did not become secular in North Carolina's antebellum legislature. Instead the state became merely Christian.

Southern ministers and reform-minded Southern politicians saw nothing intrinsically theocratic about enacting mere Christian morality through the legislative process. Tennessee's 1796 state constitution enacted relatively strident anti-clerical provisions barring Christian ministers from sitting in either house of its state legislature, although

39. Burton Alva Konkle, *John Motley Morehead and the Development of North Carolina, 1796–1866* (Philadelphia: William J. Campbell, 1922), 160.

40. Konkle, *John Motley Morehead and the Development of North Carolina*, 161.

the same constitution banned atheists from holding office. Nonetheless, Protestant divines enjoyed considerable social prestige. They intellectually led the state and taught members of the state house, and this intellectual and social authority had significant political consequences. Ministers in Tennessee and in other southern states spoke on political issues of the day expressly to affect the legislative process, and they generally got what they wanted from the legislatures. In 1831 the Tennessee General Assembly voted to remove a law banning the sale of more than one quart of alcohol. The decision enraged Tennessee's Methodist conference, and the ministers organized temperance societies throughout the state. Ministers from other Protestant sects—Baptists and Presbyterians in particular—joined the Methodists demanding the state's legislature renew the older laws. Not only did Tennessee renew the law limiting sale of alcohol to a quart; it enacted a law prohibiting alcohol being sold within certain distances from churches.[41]

Methodists and other Southern Protestants affirmed the cooperation of church and state throughout the first half of the nineteenth century, even as some Protestant intellectuals, particularly Presbyterians, articulated the doctrine of the spirituality of the church. Southern Presbyterians, most notably James Henley Thornwell (1812–1862), argued that the church was an entirely spiritual institution that did not have scriptural warrant to speak to temporal matters. The doctrine, argued Alan Strange, "specifically addressed in

---

41. Francis Newton Thorpe, *The Federal and State Constitutions, Colonial Charters, and Other Organic Laws of the States, Territories, and Colonies Now or Heretofore Forming the United States of America*, vol. 6 (Washington, DC: Government Printing Office, 1909), 3420; Joe L. Coker, *Liquor in the Land of the Lost Cause: Southern White Evangelicals and the Prohibition Movement* (Lexington: University Press of Kentucky, 2007).

terms of 'the spirituality of the church,' though of ancient origins, did not appear in that form until the 1850s in the Old School Presbyterian Church in America (which came into being in 1837 and reunited with the New School in 1869)."[42] The doctrine, noted Strange, had to do "with the question of the province of the church and the nature and limits of its power." The doctrine of the spirituality of the church contended that, "since the church is a spiritual institution, a kingdom 'not of this world,' its concern and focus should be spiritual and not civil or political." Conservative Old School Presbyterians "rather widely held convictions about the spirituality of the church, at least as to the principle that the church is a spiritual kingdom," but the application of the principle nonetheless "engendered enormous controversy."

Although Southern ministers supported the emphasis on the spirituality of the church, it would be wrong to separate the doctrine entirely from the status of slaveholding in the Presbyterian church, and it would be inaccurate to say that the spirituality of the church kept southern churches from being as political as their northern counterparts. Alec Ryrie noted that both *de facto* pro-slavery and abolitionist Protestants built defenses of their respective positions into their conceptions of political theology.[43] The few anti-slavery Southerners writing before it became socially dangerous to do so appealed to politicized language of dominion in the same way that pro-slavery Southerners did. Southern Protestants might argue that their churches did not speak

---

42. Alan D. Strange, "The Doctrine of the Spirituality of the Church in the Theology of Charles Hodge," *Mid-America Journal of Theology* 25 (2014), 102.

43. Alec Ryrie, *The Protestants: The Faith that Made the Modern World* (New York: Penguin, 2017), 206–7.

on politics not expressly dealt with in Scripture, but their delineation of what Scripture spoke to and did not speak to was in itself a political assertion that bound respective legislatures more than it bound southern pro-slavery divines.

Slavery remained at the center of American political discourse throughout the first six decades of the nineteenth century and the disagreements over human bondage between conservative Presbyterians threatened to break up the Presbyterian Church in the United States much as it had already fractured Methodists and Baptists. James O. Farmer in his biography of James Henley Thornwell, the most noted proponent of the doctrine of the spirituality of the church, argued that the doctrine helped shield Southern Presbyterians from partisan politics. Southern ministers certainly did not indulge in democratic electoral politics, but neither did they believe that the spirituality of the church removed the church from the political order in the broad sense. Religion's influence on law did not change with disestablishment.[44]

Thornwell argued that the moral law remained in force, and the church had a right and duty to declare and even enforce the moral law in society. That the church could not dictate *how* the moral law should be worked out by the civil order or the state did not mean that the church or its ministers were indifferent when the civil order failed to work it out. The church, declared Thornwell, was to "declare and enforce revealed Truth, and, among other duties, she is to enjoin obedience to the powers that be." [45] But when the

---

44. James O. Farmer Jr., *The Metaphysical Confederacy: James Henley Thornwell and the Synthesis of Southern Values* (Macon: Mercer University Press, 1986), 168.

45. James Henley Thornwell, "Reasons for Separate Organization," in *The Collected Writings of James Henley Thornwell*, vol. 4, *Ecclesiastical*,

question as to "who and what those powers are, and how far obedience must be carried, the Church must remit the answer to the civil tribunals of the land, and to the dictates of the individual conscience." The church had "no commission from her Lord to declare what form of government any people shall adopt, how long they shall continue to maintain it, or under what circumstances they shall change it." Church members, "as citizens, may and should take an active part in all discussions of the kind, but her courts, as authoritative tribunals of Christ, must be as silent as their Master." General ecclesiastical authorities "may and must announce the eternal principles of the moral law; but their concrete application to political constitutions and political changes does not fall within the limits of her power." Even Thornwell, however, could not bind himself to his own articulation of concrete application. When South Carolina seceded in December, 1861, he famously argued in very political terms that the federal Congress did not have the right to govern on slavery in the territories.[46] Debates over slavery wedded religion and politics, and Thornwell—who so vocally championed the spirituality of the church—openly admitted the connection. "The parties" in the conflict between the slave states and free states were not "merely abolitionists and slaveholders. They are atheists, socialists, communists, red republicans, Jacobins on the one side, and friends of order and regulated freedom on the other."[47] In one word, said

ed. John B. Adger and John L. Girardeau (Richmond, VA: Presbyterian Committee on Publication, 1873), 440.

46. See James Henley Thornwell, *The State of the Country: An Article Republished from The Southern Presbyterian Review* (Columbia, SC: Southern Guardian Steam Power, 1861).

47. James Henley Thornwell, "The Christian Doctrine of Slavery" in *Collected Writings*, 4:405.

Thornwell, "the world is the battleground—Christianity and Atheism the combatants; and the progress of humanity at stake."

The conflict over slavery revealed the most enduring, and in many ways disturbing, evidence of religion's enduring place in the political order and the ways in which state legislatures sought to shape political religion. In the aftermath of Gabriel's Rebellion near Richmond, Virginia, in 1800, the General Assembly of that state passed rigid laws on who and who could not receive certain types of religious instruction and who and who could not assemble for public worship. Laws passed to curtail the slaves learning the catechism ostensibly were political and not religious, but they nonetheless infringed on the duties and rights of religious ministers and church officers. Southern states decided there would definitively be a public religion mandated by the states, and they decided who participated in that same public religion. Northern states spelled out their antislavery laws in explicitly religious terms. William H. Seward (1801–1872) and others argued that positive law in the United States had to conform to a divine higher law to be truly valid. Seward was not alone in believing God had a place in northern antislavery law. Massachusetts, New York, and other states passed resolutions explicitly subordinating their state legislation to a divine higher law. Midwestern Baptists and Congregationalists appealed to higher law language, as well as New Englanders and New Yorkers. Northern legislators across the free states politicized Protestant expressions of divine sovereignty in the defense of the antislavery cause as much as southern lawmakers used Protestant theology to defend slavery; the question of Protestantism's place in state law was not *if* it existed, but *what form* it took. By 1850, anti-slavery and pro-slavery forms of institutionalized Protestantism existed in both the free states and slave states.[48]

Disestablishing churches in the Early Republic never took religion out of politics. Preexisting institutional Christianity became stronger in many states, and even those states in the South and West that endorsed Jeffersonian liberty put religion into their civil and political orders through Sabbath laws and moral reform. The overwhelmingly Protestant population of states outside the Northeast meant that state democracies built their legal and political cultures on the Protestant religion. "American national culture," as Mark Noll states in his work *The Civil War as a Theological Crisis*, "had been built in substantial part by voluntary and democratic appropriation of Scripture."[49] Noll proposes that the democratic and voluntarist nature of religion in the United States is what led to such violent disagreements over slavery and biblical interpretation. While not inaccurate, this does not take into account the institutional foundation of Christianity in the states. Noll's anarchical interpretation does not take into account the fact that appropriation of religion was not always as democratic and voluntarist as modern historians might assume, and whatever democratic and voluntarist dispositions did exist did not make the marriage of religion and law any less authoritative in the minds of nineteenth-century Americans. "The Book that made the

---

48. For studies relevant to this paragraph see Nicholas May, "Holy Rebellion: Religious Assembly Laws in Antebellum South Carolina and Virginia," *The American Journal of Legal History* 49, no. 3 (2007): 237–56; Walter Stahr, *Seward: Lincoln's Indispensable Man* (New York: Simon & Schuster, 2012), Chap. 5, Kindle; John R. McGivigan, *The War against Proslavery Religion: Abolitionism and the Northern Churches, 1830–1865* (Ithaca: Cornell University Press, 1984), 152.

49. Mark A. Noll, *The Civil War as a Theological Crisis* (Chapel Hill: University of North Carolina Press, 2006), 8.

nation," Noll writes, "was destroying the nation." In fact the contest seems to have been rooted not in Protestant anarchy but in Protestant institutionalization. Abraham Lincoln rightly noted that pro-slavery and anti-slavery Protestants read the same Bible, prayed to the same God, and invoked his aid against the other. The Civil War was less the book destroying the nation than a contest between two durable institutionalized Protestant orders: one pro-slavery, and one anti-slavery. The Union victory in the Civil War did not make Southern states' political orders any less Protestant. But it did make them free.[50]

---

50. Abraham Lincoln, "Second Inaugural Address" in *Abraham Lincoln's Speeches*, ed. L. E. Chittenden (New York: Dodd, Mead, 1896), 358–61.

CHAPTER IV

COURTS

In the cold days of January 1801, John Adams fumed at his desk in Washington City. The drafty Executive Mansion never really provided any warmth, and Adams, his wife, and their dependents in the home regularly complained about how drafty the rooms were. Adams's mood was not improved by the task before him. From the middle of summer to the beginning of November, states sent their electoral returns to the federal capital. Messengers kept arriving until the end of November bearing distinctly unwelcome news for the second president. He would not serve another term as president. What he, and the American people did not know yet was who would succeed him. Ultimately, Vice President Thomas Jefferson prevailed over Aaron Burr in an election held in the House of Representatives, but that did nothing for Adams's mood. Furious at the perfidy of his political opponents and the inconstancy of the American people, Adams nonetheless sought to use his last few weeks in office to secure some sort of political legacy. That legacy came in the form of a large number of Federalist judges appointed by Adams and confirmed by the Federalist majority in Congress. Most notably this included nominating John Marshall (1755–1835) to be the Chief Justice of the United States Supreme Court, but more local judges also shaped the Early Republic judiciary's relationship to religion in vitally important ways. Jefferson sourly complained that Federalism had retreated into the judiciary as its stronghold, and from "that battery all the works of Republicanism are to be beaten down and erased."[1] In one sense he was right: judges in every region of the new republic and across the spectrum of late eighteenth and early nineteenth century political parties upheld the place of religion—institutional and social—in American culture, politics, and society throughout the first half of the nineteenth century.

Even before the Bill of Rights' First Amendment provisions on religion went into force in 1790, courts made their presence known in the life of churches in the still young American republic. The process of disestablishment that began in Virginia in 1785 occurred in other states, but without Virginia's aggressive anti-institutional tactics. Virginia alone forbade churches to incorporate. Stuart Banner notes that "Nineteenth century American judges and lawyers often claimed that Christianity was part of the common law."[2] The oft-repeated "maxim that 'Christianity is part and parcel of the common law' (or some variant thereof) was heard so often" that later commentators referred to it "as a matter 'decided over and over again'" and one which textbook and law writers reiterated and courts affirmed. "The maxim even received an endorsement of sorts from the Supreme

---

1. Kathryn Turner, "The Midnight Judges," *University of Pennsylvania Law Review* 109, no. 4 (1961), 494.

2. Stuart Banner, "When Christianity Was Part of the Common Law," *Law and History Review* 16, no. 1 (1998), 27.

Court which in 1844 affirmed 'that the Christian religion is part of the common law of Pennsylvania.'" A British Baptist, John Howard Hinton (1791–1873), observed in 1851 that although the United States no longer sustained state churches, the courts nonetheless institutionalized Christianity. "Politically speaking," said Hinton, "the United States count themselves a Christian nation; and the courts maintain that Christianity is part and parcel of the law of the land."[3]

Judges in the United States routinely interacted with religious law from the moment the Constitution went into effect. Colonial judges, of course, served the officially Anglican or Congregationalist colonies and upheld their laws. They also bore allegiance to an Anglican monarch. The dawn of a republican regime in North America did not annihilate judges as protectors or sustainers of religion. American courts had religious identities and commitments. The legal meaning of Sabbath laws in Early Republic Massachusetts instigated a conflict between Congregationalists and Unitarians over who received the benefits of the state's establishmentarian clauses. The Unitarians won, because they managed to capture Massachusetts's supreme judicial court. In his history of American religious freedom John Noonan notes that "all public disputes in America become judicial disputes," and religious disputes were and are no different.[4] Judges regularly suppressed public criticism of

---

3. John Howard Hinton, *The Test of Experience, Or, The Voluntary Principle in the United States* (London: Albert Cockshaw, 1851), 37.

4. John T. Noonan Jr., *The Lustre of Our Country: The American Experience of Religious Freedom* (Berkeley: University of California Press, 1998), 68, 104; see also Samuel Goldman, *After Nationalism: Being American in the Age of Division* (Philadelphia: University of Pennsylvania Press, 2021), 31.

Christian doctrine and practice on the grounds of religion and keeping the public order; for nineteenth-century Americans, those two things represented a distinction without a difference. The very fact that the courts bore a Federalist stamp—even as mild a Federalism as that of John Adams at the end of his presidency—meant that the judiciary acceded to public connections between themselves and institutional Christianity.

The long-time marriage of judges and religion persisted in the United States even after disestablishment. This lingering entanglement between Christianity and the courts exasperated Marshall's political opponents, most notably Thomas Jefferson. "Interdependence of law and religion" annoyed Jefferson throughout his long political career. The third president had always been, Mark DeWolf Howe wrote, "uncomfortably aware of the closeness of the affiliation between Christianity and the common law."[5] If Jefferson hoped that through disestablishment his own maxims disconnecting law and religion would remove institutional Christianity from the courts and legal decisions rendered by federal and state judges in the American republic, he was bound to be sorely disappointed. "Jefferson's effort had little effect on the decision of cases in American courts administering common law," says DeWolf Howe.[6] Judges—both Federalists and Republicans—"found it very easy to repeat the old maxim [on the close relationship between law and Christianity] and to find reasons for discrediting the endeavor of Jefferson." Reports from courts in the Early Republic were accordingly "full of cases in which

5. Mark DeWolf Howe, *The Garden and the Wilderness: Religion and Government in American Constitutional History* (Chicago: University of Chicago Books, 1965), 27.

6. DeWolf Howe, *The Garden and the Wilderness*, 28.

decisions were affected, and sometimes controlled, by the thesis that Christianity is a part of the common law," which the United States inherited from Great Britain. This, Howe said, constituted "persuasive evidence that it was a common assumption in the first decades of the nineteenth century that state governments may properly become the supporters and friends of religion." Early Republic state governments' commitment to maintaining the connection between the courts and Christianity had profound consequences for the durability of institutional Christianity in the American legal system and, as we shall see in a later chapter, for legislatures as well.

From the moment Adams appointed Marshall, the latter put his stamp on not just the Supreme Court, but the entire federal judiciary. President Jefferson knew what Marshall's stamp looked like, and he didn't like it. Since 1789 the men had been at odds on political questions, and the fact that they were cousins gave their bad relationship a personal edge. Marshall had lampooned sympathy for the French Revolution from its beginning in 1789. France's successive republican governments, he declared, tore down every necessary cultural and social edifice for a moral society. Marshall attended church regularly and identified as a devotee of the Christian gospel, language Jefferson rejected outright. The latter believed in Jesus' teaching, but not the soteriological foundation of historic creedal Christianity. And Jefferson especially disliked religion having an institutional public voice. The reasons no doubt lay in his intellectual dislike of historic Christianity, but it also allowed him to portray his Federalist opponents as hidebound theocrats attempting to roll back American liberties.[7]

---

7. Jack L. Cross, "John Marshall on the French Revolution and on American Politics," *William and Mary Quarterly* 12, no. 4 (1955): 631–

Judges in the federal courts of the Early Republic tended to be Federalist in their political sympathies, even in states outside New England and the Mid-Atlantic. Among the most educated men of the era, judges knew that the constitutional and legal history of the United States remained deeply wedded to English common law and the *longue duree* of the Western legal tradition.

Marshall's own opinions on law, and those of judges like James Kent (1763–1847), the head of New York's early nineteenth century chancellery court, proposed that the United States' legal system lay downstream from not merely natural law, but the creation of a particularly Christian understanding of natural law. "The law of nations," he posited, "so far as it is founded on the principles of natural law, is equally binding in every age, and upon all mankind."[8] Europe's Christian nations "and their descendants on this side of the Atlantic," had through superior "attainments in arts, and science, and commerce, as well as in policy and government; and, above all, by the brighter light, the more certain truths, and the more definite sanction, which Christianity has communicated to the ethical jurisprudence of the ancients," established a Christian law of nations "peculiar" to Christian states.

Chief Justice Oliver Ellsworth (1745–1807), notes one historian of the court, "was a thoroughgoing religionist who viewed his public and private activities through the

---

49; Horace Binney, *An Eulogy on the Life and Character of John Marshall: Chief Justice of the United States* (Philadelphia: J. Crissy and G. Goodman, 1835), 69; James F. Simon, *What Kind of Nation: Thomas Jefferson, John Marshall, and the Epic Struggle to Create a United States* (New York: Simon and Schuster, 2003), 123–24.

8. James Kent, *Commentaries on American Law* (New York: O. Halsted, 1832), 1:3

lens of Calvinism."[9] Religion caused Ellsworth to act and rule in specific ways. Ellsworth served from 1796 to 1800 and oversaw a court of undeniably religious men who understood that religion was a vital part of the American republic's judicial philosophy. Ellsworth's Connecticut Congregationalism inspired a providentialist understanding of history in his public life and in his judicial philosophy. Calvinism was "the organizing philosophy of Ellsworth's life." He and his peers' judicial philosophies and rulings, noted William Casto, could not be understood if their faith was marginalized.[10] Supreme Court justices and judges in lower level courts did not view themselves as irreligious actors, nor did they separate religion from their judicial philosophy or rulings. The American judiciary of the late eighteenth century and early nineteenth century were not wedded to the twentieth-century presumptions of secular proceduralism. The courts had a religion—Christianity, and usually Protestantism—and it showed in rulings throughout the first half of the nineteenth century.[11]

The Federalist-dominated Supreme Court in 1800 included Southerners along with New Englanders and those from the Mid-Atlantic states. Justice James Iredell (1751–1799) of North Carolina did not share the establishmentarian convictions of his New England peers regarding the maintenance of state churches, but he remained convinced

---

9. Michael C. Toth, *Founding Federalist: The Life of Oliver Ellsworth* (Wilmington: ISI Books, 2014), Chap. 1, Kindle.

10. See William Casto, "Oliver Ellsworth's Calvinism: A Biographical Essay on Religion and Political Psychology in the Early Republic," *Journal of Church and State* 36 no.2, Summer 1994: 507-526.

11. See Scott Douglas Gerber, "Introduction: The Supreme Court Before John Marshall," in *Seriatim: The Supreme Court Before John Marshall*, ed. Scott Douglas Gerber (New York: NYU Press, 1998), 1–25.

that Christianity was a necessary as a defining commitment of civil servants in the United States. English-born Iredell migrated to North Carolina to take up a colonial clerk post. He studied the law and became a leading Patriot in the state during the American Revolution. After independence, his prestige was such that George Washington appointed him to the Supreme Court in 1790. To understand law, Iredell believed, a judge had to respect Christianity. His "belief and veneration of the Christian religion" meant "that he could not well brook the idea of men who hold principles confessedly inimical to the Christian religion, getting into offices and places of high trust and responsibility."[12] Religion's "sacred influence...on his own mind" qualified Iredell "for so conspicuous a discharge of public trusts, and in different grades of advancement, he was capable of setting a true estimate on that religion."[13] Christianity was for Iredell "not only as the best and surest foundation for good government, together with security for life and property, but also the safest and best foundation whereon to rest our hopes of a happy and glorious immortality beyond the grave."[14]

Maryland's Samuel Chase (1741–1811), whose ferocious Federalism later provoked Jeffersonian Republicans in the House of Representatives to successfully impeach him in a highly partisan trial (though the senate did not convict

12. Willis P. Whichard, *Justice James Iredell* (Durham: Carolina Academic Press, 2000), 26.

13. Junius Davis, Alfred Moore, and James Iredell, *Revolutionary Patriots and Associate Justices of the Supreme Court of the United States* (Raleigh: North Carolina Society of the Sons of the Revolution, 1899), 19–29.

14. Griffith J. McRee, *Life and Correspondence of James Iredell: One of the Associate Justices of the Supreme Court of the United States,* vol.2 (New York: D. Appleton, 1857), 586.

him) thought justices had a right to admonish convicts on matters of law and religion. Chase routinely drew the ire of Virginia's small but influential class of Deists and Islamophiles. It is not surprising that eccentric Virginia planter John Randolph of Roanoke (1773–1833), a notorious devotee of the French Revolution and active loather of Christianity before his stunning conversion in 1818, led Chase's prosecution in the House. Chase saw no division between religion and the law, and took the opportunity to make religious statements from the bench without hesitation. On one occasion when Chase rode circuit in 1800, he used a sentencing hearing to make soteriological pronouncements to a convict recently sentenced to death. "You have," Chase sermonized, "forfeited your life to justice."[15] He earnestly urged the accused "seriously to consider your situation" and review his past life, and "employ the very little time you are to continue in this world in endeavors to make your peace with that God whose mercy is equal to his justice." Chase assumed the convict was a Christian and addressed him as such. "Be assured, my guilty and unhappy fellow-citizen, that without serious repentance of all your sins, you cannot expect happiness in the world to come." The convict's potential repentance would "add faith and hope in the merits and mediation of Jesus Christ. These are the only terms on which pardon and forgiveness are promised to those who profess the Christian religion." Chase repeatedly entreated the condemned "to apply every moment you have left in contrition, sorrow and repentance. Your day of life is almost spent; and the night of death fast approaches. Look up to the Father of Mercies, and God of Comfort." Sounding more

---

15. United States v. John Fries, 9 F. Cas. 924 (1800), at 934, https://law. resource.org/pub/us/case/reporter/F.Cas/0009.f.cas/0009.f.cas.0924. pdf.

like a cleric than a judge, Chase exhorted the doomed that the latter still had "a great and immense work to perform, and but little time in which you must finish it." There was, warned Chase, "no repentance in the grave, for after death comes judgment; and as you die, so you must be judged." The justice told the convicted prisoner that "by repentance and faith, you are the object of God's mercy." If, however, the prisoner did not repent and did not "have faith and dependence upon the merits of the death of Christ," but died "a hardened and impenitent sinner, you will be the object of God's justice and vengeance." But, Chase, preached, even prisoners sentenced to execution could sincerely repent and believe. "God has pronounced his forgiveness; and there is no crime too great for his mercy and pardon."[16]

Jefferson actively loathed the idea that Christianity birthed the common law tradition received by the United States and blamed the Medievals for contriving a churchly origin for something he believed lay in Britain's primordial pagan Anglo-Saxon past. Judges, the third president seethed, "have usurped, in their repeated decisions, that Christianity is a part of common law."[17] The nineteenth-century United States, argues Robert Boston, "was a mild form of theocra-

---

16. For further background on Chase see James Haw, F. F. Beirne, and R. S. Jett, *Stormy Patriot: The Life of Samuel Chase* (Baltimore: Maryland Historical Society, 1980); Henry Adams, *John Randolph* (Boston: Houghton, Mifflin, 1898), 14; *Trial of Samuel Chase: An Associate Justice of the Supreme Court of the United States, Impeached by the House of Representatives for High Crimes and Misdemeanors, Before the Senate of the United States,* eds. Samuel H. Smith and Thomas Lloyd, vol. 1 (Washington D.C.: Samuel H. Smith, 1805), 1.

17. Thomas Jefferson to Major John Cartwright, Monticello, 5 June 1824 in *The Writings of Thomas Jefferson*, vol. 16, eds. Andrew A. Lipscomb and Albert Ellery Bergh (Washington, D.C.: Thomas Jefferson Memorial Association, 1904), 48.

cy."[18] Although not meaningfully a theocracy, the United States' judiciary maintained a form of Protestant institutional ascendancy through both positive action as well as inaction. When non-Christians and even non-Protestants tried to assert their rights, violence ensued, and judges rarely prosecuted cases where civil society rose up to defend socially institutionalized Protestantism. The *de facto* Protestant establishment was therefore "made possible because most Americans were Protestant and because the federal courts rarely involved themselves in church-state matters." There was, proposes Boston, "little to stop lawmakers from passing and enforcing laws that had religious veneers."

The Supreme Court did in fact protect religious veneers, and more substantively they protected religious institutions from the whims of democratic majorities in legislatures. When Jeffersonians in Virginia, led by Spencer Roane (1762–1822), moved to strengthen the Old Dominion's draconian anti-church laws that kept religious bodies from incorporating, the Supreme Court made it clear that aggressively trying to remove churches from the body politic was unconstitutional. Roane hailed from a prominent family and drank deeply of the disestablishmentarian and anti-religious rationalism that typified The College of William and Mary at in the last half of the eighteenth century. Roane and other Jeffersonians intensely disliked the social place of the Church of England in Virginia society. Even after the passage of the Virginia statute on religious liberty in 1786, Roane sought more aggressive measures to remove Anglicanism, and institutional Protestantism, from Virginia's political milieu. The enduring presence of a so-called church party, led by former governor Patrick Henry, incensed Roane. Henry,

---

18. Robert Boston, *Why the Religious Right Is Wrong About Separation of Church and State* (Amherst: Prometheus Books, 2003), 98.

a formerly moderate partisan of Jefferson, caucused with the Federalists in the late 1790s because of perceived attacks on religion from Jefferson's Republicans. Henry, a devoted and pious Anglican layman, believed that the Republican program was making Virginia less religious and therefore less virtuous. He agreed that the Church of England's particular establishment was unacceptable in a free society, but he stopped short of condoning the wholesale institutional disestablishment of churchly religion in Virgina. His own plan was for a general tax assessment for religion that established a broad Protestant establishment wherein funds could go to any denomination. The plan gained support from a broad swath of Virginia society but Jefferson and his evangelical supporters—Baptists, Methodists, and Presbyterians—killed the proposition.[19] Thomas S. Kidd notes that the essentially double-minded nature of Jefferson and evangelicals of the era on religion by pointing out that even as they killed the general assessment, they believed that the federal government could fund missionary schools on the frontier. "Even the great champion of total disestablishment believed that the government could employ religious workers to accomplish public goods" like state educational and civilizational programs.[20]

Spencer Roane exceeded even Jefferson in his zeal for disestablishment. Patrick Henry's influence worried Roane. Even more worrisome than Henry was John Marshall, whose partisans—often veterans of the Revolutionary War—re-

---

19. See "Judge Spencer Roane of Virginia: Champion of States' Rights, Foe of John Marshall," *Harvard Law Review* 66, no. 7 (1953): 1242–59; David Johnson, *Irreconcilable Founders: Spencer Roane, John Marshall, and the Nature of America's Constitutional Republic* (Baton Rouge: Louisiana State University Press, 2021), 12–13, 55–57.

20. Kidd, *Patrick Henry*, 174.

mained loyal to the legacy of Washington and Hamilton. Federalist devotees of Marshall dominated society in Richmond, and the politics of Virginia's capital mirrored the rest of the country more than it did the enthusiastic adoration of the Enlightenment among Virginia planters. Roane, therefore, used every tool at his disposal to kill off the old power bases of Federalism in Virginia. The Episcopal Church's continued ownership of land annoyed Roane because, he claimed, land was really the government's, and a church's ability to own property was a privilege to religion that the state had given churches. Roane's notion of religious institutions saw no role for religion outside that which was merely spiritual. Any institutional protection of temporal aspects of religion outside the preservation of a space for Christian worship was, he and his partisans believed, an unacceptable intrusion on the conscience rights of Americans. In this regard, Roane and more extreme Jeffersonians foreshadowed progressive and secular jurisprudence of the early twenty-first century, which treats freedom of religion as only freedom of worship. Churches should not, Roane believed, own property or anything else for that matter. Their presence in the public would, he hoped, be limited to mere soteriological proclamation.[21]

In 1815, the case of Episcopal lands in Virginia made its way to the Supreme Court in *Terrett v. Taylor*. The Court rejected Roane's proposal and issued one of its most important rulings on religion in the nineteenth century. The

---

21. See Rex Beach, "Spencer Roane and the Richmond Junto," *William and Mary Quarterly* 22, no. 1 (1942): 1–17; Timothy S. Huebner, "The Consolidation of State Judicial Power: Spencer Roane, Virginia Legal Culture, and the Southern Judicial Tradition," *Virginia Magazine of History and Biography* 102, no. 1 (1994): 47–72; Andrew T. Walker, *Liberty for All: Defending Everyone's Religious Freedom in a Pluralistic Age* (Grand Rapids: Brazos, 2021).

justices unanimously ruled that the Episcopal Church could own and dispose of property. They noted that it was a necessity of disestablishment that the Church of England—after 1789 the Protestant Episcopal Church in the United States—was no longer exclusively supported by the taxpayers. But, they argued, "although it may be true, that 'religion can be directed only by reason and conviction, not by force or violence,' and that 'all men are equally entitled to the free exercise of religion according to the dictates of conscience,'" according to the Virginia Declaration of Rights, it was nonetheless "difficult to perceive how it follows, as a consequence, that the legislature may not enact laws more effectually to enable all sects to accomplish the great objects of religion by giving them corporate rights for the management of their property, and the regulation of their temporal as well as spiritual concerns."[22] It was true, the justices wrote, that Virginia could not establish a church, but "the free exercise of religion cannot be justly deemed to be restrained by aiding with equal attention the votaries of every sect to perform their own religious duties, or by establishing funds for the support of ministers, for public charities, for the endowment of churches, or for the sepulture of the dead." The purposes of religion "could be better secured and cherished by corporate powers, cannot be doubted by any person who has attended to the difficulties which surround all voluntary associations." Therefore, ruled the court, although "the legislature might exempt the citizens from a compulsive attendance and payment of taxes in support of any particular sect," the justices did not perceive that "either public or constitutional principles required the abolition of all religious corporations." The Virginia legislature could exempt citizens from mandatory church attendance

---

22. Terret v. Taylor, 9 Cranch 43 (1815).

and "justly take away the public patronage, the exclusive cure of souls, and the compulsory taxation for the support of the church," but beyond that, argued the Court, they did not admit "the justice or authority of legislative discretion." State legislatures, therefore, could only remove exclusive principles from churches, but could not remove privileges given to churches from the state or from natural law. *Terrett v. Taylor* even posited that there was a higher law—an ostensibly divine one—that governed the United States as much as positive law did.[23]

Justice Joseph Story (1779–1845) wrote the court's unanimous decision in *Terrett v. Taylor*. Story grew up in Marblehead, Massachusetts, the son of a veteran who fought with the Sons of Liberty at the earliest battles of the American War for Independence. Story saw himself as an inheritor of the Declaration of Independence and identified with Jefferson's Democratic-Republicans. Story, however, rejected the aggressive dispositions toward religion taken by Spencer Roane and other more extreme republican ideologues. After serving in the House of Representatives, Story joined the Supreme Court in 1811. John Marshall remained an active chief justice but he regularly deputized Story to write the court's decisions in a variety of consequential cases. Story saw Christianity woven into the fabric of the American legal system. It was, he supposed, "inconceivable how any man can doubt, that Christianity is part of the Common Law of England, in the true sense of this expression, which I take to be no more than that Christianity is recognized as true, and

---

23. See also Richard Peters, ed., *Condensed Reports of Cases in the Supreme Court of the United States*, vol. 3 (Philadelphia: John Grigg, 1831), 299; J. A. C. Grant, "The Natural Law Background of Due Process," *Columbia Law Review* 31, no. 1 (1931): 56–81; Leonard W. Levy, "Terrett v. Taylor," in *Encyclopedia of the American Constitution*, ed. Leonard W. Levy (New York: Macmillan, 1986), 1877.

as the established religion of England."[24] Since the United States inherited English Common Law, religious law was a fact of life for the still young American republic. The mission of the First Amendment, as Story saw it, "was, not to countenance, much less to advance Mahometanism, or Judaism, or infidelity, by prostrating Christianity; but to exclude all rivalry among Christian sects, and to prevent any national ecclesiastical establishment."[25] The First Amendment kept ecclesiastical hierarchies from "exclusive patronage of the national government." Finally, the First Amendment "cut off the means of religious persecution, (the vice and pest of former ages,)" and it protected "the rights of conscience in matters of religion, which had been trampled upon almost from the days of the Apostles to the present age."[26]

The First Amendment provided a foundation to mitigate persecution, but Early Republic judges and officers of the law did not believe that mitigation of persecution led to political and social libertinism regarding religion. Even in Southern states, where Jefferson's disestablishmentarian rhetoric inspired frontier Baptists and Methodists to challenge the institutional commitments of Anglican grandees, enduring forms religious law were taken for granted. South Carolina's growing evangelical population supported disestablishment but stopped short of embracing revivalist spir-

---

24. Joseph Story, *Life and Letters of Joseph Story,* ed. William W. Story, vol. 1 (London: John Chapman, 1851), 430.

25. Joseph Story, *Commentaries on the Constitution of the United States: With a Preliminary Review of the Constitutional History of the Colonies and States, Before the Adoption of the Constitution,* vol. 3 (Boston: Hillard, Gray, 1833), 728.

26. See also R. Kent Newmyer, *Supreme Court Justice Joseph Story: Statesman of the Old Republic* (Chapel Hill: University of North Carolina Press, 1985), 4–20.

itualism. Even the free men's religion had to be governed. An 1810 manual for South Carolina magistrates defined blasphemy as a crime and gave a precise working definition to help officers of the court identify public blasphemy: "If any person, professing the Christian religion, within this State" wrote, printed, taught, or spoke a denial of "any one of the persons of the holy Trinity to be God," or asserted that "there are more Gods than one," or denied "the Christian religion to be true, or the holy scriptures of the Old and New Testament to be of divine authority," they were to be indicted.[27] Any person "thereof convicted in any of the courts of record of this State, by the oath of two or more credible witnesses, such person shall, for the first offence, be disabled to have or enjoy any office or employment, ecclesiastical, civil, or military." A second blasphemy conviction would result in the person being unable "to sue, prosecute, plead, or use any action or information in any court of law or equity." Persons convicted of blasphemy could not "be guardian of any child, or executor or administrator of any person, or capable of any legacy or deed of gift, or bear any office, civil, military, or ecclesiastical, or be capable of being a member of assembly, for ever within this State." Blasphemy carried a jail sentence of three years "without bail or mainprize."[28]

---

27. *The South-Carolina Justice of Peace: Containing All the Duties, Powers, and Authorities of That Office, as Regulated by the Laws Now of Force in This State, and Adapted to the Parish and County Magistrate* (New York: T. & J. Swords, 1810), 72–73.

28. See also Lacy K. Ford, *Origins of Southern Radicalism: The South Carolina Upcountry, 1800–1860* (New York: Oxford University Press, 1988), Chap. 1, Kindle; Rachel N. Klein, *Unification of a Slave State: The Rise of the Planter Class in the South Carolina Backcountry, 1760–1808* (London: University of North Carolina Press, 1990), Chap. 9, Kindle.

Judges used justices of the peace and magistrates to help prosecute blasphemy in the Early Republic. One of the most famous cases involved James Kent, the chancellor of New York, who upheld the conviction of a man named John Ruggles for blasphemy in 1811. Ruggles called Christ a bastard and Mary a whore. He was arraigned by a magistrate and a jury quickly found him guilty of blasphemy. They argued that his statements constituted behavior toward Christianity that was unacceptable in the United States. James Kent oversaw New York's chancellery court, the early nineteenth-century analog of a state supreme court. He was a conservative Federalist in the mode of Washington and Hamilton who did not see Christianity's place in politics or society as negotiable, nor did he see public criticism of Christianity as a moral or legal *adiaphora*. Americans, he argued, were "a Christian people, and the morality of the country is deeply ingrafted upon Christianity, and not upon the doctrines or worship of those imposters."[29] A year earlier a case in Maine prompted judges in Massachusetts to make a similar proclamation. Because Christianity had the "promise not only of this, but of a future life, it cannot be denied that public instruction in piety, religion, and morality, by Protestant teachers, may have a beneficial effect beyond the present state of existence."[30] Christian people, the court said, were "to be applauded" for "their benevolence as for their wisdom…in selecting a religion whose precepts and sanctions might supply the defects in civil government." Christianity was a foundational support for government

---

29. *Reports of Cases Adjudged and Determined in the Supreme Court of Judicature and Court for the Trial of Impeachments and Correction of Errors of the State of New York,* eds. Edwin Burritt Smith and Ernest Hitchcock, vol. 4 (Newark: Lawyer's Cooperative Publishing, 1833), 546.

30. Barnes v. Inhabitants of First Par. in Falmouth, 6 Mass. 401 (1810);

"necessarily limited in its power." Supporting Christianity through temporal civil penalties was limited government, the judges argued, that allowed men the right to their consciences. Nonetheless, it was right that citizens should have the state support Christianity because Christianity was "founded in truth" and its precepts could "protect our property." There were also social benefits to established Christianity. Protestant Christianity made "every man submitting to its influence, a better husband, parent, child, neighbor, citizen, and magistrate." For this reason, Protestantism was established by the people "as a fundamental and essential part of their constitution." The head of the Massachusetts Supreme Court, Theophilus Parsons (1750–1813), saw Christianity and the state as being inseparable to the point that he called the idea of state recognition of voluntarist religion "too absurd to be admitted."[31] The state-supported Congregationalist church was a public institution that served the common good, he argued, not a private voluntarist organization. Parsons and like-minded judges, Johann N. Neem notes, thought non-established churches "served no positive civic good."[32]

States outside of New England never had the enduring establishmentarian culture that the Early Republic did, but they still saw Christianity as a social institution that needed protection. In 1824 the Pennsylvania Court affirmed

31. Johann N. Neem, "The Elusive Common Good: Religion and Civil Society in Massachusetts, 1780–1833," *Journal of the Early Republic* 24, no. 3 (2004), 381.

32. Neem, "The Elusive Common Good," 382. See also Sarah Barringer Gordon, "Blasphemy and the Law of Religious Liberty in Nineteenth-Century America," *American Quarterly* 52, no. 4 (2000): 682–719; Nathan S. Rives, "'Is Not This a Paradox?' Public Morality and the Unitarian Defense of State-Supported Religion in Massachusetts, 1806–1833," *New England Quarterly* 86, no. 2 (2013): 232–65.

that the state prosecuted blasphemy because Christianity formed a primary pillar of English Common Law, and because Christian citizens retained a natural right to punish blasphemy, but they needed institutions to do so in an orderly fashion. The courts ordered the populace's religion in its political context. The courts did not necessarily depoliticize the populace's religion. A municipal court in Philadelphia convicted a man named Murray of "a most scandalous blasphemy" in 1818 after he "attempted by advertisement to call a meeting of the enemies of persecution."[33] His attempt to agitate against religion ended, in words of a contemporary journalist, "in mere vapour; the good sense of the people frowned upon it, and he was most justly sentenced." If every form of what freethinkers called persecution ended, "impiety and profanity must reach their acme with impunity, and every debating club might dedicate the club room to the worship of the Goddess of Reason, and adore the deity in the person of a naked prostitute." The people, argued the Pennsylvania justices, would not tolerate "flagitious acts, and would themselves punish; and it is for this, among other reasons, that the law interposes to prevent the disturbance of the public peace." The judges knew that was "sometimes asked with a sneer, 'Why not leave it to Almighty God to revenge his own cause?'" The Supreme Court noted that temporal courts did in fact let God defend himself: "Bold and presumptuous would be the man who would attempt to arrest the thunder of heaven from the hand of God, and direct the bolts of vengeance where to fall.". It was not from an attempt to protect God that the courts acted, "but on the dangerous temporal consequences

---

33. *Reports of Cases Adjudged in the Supreme Court of Pennsylvania: 1824,* eds. Thomas Sergeant and Abraham Small, vol. 3 (Philadelphia: Abraham Small, 1824), 404.

likely to proceed from the removal of religious and moral restraints." Blasphemy convictions were upheld on the "the ground of punishment for blasphemous and criminal publications; and without out any view to spiritual correction of the offender."

States between 1800 and 1860 oversaw blasphemy laws, and they even took notice of the inner workings of churches. American churches did not have public and private distinctions in the nineteenth century to the same degree that we do today. When a Dutch Reformed Church in Albany suspended their minister, the aggrieved cleric, Bradford, attempted to regain his salary, arguing that his vocational entitlements were tied only to his actions in church services, and could not be withheld because of his private actions of beliefs. The New York high court obliterated the idea of privatized religion in their decision rejecting his case: "The obligations imposed on the minister by the call, are not confined to the actual services he was to render to the congregation immediately under his charge."[34] Ministerial duties "extend also to his own private life, and his moral and religious conduct." The court ruled that a man of God was "faithfully to officiate, in his character of pastor for his congregation, in all the services of the church, and to fulfill the whole work of the gospel ministry." Divines were to "observe, in all the relations of private life and his own demeanor, a line of conduct consistent with his moral obligations and religious duties." The court saw itself as competent enough to demand, in the name of religion, public behavior "calculated and tending to maintain the honor of religion,

---

34. "Dutch Church of Albany v Bradford, Dec. 1826," in *Reports of Cases Argued and Determined in the Supreme Court, and in the Court for the Trial of Impeachment and Correction of Errors in the State of New York,* ed. Esek Cowen, vol. 8 (Albany: William Gould, 1829), 505.

and promote the success of the gospel." Necessary "obligations and duties partake so largely of a religious and moral character, and are so intimately connected with the relations of domestic life and the moral conduct of the pastor," that church officials had to inquire "into charges of misconduct in those respects" because church courts were entitled to rule on them. The New York high court believed it had a right to protect church courts in the pursuance of their ecclesiastical duties. In fact it was vitally important for state courts to protect church courts because it would be harmful for public perception of religion to litigate ecclesiastical cases in state courts. "To expose the infidelity and immorality of a minister of the gospel" in public trials before courts and juries in actions regarding salaries, or to "conduct an inquiry into the soundness of his faith and religious opinions before a court of justice, would tend to produce unfavorable impressions of religion on the public mind." In aggravated cases, warned the judges, "the disclosures would too often scandalize the public ministry of the gospel." State courts rightly protected religious courts because the controversies regarding the latter "so important to the well being of society," and controversy surrounding doctrine making its way into a state court "might materially impede its success in the great and interesting work to which it is devoted."[35]

The protection of religious courts and the separation of state and church courts into separate spheres of adjudication did not mean that judges did not issue religious rulings. States continued to pass blasphemy laws after the disestablishment of state churches and state courts prose-

---

35. For similar instances, see I. F. R. and M. W. Fuller. "Supreme Court of Illinois. Samuel Chase et al. v. Charles E. Cheney," *American Law Register* 19, no. 5 (1871): 295–319; Charles Z. Lincoln, *The Civil Law and the Church* (New York: Abingdon, 1916), 12.

cuted those laws. Blasphemy laws were neither quaint nor toothless, and judges regularly enforced them. Massachusetts disestablished its state Congregationalist church in 1833 but continued to prosecute blasphemy laws. In 1833 Abner Kneeland (1774–1844), a Baptist turned Universalist turned pantheist, began attacking Christianity publicly and publishing literature denouncing historical Christian doctrines. In particular he denied the divinity of Christ and the virginity of Mary, and generally engaged in rhetorically sensational attacks on Christian dogma.[36]

The Kneeland trial exposed the innate tensions between religious disestablishment and the enduring Christian institutional foundations in the American republic's courts, legislatures, and colleges. Devotees of Kneeland argued that "the entire severance of church and state is the great boast of American liberty."[37] Every other country continued the "disastrous alliance" of religion and government, "fatal to all the best interests of mankind." Whenever the church was "the stronger party, the civil power is employed in persecuting heretics and enriching the clergy." If the civil power predominated, "the clergy are converted into the mere tools of the government, and constitute a standing army, on which, tyranny relies, as much as on its bayonets, and which, liberty and reform have infinitely more cause to dread." Kneeland and his allies believed that any interaction between church and state led to either a religious theocra-

---

36. Henry Steele Commager, "The Blasphemy of Abner Kneeland," *New England Quarterly* 8, no. 1 (1935): 29–41; Abner Kneeland, *A Review of the Evidences of Christianity: in a Series of Lectures* (Boston, 1831).

37. *An Appeal to Common Sense and the Constitution, in Behalf of the Unlimited Public Discussion: Occasioned by the Late Trial of Rev. Abner Kneeland for Blasphemy* (Boston, 1834), 3.

cy or a political despotism wherein churchmen were useful stooges for tyranny. Kneeland and Americans who believed in an absolute right to say and print anything without legal repercussions were "jealous of anything that savors of an intention to revive among us, a system, from which we have gradually, and almost imperceptibly, escaped." Massachusetts's blasphemy prosecutions were "a late attempt to employ the aid of the civil arm in silencing the free discussion of Religious dogmas."[38]

Open admittance of making the statements and publishing similar sentiments did not help Kneeland's case with the public, and it guaranteed his conviction by state courts. Massachusetts's legal system prosecuted him, not for attacking churches, but for breaking Massachusetts law. S. D. Parker, the Commonwealth Attorney for Massachusetts, claimed that he was not engaging in a philosophical debate over the necessity of religion in society. The case was not "the time or place for me to discuss, and pronounce an eulogium upon the merits or evidences of religion in general, or of Christianity in particular."[39] Nonetheless, Parker declared Christianity to be "the wisest, best, and most fully evidenced of all religions the world ever knew," and "the religion of the men of the most enlarged, acute, patient, scrutinizing, and capacious intellects the world has ever seen, Philosophers, Scholars, Judges, Poets, Moralists, and Statesmen." The case remained the province of Boston's criminal courts;

---

38. See also Rodrick S. French, "Liberation from Man and God in Boston: Abner Kneeland's Free-Thought Campaign, 1830–1839," *American Quarterly* 32, no. 2 (1980): 202–21.

39. *Report of the Arguments of the Attorney of the Commonwealth, at the Trials of Abner Kneeland, for Blasphemy, in the Municipal and Supreme Courts in Boston, January and May, 1834* (Boston: Beals, Homer, 1834), 5.

Kneeland received a trial by jury in the Boston municipal court. Parker repeated an older admonition to the seated jurors that called "for reverence to the sacred scriptures, not from their merits, unbounded as they are, but from their authority in a Christian country—not from the obligations of conscience, but from the rules of law."

Parker appealed to an organic institutional Christian establishment that transcended federal and state disestablishment. Democratic law also upheld institutionalized Christianity in the Early National United States. "The business of a Juror," explained Parker, "is not to consider what is the kind or degree of toleration which he would himself be inclined to extend, but what is that which the law has granted—not what he would do if the question were left to his own discretion in the exercise of his duty—but what the Legislature has authorized or forbidden."[40] He reminded the jurors that the "general faith is the sanction of all our moral duties, and the pledge of our submission to the system which constitutes the State." If the Constitution and Laws were to be preserved, "it must be by preserving that general faith on which they are based. We have then a positive, definite Statute Law, which it is our duty to enforce. It was passed on the 3d July, 1782, and is entitled 'an Act against Blasphemy.'" Massachusetts might have disestablished its state church, but it had not disestablished public Christianity. Citizens of Boston in 1834 lived in the most educated and in many ways the most liberal city in the American republic. The numerous colleges in Boston and its hinterland brought a cosmopolitan flourish to New England's largest city. Few cities seemed more invested in the cause of human freedom. Unlike New York or Philadelphia, abolitionist

40. *Report of the Arguments of the Attorney of the Commonwealth, at the Trials of Abner Kneeland*, 5.

newspapers enjoyed a sizable readership in Boston, although even Boston could hardly be called abolitionist-friendly until the 1850s. Immigration attracted a worldly population to the city as the nineteenth century progressed. Boston of 1834 had changed considerably from the provincial capital of conservative Massachusetts Federalism of 1800, but Massachusetts's willingness to use the state to maintain the privileged position of Christianity had not ceased, nor were the courts of Massachusetts willing to accommodate a supposed "apostle of Satan" in the Commonwealth. State churches ceased in Massachusetts in 1833, but forms of established religion did not.[41]

Four years after Kneeland's conviction, the Supreme Court of Delaware prosecuted blasphemy on the grounds that it went against the preferences of the people. In 1837 the aptly named Thomas Jefferson Chandler had the Delaware court acknowledge that what they argued was plentiful legal evidence that Christianity "has been and now is the religion preferred by the people of Delaware." With independent "evidence existing on the statute book of the state," the court felt "bound to notice as judges acting under the authority of the people at all times, what is that religion which they have voluntarily preferred."[42] They knew that "not only from the oaths that are administered by our authority to witnesses and jurors," but also "from that ev-

41. See Mark Peterson, *The City-State of Boston: The Rise and Fall of an Atlantic Power, 1630–1865* (Princeton: Princeton University Press, 2019), 461–89; Leonard W. Levy, "Satan's Last Apostle in Massachusetts," *American Quarterly* 5, no. 1 (1953): 16–30.

42. Samuel H. Harrington, ed., *Reports of Cases Argued and Adjudged in the Superior Court and Court of Errors and Appeals of the State of Delaware Under the Amended Constitution*, vol. 2 (Dover: S. Kimmey, 1841), 567.

idence to which every man may resort beyond these walls, that the religion of the people of Delaware *is Christian*." The Delaware Supreme Court proposed "that the people have secured to them by their constitution and laws the full and perfect right of conscience, the right to prefer any religion they think proper." Conscience rights did not, therefore, negate the possibility of some sort of established religion. The rights of the people to their preferences in religion annexed "the corresponding and correlative right to protection in the exercise of this and all other their religious principles." There was a sound distinction, noted the court, "between a religion preferred by law, and a religion preferred by the people, without the coercion of law." There was also a difference, the judges opined, "between a legal establishment which the present constitution expressly forbids in the 1ˢᵗ article already quoted, and a religious creed freely chosen by the people for themselves." The people of Delaware had a right to "the full and perfect enjoyment" of their freely chosen religion, "without interruption or disturbance, they may claim the protection of law guaranteed to them by the constitution itself." According to the Delaware Supreme Court, government by the people and for the people meant that self-identified Christian peoples of the Union had a duty and a right to protect the religion of the people through the political process.[43]

Delaware's judges made it clear that a government by the people and for the people would also be by and for the people's religion. Court protection of the civil and social spheres meant institutional protection for the religion of the people. Historians and laypeople looking for states' declara-

---

43. See also A.H. Wintersteen, "Christianity and the Common Law," *American Law Register* 38, no. 5 (1890): 273–85; State v. Chandler, 2 Del. 553 (Del. Gen. Sess. 1837).

tions regarding Christianity's place in the American courts won't find any. But there are plenty of reasons to think that the protection of institutional religion remained a priority for the American judiciary well into the middle of the nineteenth century.

American courts' retention of positive and natural law grounded in historically Christian sensibilities was especially clear in their dealings with the Latter Day Saint movement. Courts ruled against Mormons in trials regarding the practice of polygamy, and they did so through positive law. Nonetheless courts also harbored a distinct dislike of the Latter Day Saints for other cultural and religious reasons. The Marshall Court's sensibilities on religion's place in law was unambiguous, but even justices like Stephen Field (1816–1899), who joined the court in 1863, grounded their opposition to Mormons not in positive law but in Christian rhetorical expressions of natural law. Field said as late as 1890 that Mormon appeals to religious freedom to justify polygamy were invalid because "bigamy and polygamy are crimes by the laws of all civilized and Christian countries."[44] Religious liberty had limits within a Christian civilizational order, and Field argued that probably never before in the history of this country has it been seriously contended that the "whole punitive power of the government for acts, recognized by the general consent of the Christian world in modern times as proper matters for prohibitory legislation," could not be "suspended in order that the tenets of a religious sect encouraging crime may be carried out without hindrance."[45]

---

44. Philip B. Kurland, *Religion and the Law: of Church and State and the Supreme Court* (Chicago: Aldine, 1961), 24.

45. Davis v. Beason, Sheriff, 133 U.S. 333 (1890), in Legal Information Institute, https://www.law.cornell.edu/supremecourt/text/133/333.

The social and legal treatment of Early Republic Mormons in Missouri did not occur in a vacuum. The state's supreme courts held that Christianity—and we can safely assume this definition of Christianity did not include the Latter-Day Saint movement in antebellum Missouri—had a legally institutionalized and privileged place in the Show Me State's laws. The Court made it clear in 1854 that the state's laws were crafted for and by a "people professing Christianity."[46] Christianity was so deeply imbedded in the legal and social order of the American that removing the Sabbath, for example, was a socio-political impossibility. Those who questioned the constitutionality of Missouri's Sunday laws, "seem to imagine that the constitution is to be regarded as an instrument framed for a state composed of strangers collected from all quarters of the globe," that each had a religion of their own, "bound by no previous social ties, nor sympathizing in any common reminiscences of the past."[47] Treating law this way, argued Missouri's high court, was ahistorical, "unlike ordinary laws." It was untenable, the judges argued, to construe law without "reference to the state and condition of those for whom it was intended." It was a legal impossibility to see law as merely "words" that were to be comprehended "alone" "without respect to the history of the people for whom it was made." Law in the United States, therefore, had to be measured against the people who made it and be understood in the context of their beliefs. Courts had to "regard the people" for whom the Constitution was ordained. While the judges did not want to have the interposing arm of the civil power, they declared that

46. *Reports of Cases Argued and Determined in the Supreme Court of the State of Missouri*, vol. 20 (St. Louis: George Knapp, 1855), 219.

47. *Reports of Cases Argued and Determined in the Supreme Court of the State of Missouri*, 20:216.

"Christian men" made the Constitution, and that Christianity was the religion of the Founders.[48] The "softening influences of Christianity" "tempered" law in Missouri, and that tempering gave social life in the state specific "social advantages."[49] How, asked the court, "can we reconcile the idea to our understanding, that a people professing Christianity would make a fundamental law by which they would convert Sunday into a worldly day?" Removing the Sabbath would be an "act of deadly hostility to the religion they professed, exposing it to the danger of being reduced to the condition in which it was before the Roman world was governed by Christian princes." Although Christianity might not be "persecuted by the arm of the civil power," without courts upholding Christian law, removing Sabbath laws and other legislation would allow Christianity to be "driven by the annoyances and interruptions of the world to corners and by-places, in which to find a retreat for its undisturbed exercise."

Judges in Michigan likewise worried about the place of Christianity in the 1850s and its effect on the relationship of the people to the law. The Michigan supreme court stated in their proceedings that it was a matter of deep regret "to see citizens of age, intellect and influence, and among them moral and religious teachers" forget their "duties as such citizens."[50] Shirking the duties of citizens lay downstream from losing sight of the "great value of our constituted sys-

48. *Reports of Cases Argued and Determined in the Supreme Court of the State of Missouri*, 20:217.

49. *Reports of Cases Argued and Determined in the Supreme Court of the State of Missouri*, 20:219.

50. *Reports of Cases Argued and Determined in the Supreme Court of the State of Michigan*, ed. George C. Gibbs, vol. 3 (Detroit: S. D. Elwood, 1856), 99.

tem of government and the fundamental principles of the Christian religion." The judges wedded the affection for the Constitution and reverence for Christianity together. Those who cared for neither, they lamented, cared little for constitutional rule of law.

Court-protected Christianity did not cease with the American Civil War in 1861, but it did change. After the Civil War Darwinist theory and that of Herbert Spencer (1820–1903) became more common even in Protestant universities, changing the way in which Protestantism related to the courts. Jackson Lears rightly reminds us that "as early as the 1880s, older Christian ideas had ceded significant ground to scientific racism."[51] The Protestant judicial establishment remained after the Civil War, but with substantially different theological commitments. For nearly a hundred years some protection of Christianity in the courts lingered, but by the 1960s Darwinism and secularism changed the American judiciary's relationship to institutional public Christianity. Historians wrongly assumed, however, that secularist commitments of the courts lasted for generations. They didn't, and the evangelical legal response to state-enforced secularism in the courts began almost immediately after the landmark decision of the Supreme Court in 1962 that took prayer out of state schools. Daniel Bennett argues in his book on the Christian legal movement that for the Christian Right, which he dates to Reagan's election in 1980, "advocating for religion's place in the public square has always been a priority."[52] Bennett is right, in more ways

51. Jackson Lears, *Rebirth of a Nation: The Making of Modern America, 1877–1920* (New York: HarperCollins, 2009), 121.

52. Daniel Bennett, *Defending Faith: The Politics of the Christian Conservative Legal Movement* (Lawrence: University Press of Kansas, 2017), 7.

than he knows. Throughout the *longue durée* of American history, the courts protected the identifiable religion of the American people. Only when the courts stopped doing so did the late twentieth-century Christian legal movement begin, ostensibly not to force religion on the people, but to restore the constitutional settlement between the judiciary and religion that that began in 1789 and lasted throughout the nineteenth century.

CHAPTER V

SABBATH

In the summer of 1832, James R. Willson (1780–1853) enjoyed his fifteenth year of pastoring a Reformed Presbyterian—or Covenanter—church in Newburgh, New York. New Yorkers in Orange County and most of the region north and west of the Hudson River all the way to the Canadian borderlands along the Niagara River went to church at higher rates than any others in the rest of the Union. Not only did they go to church, but they also went to church as often as they could and in as many places as they could.[1]

In the preceding decade revival after revival swept the so-called Burned Over District.[2] Respectable religious opinion varied on how the revivals were received. Those less inclined toward the fires of religious enthusiasm called

---

1. William M. Glasgow, *History of the Reformed Presbyterian Church in America* (Baltimore: Hill & Harvey, 1888), 723–24.

2. See Judith Wellman, *Grassroots Reform in the Burned-Over District of Upstate New York: Religion, Abolitionism, and Democracy* (New York: Routledge, 2000), 27–40.

Upstate New York "infected."[3] Charles G. Finney (1792–1875), perhaps the best-known revivalist from the era, used the term "burned" or "burnt over" not as a pejorative but as a metaphor for fires of the Holy Spirit that swept across the prairies of the Early Republic.[4] Sometimes the fires burned too far and took with them the standards of orthodoxy that Protestants had used for hundreds of years, or so thought educated ministers at Princeton or Yale. Even those who supported the revivals felt they had gotten out of hand. Famed revivalist Alexander Campbell (1788–1866), for example, denounced a charismatic leader of a revivalist sect in Palmyra, New York, as a complete charlatan and "as impudent and ignorant a knave as ever wrote a book."[5] Joseph Smith Jr's (1805–1844) Church of Christ—soon to be renamed the Church of Jesus Christ of Latter Day Saints—shocked local Protestants, and soon enough would scandalize the rest of the republic.

But revivals, strange as they were, didn't take up much of Willson's mental energy. Something far more worrisome kept him up at nights. The Christian Sabbath, he feared, was "very grossly and scandalously violated in all parts of the United States."[6] He conceded that "the federal and state legislatures, and the courts of justice, do yet adjourn, on

---

3. Whitney R. Cross, *The Burned-over District : The Social and Intellectual History of Enthusiastic Religion in Western New York, 1800–1850* (Ithaca: Cornell University Press, 2015), 3

4. Charles G. Finney, *Memoirs of Rev. Charles G. Finney* (New York: Fleming H. Revell, 1876), 78.

5. Paul C. Gutjahr, *The Book of Mormon: A Biography* (Princeton: Princeton University Press, 2012), 44

6. James R. Willson, *Prince Messiah›s Claims to Dominion Over All Governments; and the Disregard of His Authority by the United States, in the Federal Constitution* (Albany: Packard, Hoffman, and White, 1832), 37.

the Lord's holy day." But how, he watchfully inquired, "do the officers of government spend their Sabbaths? Which of them reads the Holy Scriptures, 'spending the whole time in the public and private exercises of religion'?" Closing state houses and the federal Congress on Sundays was a lukewarm concession to the Almighty. "The transportation of the mails—the opening of the post-offices, and the diffusion of political and other secular intelligence" on Sundays, Willson raged, "profane the Sabbath, and corrupt the public mind." While "the friends of Christian morality" had done much "to instruct the public in relation to the claims of the Sabbath, and other institutions of heaven, upon all classes of the citizens" their efforts had not "done much more than to stay a little the progress of irreligion." More effort was needed. And the necessary step to take was to halt the government from carrying its own mail on Sunday.

The United States government had only been running mail on Sunday since 1810. That year Congress passed a series of measures to reform and expand the post offices, only one of which actually opened post offices on Sundays. Congress also added new post offices, employed new postmen, amended rates of postage, and revised criminal penalties for robbing the mail. The public at large wanted a more efficient post office that provided more services, but there wasn't a significant constituency for Sunday mail and it immediately proved to be controversial. The postmaster of Philadelphia, reputed to be a serious Protestant, publicly said he would resign if the government forced postmasters to work on Sunday. The Sunday mail question vexed religious Americans, particularly those who held to a strict and usually particularly Calvinist interpretation of what constituted necessary or allowable works for Christians to do on Sunday. When, in 1808, Presbyterians in Pennsylvania barred a local postmaster from communion and suspended his membership for following a directive from his superior to open mail on Sunday, they initiated a sectarian feud that ultimately forced the government to weigh in on the question of the rights of conscience in its relationship to the Christian Sabbath. The government appealed not to abstract natural law, but to Christian principles. Even when the United States acted against sectarian interests, then, it did so in a self-consciously Christian way. In the 1830s, that meant the government would not force mail carriers to be beholden to particular Calvinist conceptions of the Christian Sabbath. These niche Sabbatarians wanted a government that *would* not and *could* not carry its own mail on Sundays, while most American Protestants—even Sabbatarian Protestants—were satisfied with a government that *should* not.[7]

Clerical responses to the 1810 post office law varied, but the change did not garner enthusiasm from any major Protestant group. Petitions circulated in major northern cities. In Philadelphia, Protestant clergymen from a variety of sects—including decidedly non-Sabbatarian groups like Episcopalians and Lutherans—nonetheless signed what has been often perceived by later generations to be a petition demanding a return to a moral Sabbatarian past. This, however, was far from the case. Clerics from diverse denominations—Baptists, Congregationalists, Episcopalians, German Reformed, Lutherans, and Methodists—all felt comfortable signing the Philadelphia petition because it was "the work of clerical moderates intent on redressing

---

7. See Wayne E. Fuller, *Morality and the Mail in Nineteenth-Century America* (Urbana: University of Illinois Press, 2003), 1–3; Alexis McCrossen, *Holy Day, Holiday: The American Sunday* (Ithaca: Cornell University Press, 2000), 22–23; James R. Rohrer, "Sunday Mails and the Church-State Theme in Jacksonian America," *Journal of the Early Republic* 7, no. 1 (1987): 53–74.

the shortcomings of a specific piece of legislation."[8] The position of certain Presbyterians and Congregationalists in the succeeding years was neither moderate nor nuanced. Richard R. John helpfully notes that the Pittsburgh Synod of the Presbyterian church pushed a petition to Congress that was "far more radical and uncompromising" than that adopted by the irenic collection of Protestant ministers in Philadelphia. Pittsburgh Presbyterians wrote to Congress to abrogate the law allowing the distribution of Sunday mail and to dismantle any and every regulation that could possibly lead to any post office official doing anything on Sunday. This would even have included some actions pertaining to the United States military.[9]

The elders of the Pittsburgh Presbytery gained a reputation for being Sabbath sticklers among their fellow Presbyterians. An 1864 history of Presbyterian churches in the United States recorded that the Pittsburgh Synod prioritized "Sabbath-observance" among other social causes.[10] The Pittsburgh Presbyterian position (and that of Calvinist hardliners like James Willson and the more famous Lyman Beecher) would have been disruptive and innovative. Before 1810 the federal government allowed wide latitude among postmasters. Many chose to open their post offices on Sunday long before 1810. Sunday mail delivery had

---

8. Richard R. John, "Taking Sabbatarianism Seriously: The Postal System, the Sabbath, and the Transformation of American Political Culture," *Journal of the Early Republic* 10, no. 4 (1990), 523.

9. Tim Verhoeven, "The Case for Sunday Mails: Sabbath Laws and the Separation of Church and State in Jacksonian America," *Journal of Church and State* 55, no. 1 (2013): 71–91.

10. E. H. Gillett, *History of the Presbyterian Church in the United States of America,* vol. 1 (Philadelphia: Presbyterian Publishing Committee, 1864), 540.

been a reality in a significant number of locales since before the Constitution's promulgation in 1789. Richard R. John helpfully notes that "Enthusiastic as Pittsburgh's Presbyterians might have been, their position negotiated the limits of acts of necessity regarding the Christian Sabbath in a way that made other Protestants uncomfortable, even those who supported institutionalizing religion in government."[11] Although carrying the mail on Sunday "lacked a specific legislative mandate, it had long been presumed to serve the public good." Pittsburgh Presbyterians and Sabbatarian hardliners "challenged" a federal consensus and attacked a "central premise of American postal policy." The federal consensus they attacked was hardly anti-Christian or secular. A court in Massachusetts made it clear that while mail carriers who took on passengers on Sundays as part-time stage coach drivers could be prosecuted under state Sabbatarian laws, post officers carrying the mail could not, because even establishmentarian Massachusetts allowed that carrying government mail might fall under an act of necessity allowed on the Sabbath by the Christian Scriptures.[12] The strict Sabbatarian party was in fact fighting an already comfortably Sabbatarian post office regime.

Protestants who supported prohibition of commerce on Sundays were less reflexively convinced about mail. Since the 1780s the ideas of William Paley (1743–1805) had percolated in the new American republic. Paley, the Church of England archdeacon most famous for his apologetical "watchmaker analogy," had argued that the Jewish Sabbath wasn't binding on Christians. While Paley didn't argue that

---

11. John, "Taking Sabbatarianism Seriously," 524.

12. Oliver W. Holmes, "Sunday Travel and Sunday Mails: A Question Which Troubled Our Forefathers," *New York History* 20, no. 4 (1939): 413–24.

the Sabbath should be done away with entirely, he certainly believed its practice should be liberalized and modernized.[13]

Prohibitions against Sabbath commerce and travel endured well into the nineteenth century. Relatively strict Sunday customs and laws even managed to subdue, if only for one day a week, the rise of the railroad with all its raw mechanized power. Railroad schedules adhered to long-standing Sunday legislation, and not even the advent of passenger rail could overawe the Christian Sabbath. In Connecticut, mail trains were the only trains to run on Sundays until after the American Civil War; passenger trains sat idle on Sundays. The fact that mail trains ran on Sunday even in states with severe limitations on Sunday travel showed that even the scions of the Puritans in New England thought mail, and particularly government mail, sat comfortably in the category of a necessary action that was allowable on the Christian Sabbath. New England, however, remained the region most uncomfortable with Sunday mail, and it was New Englanders who led the charge to prohibit Sunday mail.[14]

In May 1828 a mass meeting of clergymen held in Boston resolved that the "violation of the Sabbath is eminently injurious to the community and tends to prostrate the interests of true religion."[15] Sabbath violation demanded "immediate attention" and concerted efforts by friends of

---

13. William Paley, *The Works of William Paley: With a Life of the Author,* vol. 2 (London: Thomas Tegg, 1825), 260.

14. Carl Russell Fish, *The Rise of the Common Man* (New York: Macmillan, 1927), 179.

15. *Proceedings in Relation to the Formation of the Auxiliary Union of the City of Boston, for Promoting the Observance of the Christian Sabbath, with the Address of the General Union to the People of the United States* (Boston: T.R. Marvin, 1828), 3.

true morality to halt the rise of anti-Sabbath activity.[16] "The great and increasing disregard of the Lord's day, throughout our land," warned the gathered ministers and laymen, "imperiously" required "every patriot and present to do all in his power by personal example, associated influence, and appeals to his fellow men, to stem the current of evil." They would leave "to civil magistrates the execution of the laws of the land on the observance of the Sabbath, as a civil institution," but they nonetheless urged Christians to "use spiritual weapons, not carnal, remembering that religious institutions must be sustained" by appeals to Scripture "and addressed to the understandings, consciences and hearts of men."[17] It was not the plan of the new Sabbath Union, as it called itself, "to enforce the laws of the several States in favour of the Sabbath. We have not the madness to think of coercion merely."[18] Men could "violate the Sabbath if they will; and our only hope is, that, by the blessing of God, we shall be able to persuade them not to do it." The Sabbath Union wanted to renovate "vigilance in families and among the ministers of Christ and the professors of his religion." They also urged Bostonians to withdraw their "capital and patronage, as fast as may be, from all participation in the violation of the Sabbath," in the hope of convincing "the understandings of our countrymen," and awakening "their consciences," and convince them to "abstain voluntarily and entirely from the violation of that day which God has given to us as the token of his love, and upon which he has suspended all our hopes for time and eternity."

---

16. *Proceedings in Relation to the Formation of the Auxiliary Union*, 4.

17. *Proceedings in Relation to the Formation of the Auxiliary Union*, 4-5.

18. *Proceedings in Relation to the Formation of the Auxiliary Union*, 11.

New Englanders' penchant for their own strict Sabbath observances may seem to imply that other regions of
the United States were veritable free-for-all carnivals of license on Sundays, but that was hardly the case. Cyril Pearl,
a Maine Congregationalist minister and teach, sneered at
the "theology" of Massachusetts Chief Justice Isaac Parker
(1768–1830), British archdeacon William Paley, and Baptist Senator Richard Mentor Johnson (1780–1850) of Kentucky, and "party newspapers."[19] Parker, an establishmentarian and Sabbatarian, nonetheless believed that opening
mail services did not impose an undue burden on the conscience of Christians. Anglican Paley disliked the Calvinist position on the Sabbath altogether. Johnson, a devout
Baptist, agreed with most of his fellow co-religionists that
excluding the mail from being delivered on Sunday represented a sectarian invasion of long-established government
practice. While Parker, Paley, and Johnson all differed from
Pearl's position on the Sabbath, none rejected a state's ability
to regulate commerce on Sunday in the abstract and none
argued for the dismantling of Sunday laws in states. Pearl's
inclusion of party newspapers—Democratic party organs
that treated anti-mail Sabbatarianism as a sectarian—and
his association of them with the three other positions on
the Sabbath showed his belief that any position on Sunday mails that differed from his own was little better than
"sophistry," "misrepresentation," and political hackery. Pearl
was not alone in his narrow understanding of the Sabbath.
Lyman Beecher (1775–1863) so wanted mail coaches and

---

19. Cyril Pearl, *The Sabbath a Divine Institution. A Reply to Arguments
on the Negative of the Question "Ought the Law Requiring the Opening
of our Post Offices and the Transportation of Our Mails on the Christian
Sabbath be Repealed?" Delivered before the Bangor Forensic Club, January
1831* (Boston: Pierce and Parker, 1831), 4, 27.

stage coaches to keep the Sabbath in still conservative and still largely Sabbatarian central New York that he took money from his wife without asking her when a salesman proposing a Sabbath-keeping stage line came to his home.[20]

For Pearl, Beecher, and their tribe, long-settled Sabbath practice on mail in the American republic was not sufficient to make a truly godly society. "So long as one steam boat, or one stage," wailed the General Union for Promoting the Observance of the Christian Sabbath that Beecher helped start, "can plead an United States' contract and legislative injunction for sabbath breaking, and thus run over State rights, the rights of conscience, and the rights of God," every citizen of the United States was party "to a flagrant violation of the divine law, and to a wide source of temporal and spiritual calamity."[21] The General Union built their argument firmly on the perceived foundation of widespread popular support for their position. They inferred from the "moral electricity" of their position that the "whole question whether this country shall or shall not have a sabbath, is not gone against us." The Union did not "believe that even a majority of our fellow citizens are willing to sacrifice this guardian of their prosperity, or that they can consent to lose the essential Institute of Christianity." The essential Christian nature of the American republic, they groaned, was at stake. Christianity could exist only "where the sabbath is reverenced, and Christianity has here introduced free government and general happiness." The heavenly spirit of Christianity "alone ever civilized and beautified any region of the globe, and it has done its wonders in soils

---

20. Stuart C. Henry, *Unvanquished Puritan: A Portrait of Lyman Beecher* (Grand Rapids: Eerdmans, 1973), 268–69.

21. *First Annual Report of the General Union for Promoting the Observance of the Christian Sabbath* (New York: J. Collord, 1829), 13.

most uncongenial." Christianity "has given the sceptre of this world's opinions to the descendant of the Goth, and of the dwellers in northern wilds, and seems to have entrusted itself for safety, and for universal propagation, to our native language." None of the Union's then twenty-four states grew "out of heathenism." Christianity, and in the case of the United States, Protestant Christianity, "founded all our glorious institutions; and with no other compulsory sway than that of light and love, as the sun reigns over the world, will pour its temporal and eternal riches upon our canals and our rivers, our plains and our mountains."

Lyman Beecher was less convinced that his fellow citizens, even the Protestant ones friendly to the idea of a Christian nation, would rise up and defend the Sabbath in a manner to his liking:

> [I] Have heard, in this land of freedom, the movements of the nation to rescue the Sabbath ascribed to priestcraft! But is it such a crime to be a minister of Christ, as creates presumptive evidence of guile, when he performs a professional duty? Who is bound to watch and sound the alarm, if not the watchmen of Zion? Or is the Sabbath such a remnant of papal superstition, that he must needs be an ambitious hypocrite, who excites his countrymen to care for and preserve it? Is religion high-treason? Are ministers disfranchised? Are we not citizens, and blessed with equal rights? And have we not families upon whose neck must come the yoke of that despotism, which vice and irreligion never fail to create? But it is not ministers alone that have awakened the solicitude which pervades the nation, and which extends and deepens, every month, and day, and hour. This is an intelligent nation, and to some extent a

religious nation; and thousands of Christian patriots appreciate the civil blessings of the Sabbath, and
perceive the certain destruction of our republican
institutions which must follow its extended and
general profanation. It is the sober, reflecting, judicious, pious part of the nation, that sees and thinks,
and feels and petitions.[22]

He poured cold water on the idea that Congress could
not legislate on the question of the Sabbath: "It is said, that
Congress have no right to legislate for religion. It is true,
and let God be praised that there is at length one nation
under heaven, one mighty nation, where church and state
are not united, and where reason and conscience are free."
But Beecher tried to convince his readers that the petitions
regarding the Sabbath were not to ask Congress to do anything for religion, "but, simply, that by legislation they will
do nothing against religion—simply that they will not, with
the people's money, hire their twenty-six thousand Mail-car-
riers, Post-masters and assistants, to unite with the wicked in
prostrating the holy Sabbath!" Beecher said he wasn't asking
for "union of church and state: but, simply, that the moral
influence of the Sabbath may not be thus bartered away
for secular gain." Sabbath breakers—in this case government mail carriers—were moral blights on society. Beecher
accused "every sabbath breaker, in addition to the ruin he
brings on himself," of impairing "the moral principle of the
community in which I live, and the obligation of an oath."
This meant that those who carried the government's mail on

22. Lyman Beecher, "The Preeminent Importance of the Christian Sabbath," in *The American National Preacher: Or, Orginal Monthly Sermons
from Living Ministers of the United States*, ed. Austin Dickinson, vols.
3–4 (New York: J.&J. Harper, 1828), 159–60.

Sundays impaired "the security of my life, and property, and character, and multiplies temptation around my family—increasing the difficulties of a virtuous education, and the chances of destruction to my children." Sunday mail carriers augmented "the power of licentiousness, and impairing that of moral principle," they prepared "to rob my children of the birth-right of liberty, and to bring upon them the yoke of a grievous bondage;—and is all this nothing to me?" Beecher went further than most Protestants when he imputed the government's sins in allowing Sunday mail carriers to every citizen. The act of the government, Beecher lamented, "is to a certain extent my own act: my suffrage, and the taxes I pay, all go in support of a national act of Sabbath day violation." Why, he groaned, "shall my rights of conscience be thus sported with, for purposes of secular convenience or gain, to that small portion of the nation, who think that they are benefited by a Sabbath mail?"

The issue at hand in the Sunday mail controversy, despite the mewling of Beecher and others, was never secularism versus Christianity on the civil order but the question of standardizing the United States Post Office's practice across an already Christian and largely Sabbatarian republic. Daniel Dreisbach helpfully notes that before the Sunday mail report was issued there was not a standard for Sunday openings or closings, and delivery of mail on Sunday was not ever intended to attack Sabbath observance broadly.[23] Nonetheless, Beecher and the opponents of Sunday mail had powerful allies in Congress. Theodore Frelinghuysen (1787–1862) and William McCreery (1786–1841) led the charge to stop Sunday mail. McCreery helped to write a

---

23. Daniel L. Dreisbach, *Religion and Politics in the Early Republic: Jasper Adams and the Church-State Debate* (Lexington: The University of Kentucky Press, 1996), 5–8

report arguing that "all Christian nations acknowledge the first day of the week, to be the Sabbath."[24] Most of the states had "by positive legislation, not only recognized this day as sacred, but…forbidden its profanation under penalties imposed by law." McCreery rightly reminded his colleagues that it "was never considered, by any of those States, as an encroachment upon the rights of conscience, or as an improper interference with the opinions of the few, to guard the sacredness of that portion of time acknowledged to be holy by the many." Sunday mail petitioners were not asking Congress "to expound the moral law" nor were they asking Congress "to meddle with theological controversies, much less to interfere with the rights of the Jew or the Sabbatarian, or to treat with the least disrespect the religious feelings of any portion of the inhabitants of the Union." They asked for the introduction "of no religious coercion into our civil institutions; no blending of religion and civil affairs." What they did ask was "that the agents of Government, employed in the Post Office Department…be permitted to enjoy the same opportunities of attending to moral and religious instruction, or intellectual improvement, on that day, which is enjoyed by the rest of their fellow citizens."

One thing McCreery noted in his minority report—and this particular point is important particularly for the purposes of this book—was that the petitioners were not asking to enact a law "establishing the first day of the week as the Christian Sabbath; they only ask the extension and application, to one department of government, of a principle which is recognized, and has, since the foundation of our government, been acknowledged in every other de-

---

24. *The Religious Monitor, and Evangelical Repository,* vol. 6 (Albany: Webster and Wood, 1829–30), 526.

partment." [25] They appealed to a "principle embraced in the petitions that had always been recognized by Congress, by adjourning on Sundays." To make this point McCreery appealed to "the first session of the first Congress," where "a law was passed establishing judicial courts, and in that law Sunday is excepted from the days on which that court may commence its sessions. All the other executive departments of government are closed on that day." Congress had never by those actions that institutionalized Christian practice— prayers, chaplains, Sunday observance, etc.—"considered itself as expounding the moral law" in a sectarian way or "introducing any religious coercion into our civil institutions, or making any innovations on the religious rights of the citizens, or settling by legislation any theological question that may exist between Jews, Sabbatarians, and other denominations." Rather, the good of society required "the strict observance of one day in seven." William Paley, and other Christian writers on moral philosophy showed that by resting men every seventh day, and by "winding up their labours and concerns once in seven days; their abstraction from the affairs of the world" improved their minds and helped them converse with God. "Orderly attendances upon the ordinances of public worship and instruction, have a direct and powerful tendency to improve the morals and temporal happiness of mankind." McCreery appealed to the idea of a natural Sabbath built into creation that didn't need sectarian sponsorship and could still be upheld by the state as a part of the moral law much in the same way the state regulated theft or adultery. By appealing to Paley, McCreery tried to make the case that his position wasn't sectarian or even meaningfully attached to an Abrahamic tradition. It

---

25. *The Christian Index and Columbian Star,* vol. 1 (Philadelphia, PA: Marten and Boden, 1829), 207.

was in nature, and therefore the government should feel as free to uphold the Sabbath as it would to prosecute murder.

Congressmen and newspaper editors and citizens who disagreed with McCreery and Sunday mail prohibitionists found a champion in Col. Richard Mentor Johnson of Kentucky. Johnson's Jeffersonian beliefs made him a perfect foil to Beecher, McCreery, and their partisans. He lived in Kentucky on a farm and devotedly attended the local Baptist church. His domestic arrangement was even less conventional. He lived openly with one of the enslaved women on his farm—Julia Chinn—and had two daughters by her in what was widely seen to be a common law marriage by his Kentucky neighbors. He built a school and educated Indian youths even as he helped shepherd Indian Removal through Congress. An extreme democrat in his views on government, he turned into an early champion of working-class voters and immigrants in major cities along the United States' eastern seaboard and in the river cities of the Midwest. Johnson, like most followers of Jefferson and Jackson—they would only start calling themselves Democrats or The Democracy after 1832—loathed establishmentarianism or sectarian intrusion into the federal government, no matter what form it took. Johnson headed the committee that told Sunday mail prohibitionists in no uncertain terms that not only would the government keep running its mail on Sundays, but also that the government would not be bullied by religious sectarians.[26]

---

26. Robert Bolt, "Vice President Richard M. Johnson of Kentucky: Hero of the Thames—or the Great Amalgamator?" *The Register of the Kentucky Historical Society* 75, no. 3 (1977): 191–203; Christina Snyder, *Great Crossings: Indians, Settlers, and Slaves in the Age of Jackson* (Oxford: Oxford University Press, 2017), 4–15; Miles Smith, "'Turning Up Their Noses at the Colonel': Eastern Aristocracy, Western Democracy, and Richard Mentor Johnson," *The Register of the Kentucky Historical*

Johnson's report conceded that there was a proper sphere for Sunday observance and that it could and should be publicly recognized, but to choose to legitimize a particular anti-Sunday-mail form of Calvinist Sabbatarianism would be an obvious breach of the establishment clause. The squabble, then, was interdenominational, not a fight between religion and secularism. "One denomination of Christians among us, justly celebrated for their piety, and certainly as good citizens as any other class, agree with the Jews in the moral obligation of the Sabbath, and observe the same day," said Johnson's committee.[27] There were, the committee noted, "many Christians among us who derive not their obligation to observe the Sabbath from the decalogue, but regard the Jewish Sabbath as abrogated." Johnson's committee did in fact do a bit of biblical interpretation when they announced that "neither their Lord nor his disciples, though often censured by their accusers for a violation of the Sabbath, ever enjoined its observance, they regard it as a subject on which every person should be fully persuaded in his own mind." Christians and Congress, even a Congress of Christians, could not force one sect's beliefs on the country. "It should," declared Johnson, "be kept in mind, that the proper object of government is, to protect all persons in the enjoyment of their religious, as well as civil rights; and not to determine for any, whether they shall esteem one day above another, or esteem all days alike holy." His committee was "aware, that a variety of sentiment exists

Society 111, no. 4 (2013): 525–61.

27. "Report on Stopping the United States Mail, and Closing the Post-offices on Sunday," January 19, 1829, 20th Cong., 2d sess., Senate Doc. 46, 19 Jan. 1829 in *American State Papers, Class VII: Post Office Dept*, ed., Walter Lowrie and Walter S. Franklin (Washington, DC: Gales and Seaton, 1834), 211.

among the good citizens of this nation, on the subject of the Sabbath day." The United States government was "designed for the protection of one, as much as for another." Congress could not interfere and pick which definition of the Sabbath would be upheld because it was not "the legitimate province of the legislature to determine what religion is true, or what is false. Our government is a civil, and not a religious, institution."

Johnson's report made the House of Representatives' position on Sunday mail clear. The Senate's report affirmed in nearly identical language to the House's that the government was a civil and not a religious institution and it would not take a side on the rightness or wrongness of the Sunday mails. Daniel Dreisbach calls the congressional reports a "classic defense of church-state separation and a powerful manifesto for a secular political order."[28] This is perhaps because of the civil libertarian language used by Baptists like Johnson and Baptist divines like the ultra-Jeffersonian John Leland who saw Sunday mail prohibition as an attempt to create a pseudo-establishmentarian Presbyterian national religion. Leland saw religion and the state as entirely separated, but that position was not even representative of most Early Republic Baptists.[29] Jonathan Maxcy (1768–1820), a leading Baptist intellectual who served as president of Brown, Union College, and finally South Carolina College, argued that Christianity formed a necessary influence on the laws of the United States.[30]

---

28. Dreisbach, *Religion and Politics in the Early Republic*, 5.

29. Smith, *John Leland*, 94.

30. Jonathan Maxcy, "An Oration Delivered at the First Congregational Meeting House, in Providence, on the Fourth of July, 1799," in *The Literary Remains of the Rev. Jonathan Maxcy, D.D.*, ed. Romeo Elton

In the sense that the government was not going to uphold a particularly sectarian expression of the Christian Sabbath or assume to itself the prerogatives of churchly actions,
Johnson's report could be termed secular, but only in that
narrow sense of the term. The Senate did not let Sunday
mail prohibitionists off so easily in their assumption of the
moral or religious high ground; in fact the Senate insisted
they already protected and privileged Christianity. Congress
and the United Staes were already Christian and already
reverenced the Sabbath. Sunday mail prohibitionists were
asking for a denominational establishment. "In all Christian countries," the senate said in its report, "it is considered
not only as a day of rest from secular employment, but one
that should be set apart for religious observances."[31] Sabbath
observance was so "intimately...interwoven with the doctrines of Christianity, that it forms an important part of the
creed of every Christian denomination. They agree in the
principle, though some of them differ as to the day." The
committee believed that "proper observance of the sabbath
is calculated to elevate the moral condition of society." They
affirmed "the recorded example of the Creator of the Universe, and enforced by scripture precepts," that "one day in
seven should be abstracted from ordinary business, and devoted to moral and religious exercises." When those duties
were "regarded in the true spirit of Christianity, a moral influence has imposed salutary restraints upon the licentious
propensities of men. It has made them better citizens, and
better men in all the relations of society, both public and
private." The institution of the Sabbath was already, they
reminded the petitioners, "respected in various operations

(New York: A. V. Blake, 1844), 381–84.

31. "Report on Stopping the United States Mail," 212.

of our Government." The senators rejected flatly the idea that they were deficient in reverencing the Sabbath: "In the halls of legislation, the courts of justice, and the executive departments, except under peculiar emergencies, business is suspended, not by legal provision, but by force of public opinion." Institutionalized custom, and not laws, nonetheless established Christian Sabbath observance in the halls of Congress. "Restraints imposed on the consciences of individuals by human laws, sanctioned by severe penalties, have always failed to produce reformation. They have generally, if not always, made men worse instead of better." The committee was as "citizens and legislators...ready to repel any attempt to bring the consciences of men under legislative control in this country. A disposition to do so can never proceed from the pure principles of Christianity."

The reaction to Congress's reports ranged from anger to celebration of various kinds. In 1830 *The American Quarterly Review* clouded Protestant opinion by publishing an article broadly perceived to posit that the Sabbath was actually a pagan celebration, an opinion that infuriated many, and the article was perceived as disrespectful to prominent Protestant clergymen, particularly William White, the presiding bishop of the Episcopal Church. *The American Quarterly*'s editors made clear they believed the petitioners were religious fanatics looking to enforce a religious test that was unconstitutional.

> These good people who prescribe to others how they shall keep the Sabbath, and are endeavouring to enforce the adoption of their tenets by the compulsion of menacing resolutions, by town meetings, by associations and combinations for the purposes of direct coercion, and by the authority of legislative enactments, would deem themselves and their dear-

est rights to be outraged beyond endurance, if any such attempts were made to direct and control their opinions and conduct. Should they be required by such means to do on Sunday what they believe ought not to be done, or what they do not choose to do; if they were to be told that the true construction of the Mosaic law is, that the Sabbath should be kept as a day of festivity and gladness, and not by gloomy lectures and religious worship, and they should be ordered by an act of congress to deport themselves accordingly; to shut up their churches and give over their preaching and praying, which darkens the joyousness of the festival, we should at once hear the loud clamour of oppression, intolerance, and an unconstitutional interference with the freedom of opinion and the rights of conscience. And so it would be. But it never occurs to them that they are exercising the same tyranny over the freedom of opinion and the rights of conscience, when they would prohibit others from doing what they as truly and conscientiously believe to be innocent and useful. Whether the constraint, in such cases, is applied to compel me to do what I disapprove, or to prevent me from doing what I think right and beneficial, the interference is equally unjust and unauthorized. On all questions of religious belief—of the obligations of religious duty, we hold ourselves to be protected, by our Constitution and institutions, from the dominion and dictation of man. If there be any thing guaranteed to us by our civil compact, this is pre-eminently so. But men, honest and sincere men, become so absorbed and infatuated with their own notions of right and wrong, that they cannot persuade themselves there can be an honest and safe

difference with them; and it does not occur to them
that they are doing the greatest wrong, by forcing
their opinions and conduct upon others.[32]

Most devotees of Sunday mail prohibition perceived
themselves as staking their position on a position of relative strength. In many ways this wasn't a sensational belief.
Sean Wilentz notes that during the 1820s businessmen and
merchants began to take the Sabbath more seriously.[33] New
School Presbyterians who prioritized inner sanctification,
moral choice, stewardship, and the necessity of moral progress joined with Methodists and some Baptists and even a
few Episcopalians to urge the American republic towards
greater societal holiness.

 Not all Protestant defenses of the Sabbath were synonymous with defenses of Sunday mail prohibition. A Methodist magazine warned that the *American Quarterly* "attempted to introduce into this country, and to spread through the
Christian community of this nation, the licentious abuse
of the Lord's day practiced by Romanists, particularly in
foreign countries, and extensively we fear even in this."[34]
The Methodists did not advocate a definitive prohibition
on Sunday mail. They had "no design to add any thing to
what we have heretofore said on the Sunday mail question
as such." All they hoped was to encourage "the proper and
religious observance of the Lord's day." The definition of

_____

32. *American Quarterly Review* 8 (Sept. & Dec. 1830): 178–79.

33. Sean Wilentz, *The Rise of American Democracy: Jefferson to Lincoln*
(New York: Norton, 2005), 271–72.

34. *The Methodist Magazine and Quarterly Review* XIII (1831), 60;
Daniel Aron, *Cincinnati: Queen City of the West* (Columbus: The Ohio
State University Press, 1992), 180.

the Lord's Day used by the prohibitionists, however, was in many ways a sectarian one, and the Sunday mail campaign was in many ways a misguided attempt to force the United States not into a rejection of secularism but into an explicit adoption of a Calvinist doctrinal expression aimed to precluding Roman Catholics from social life in the United States. That Lyman Beecher figured so prominently in the Sunday mail controversy should not be surprising, given the publication of the anti-Catholic *A Plea for the West* in 1835 and his handwringing over Roman Catholic immigration to Cincinnati and other cities along the Ohio River, as well as Lutheran immigration to Missouri and Ohio. Beecher was not an evangelical innovator trying to remake the United States in his image; he was a member of a *de facto* established religion at the height of its power who feared a potential disordering of the American republic through the introduction of Roman Catholics and non-Anglophone Protestants into the body politic of the United States. Beecher wasn't trying to make a Christian America; he was worried about an already Calvinist America falling into moral decay.

Beecher and the Sunday mail prohibitionists represented a foundational Protestant aristocracy that ruled the United States through its power in influencing legislative bodies. States had preexisting religious laws that remained on the books, but for Beecher and Princeton's Charles Hodge, these customary and even sometimes formalized establishments were insufficient to preserve the American republic from foreign immigrants. Hodge did not object to foreigners for their own sake, but he, like Beecher, objected to what he perceived as a predilection toward autocracy in Roman Catholic religiosity. He named John Hughes, Roman Catholic Archbishop of New York, as a smart man who cunningly "confounds two very different things: opposition to foreigners, as foreigners, governing the country, and opposition to

Papists, as Papists."[35] Hodge conceded that "most of these objectionable foreigners are Papists, but the opposition to them is as foreigners." It was also true, Hodge wrote, "that they are mostly Irish, but the opposition is not to them as Irish." Hodge believed the question over foreigners would "do good, and that a majority of all parties will soon unite in calling for an alteration of our naturalization laws." He accused Bishop Hughes of artfully representing "the American party as leagued to deny liberty of conscience, and to infringe on the rights of a particular class of citizens." But what right, demanded Hodge, "have the paupers of Europe to be citizens of America? We must take care of ourselves, or we shall have all our affairs under the control of the mob of foreigners who swarm our cities."

John Hughes, Roman Catholics, and some Protestants saw the Sunday mail prohibition as an attempt to set up a *de facto* national Presbyterian establishment. "Dagger" John Hughes was a native of Ireland and a champion of Irish Catholics and Catholics in general in antebellum America. He was a warm champion of religious liberty and also saw Christianity as essential to the success of American society. He did not, however, concede that Christian America would be an explicitly Calvinist Sabbatarian America. The Catholic prelate earned the goodwill of Catholics and even some Protestants for facing down Presbyterians publicly. Hughes warned that "Presbyterians in every instance, where their numbers gave hope of success, aimed, and often successfully, at the supreme civil power of the state; perfectly indifferent

---

35. A. A. Hodge, *The Life of Charles Hodge D.D. LL.D. Professor in the Theological Seminary Princeton N.J.* (New York: Charles Scribner's Sons. 1880), 348. See also Walter H. Conser Jr., *God and the Natural World: Religion and Science in Antebellum America* (Columbia: University of South Carolina Press, 1993), 106.

as to the means by which it might be acquired."[36] A desire for political power led Presbyterians to libel governments, "which they wished to overturn." They would bring about a "civil war to be followed by defeat or victory." Presbyterians "excited popular commotion," circulated libels, and inflamed "the passions of the multitude," in order to bring about some "political stroke which should place Presbyterians uppermost."[37] The attack on Roman Catholics "which they are now exciting the people to make, is not their first attempt in this country, to obtain the control and direction of the civil government." The first attempt, and most notable to Hughes and Roman Catholics, was the Sunday mail controversy. "We all remember the effort made by them, as a trial of strength, to have the Sunday mail stopped, and by an act of Congress, save the country from the national sin of transporting letters on the Sabbath-day. The experiment failed."[38] The "untiring, indomitable spirit of Presbyterian ambition returns to the onset, and, out of pure, disinterested zeal 'for civil and religious liberty' undertakes to deprive Catholics of both." Hughes predicted, rightly, that Presbyterian ambitions would be "defeated; as soon as it will be discovered that there is an ulterior object towards which the putting down of the Catholics is but the first stepping stone."[39]

Other Protestants joined Roman Catholics in the fight against Sunday mail prohibition. Lutherans and German Reformed Christians rejected entirely the attempts by Pres-

36. John Loughery, *Dagger John: Archbishop John Hughes and the Making of Irish America* (Ithaca: Cornell University Press, 2018), 89.

37. Hughes and Breckenridge, *A Discussion of the Question*, 288.

38. Hughes and Breckenridge, *A Discussion of the Question*, 289.

39. See Loughery, *Dagger John*, 89.

byterians, Congregationalists, and their evangelical allies to institutionalize the latter group's Sunday practices into federal law. At public meetings in eastern Pennsylvania German Reformed and Lutheran laypeople and ministers gathered to protest voluntarist societies like the Sunday School Union and the wish to institutionalize the particular Calvinist (and in their minds New England) Sabbath nationally. They furiously scorned what they saw as fanatical asceticism infected with overzealous and "erroneous opinions of over-heated enthusiasm."[40] Sunday mail prohibitionists were nothing better than moralistic scolds intent on foisting their benighted religion on the liberty-loving American republic. Beecher, Hodge, and the like targeted "innocent amusements." Steven M. Nolt found that hundreds of Lutherans and German Reformed protested Sunday mail prohibition in 1828 and 1829. He noted that while the German-Americans upheld the Sabbath as a day of worship and rest, they rejected Sabbatarianism *à la* Sunday mail prohibition as "incipient steps towards the attainment of an object fatal to religious freedom."[41]

Opposition to Sunday mail never meant opposition to public Christianity or even to institutionalized Christianity. The actual writer of Richard Mentor Johnson's report was the Reverend Obadiah Brown (1779–1852), a Baptist and confidante of Johnson. Brown served as a congressional chaplain and Johnson used his patronage to get Baptists placed in federal chaplaincy posts. James Kabala notes that the "failure of the campaign against Sunday mail might seem to be a notable defeat for the Protestant non-sectari-

---

40. Steven M. Nolt, *Foreigners in Their Own Land: Pennsylvania Germans in the Early Republic* (University Park: Pennsylvania State University Press, 2002), 97.

41. Nolt, *Foreigners in Their Own Land*, 98.

an consensus and a victory for a policy of secularism."[42] In many ways, "it was a long-lasting victory, as Sunday mail, although occasionally placed under further restrictions, continued to be delivered even in Whig and Republican administrations more sympathetic to the evangelical cause." Still, Kabala notes that running the mail on Sunday was aberrant and an anomaly relative to the government's commitment to not doing business on Sunday. Historians have tended to look at the Johnson's report and treat it as the entirety of the government's position in favor of secularism without considering the senate's statements as well. Yes, the house report claimed that there could never be too strongly drawn a line between church and state. The senate agreed, precisely because the state already acted Christian enough and didn't need to prove its providing and protection of Christianity by shutting down Sunday mail delivery.

42. James A. Kabala, *Church-State Relations in the Early American Republic, 1787–1846* (London: Routledge, 2016), 39.

CHAPTER VI

WORLD

In the late summer of 1851, Robert Baird, a well-known Presbyterian minister and author, addressed a meeting of the international Evangelical Alliance. The Alliance heard reports on the state of evangelical Protestantism around the world. There was some good news, and there was some bad news, but the report from Baird concerning religion in the United States told a British audience that the period between 1815 and 1851 had been the most prosperous era in America history, "especially in regards to religion."[1] The United States' secure place in the world allowed religion to flourish and the republic's moral order to solidify. "With the exception of two or three commercial crises, one or two of which were very severe, the country has enjoyed great temporal or material prosperity. There were no wars that

---

1. Robert Baird, "United States of America: Progress and Prospects of Christianity in the United States of America," in *The Religious Condition of Christendom Exhibited in a Series of Papers Prepared at the Instance of the British Organization of the Evangelical Alliance as Read at its Fifth Annual Conference Held in Freemason's Hall, London, August 20 to September 3, 1851*, ed. Edward Steane (London: James Nesbit, 1852), 592.

greatly troubled the country." Baird admitted "a few Indian wars, of no great importance; a war of a few months with one of the Barbary powers, and one with Mexico of some two years' duration." The Mexican War, Baird submitted, was a minor affair: "Although it produced some excitement, it cannot be said to have agitated the country very greatly, because the scene of it was remote. It was greatly deplored by many of our best people." The first half of the nineteenth century was "one of great spiritual as well as material progress. During that time, the increase of our churches, and of the means of religious instruction, was wonderful." Baird perceived "many instances of the outpouring of the Spirit in all parts of the country." Formation and growth of "societies for spreading the gospel at home and abroad, for increasing the staff of the ministry, for the promotion of temperance," and "for the reforming of the criminal" continued unabated. "In a word," extolled Baird, "great progress in all that concerns the moral and religious as well as material interests of the nation" could be traced in the security of the American republic in the year 1851. Four years later Philip Schaff explained to a German audience what he perceived to be the global importance for religion of the rise of the United States. For anyone, he said, "interested, as every man of intelligence and cultivation should be, in the future history of the world and the church, the name of the United States awakened either deep sympathies or as deep antipathies, joyful hopes, or desponding fears, or perhaps a strange mixture of bright anticipations and dark forebodings."[2]

That same year, Richard Rush (1780–1859) surveyed the recent happenings in Paris, where he served from 1847

2. Philip Schaff, *America: A Sketch of the Political, Social, and Religious Character of the United States, in Two Lectures* (New York: C. Scribner, 1855), 26.

to 1849 as the United States Envoy Extraordinary and Minister Plenipotentiary to the Court of the Tuileries, the official title of the American republic's minister to France.[3] Richard was the son of the famed physician Benjamin Rush, a Founding Father who regularly noted the "connection between religion and good government."[4] The younger Rush inherited his father's piety and sense of American destiny. In February 1848 Parisian radicals overthrew France's last king and replaced him with a short-lived republic, which was overthrown three years later in a coup led by the then president of the French republic, Louis Napoleon Bonaparte (1808–1873), Napoleon's nephew. Rush understood that the American republic in that era never stood apart from happenings in Europe. Mass migration to the United States rose to a breakneck pace in the aftermath of the Irish famine and continued at a rapid rate as the revolution in Paris spread across the continent. Americans took security for granted, thought Richard Rush. As the United States grew more powerful, he knew it would also have to understand its role as a Christian society among other Christian societies. "We are," wrote Rush, "part and parcel of Christendom, and it is no longer possible that a great nation like this can be wholly detached from its movements."

The contribution this chapter makes to the historiography of religion in nineteenth-century United States is a

---

3. J. H. Powell, *Richard Rush: Republican Diplomat, 1780–1859* (Philadelphia: University of Pennsylvania Press, 1942), 268–71. See also Stephen Fried, *Rush: Revolution, Madness, and Benjamin Rush, the Visionary Doctor Who Became a Founding Father* (New York: Broadway, 2018).

4. Benjamin Rush to Elias Boudinot, 9 July 1788 in *The Sacred Rights of Conscience: Selected Readings on Church-State Relations in the American Founding*, ed. Daniel L. Dreisbach and Mark David Hall (Indianapolis: Liberty Fund, 2009), 354.

narrow but substantive one: America was still perceived as Christian in what passed for world politics in the nineteenth century, and few if any substantive protestations about that perception were made by American diplomats. Scholars of American diplomacy like Andrew Preston and George C. Herring identify the beginning of substantial religious influences on American foreign policy with the moral reformist movements of the 1830s.[5] Christianity, in this reading of diplomatic history, affected the United States' interactions with the world only in the aftermath of the Second Great Awakening. It is argued that Early Republic diplomats in the Washington and Adams administrations saw their actions as part of the fulfillment of a divine plan for the world, and that they believed the United States was a Christian political instrument to realize God's will on earth. Christianity, and more particularly Protestantism, was deeply embedded in the institutional life of American diplomacy before the revivals of the early nineteenth century, and it continued to be a vital part of American diplomacy throughout that century. Walter L. Hixson's work on American diplomacy theorizes that the "emotional Second Great Awakening *reaffirmed* national destiny" (emphasis added).[6] That era, says Hixson, fused religious zealotry with patriotic identity to form a type of millennialism that dominated religious culture in the United States until the end of the nineteenth century. He

---

5. See Andrew Preston, *Sword of the Spirit, Shield of Faith: Religion in American War and Diplomacy* (New York: Alfred A. Knopf, 2012) and *American Foreign Relations: A Very Short Introduction* (New York: Oxford University Press, 2019); see also George C. Herring, *From Colony to Superpower: U.S. Foreign Relations Since 1776* (New York: Oxford University Press, 2008).

6. Walter L. Hixson, *The Myth of American Diplomacy: National Identity and U.S. Foreign Policy* (New Haven: Yale University Press, 2008), 59.

offers as proof Lyman Beecher's 1835 declaration that providence had destined America to lead the way in the moral and political emancipation of the world.[7] Beecher, the father of Harriet Beecher Stowe (1811–1892), the famed author of *Uncle Tom's Cabin*, and a Congregationalist-turned Presbyterian whose fears over the rise of Roman Catholic influence led him to found Lane Seminary in Cincinnati, certainly articulated the millennialism of the Second Great Awakening. But the inference Hixson makes is that Beecher was *reviving* a religious identify and self-conception that had been in abeyance, not instigating something new as Preston and Herring suggest. In fact, throughout the Early Republic religion played a role in diplomatic actors' conceptions of their role as agents of the American republic. "The first well delineated versions of American destiny," notes Conrad Cherry, were Protestant; Protestant ministers in the late eighteenth century regularly exclaimed that the United States' role in the world was providentially mandated, and their views were widely shared in the Early Republic diplomatic corps.[8] It didn't take a revival for America to conceive of itself as a Christian nation in the world. The American Union acted as a Protestant polity on the global stage from the beginning of its life as a constitutional republic.

The American Union's place in the international order during the Federalist Era of the 1790s seemed precarious given the Revolutionary Wars in Europe and the intransigence of Great Britain, who happened to be the United States' most important trading partner. The war between Great Britain and her allies and Revolutionary France divid-

---

7. Hixson, *The Myth of American Diplomacy*, 59-60.

8. Conrad Cherry, *God's New Israel: Religious Interpretations of American Destiny* (Chapel Hill: University of North Carolina Press, 1998), x.

ed Americans. The increasingly obvious anti-Christian commitments of the Jacobins in France convinced even most
American Republican devotees of Thomas Jefferson that the
anti-religious nature of the French Revolution destroyed ordered liberty and represented a form of despotism at least as
worrisome as monarchy. The Founders' fear of concentrated
power as a primary form of despotism, argues Andrew Preston, was a particular Protestant fear that in the United States
eventually helped the codify "a very old and very Protestant
tradition of hostility to arbitrary power" in the Union's diplomacy during the first half of the nineteenth century.[9] The
Protestant ethic that feared consolidation of political power,
Preston states, "made America suspicious about other nations that relied too heavily on concentrations of power."
In the Early Republic, this often took the form of anti-mo-
narchical tendencies and a suspicion of states perceived to
be influenced by the Roman Catholic hierarchy, but it was
not limited to that. What was undeniable, however, was the
United States' singular commitment to religious liberty in
its foreign policy. Support for religious liberty and distrust
of absolutism both confirmed Protestantism's continued influence on the Early National United States' foreign policy.

    Diplomatic agents of the United States saw the Ear-
ly American republic as playing an important role in the
Christian God's divine plan for the ordering of the human
race and even the spiritual salvation of the world. Providentialism—the belief that God specifically protected the
United States—was not a product of Second Great Awakening, the Fundamentalist-Modernist Controversy of the early
twentieth century, or the rise of the Religious Right in the
age of Reagan. Providentialism, and a particularly Protestant strain of it, says Nicholas Guyatt, "played a leading role

9. Preston, *Sword of the Spirit, Shield of Faith*, 101.

in the invention of American national identity before 1865 and…its role was neither static nor timeless."[10] American politicians, literati, clerics, soldiers, and diplomats "used the idea of God's involvement in history to influence some of the most important political debates in antebellum America." Wedded to providentialism was the United States' open and often violent populist anti-Catholicism. Amy S. Greenberg proposes that the United States in the first half of the nineteenth century was a "virulently Protestant nation."[11] Because of this, critiques of Roman Catholicism became a mainstay of travelogues and memoirs written by United States diplomats and American travelers. While few if any of the United States official diplomats in the Early Republic engaged in open bigotry of the type that typified anti-Catholic mobs in large American cities, nor did they spend their time in foreign capitals extolling the virtues of American pluralism, Americans remained suspicious of the Vatican's diplomatic apparatus and potential Roman Catholic infiltration of American society. Until the formation of the Kingdom of Italy in 1861, the Pope ruled most of central Italy as a temporal sovereign; and while the United States appointed a consul to Rome in 1797, the Protestant nature of the United States' diplomatic statecraft meant that the United States refused to send a more official representative to the Papal States for over half a century.[12]

10. Nicholas Guyatt, *Providence and the Invention of the United States, 1607–1876* (Cambridge: Cambridge University Press, 2007), 3.

11. Amy S. Greenberg, *Manifest Manhood and the Antebellum American Empire* (Cambridge: Cambridge University Press, 2005) 98.

12. See George Barany, "A Note on the Prehistory of American Diplomatic Relations with the Papal States," *Catholic Historical Review* 47, no. 4 (1962): 508–13; David J. Alvarez, "American Recognition of the Papal States: A Reconsideration," *Records of the American Catholic His-*

The relationship between the Protestant colonies of British North America and Roman Catholicism was a foundational aspect of the way in which Americans viewed their place in the world. English Protestants since the seventeenth century had believed that God offered special protection to colonists against Roman Catholic France and Spain. The foundations of American diplomacy lay in colonial fears of centralization of power in the British Empire, and the potential of Roman Catholicism—perceived as synonymous with autocracy and religious intolerance by British North Americans of the eighteenth century—to gain a diplomatic or geographic foothold in North America. Elizabeth Fenton argues that the concept of national religious pluralism that the United States defended domestically and internationally, and that eventually underpinned American liberal democracy, "developed in opposition to Anglo-American Protestant imaginings of French Catholicism."[13] The Quebec Act of 1774, which gave only limited civil rights to Roman Catholics in British Canada, terrified Protestant colonists in the thirteen colonies and served as a catalyst for Patriot action in the 1770s. Washington and Benjamin Franklin, among others, protested the act. John Jay rebuked the British government for *de facto* establishing a religion "fraught with sanguinary and impious tenets" that had deluged the island of Great Britain "in blood, and dispersed impiety, bigotry, persecution, and rebellion throughout the

---

torical Society of Philadelphia 91, no. 1/4 (1980): 49–57; Martin Hastings, "United States-Vatican Relations," *Records of the American Catholic Historical Society of Philadelphia* 69, no. 1/2 (1958): 20–55.

13. Elizabeth Fenton, "Birth of a Protestant Nation: Catholic Canadians, Religious Pluralism, and National Unity in the Early U.S. Republic," *Early American Literature* 41, no. 1 (2006), 30.

world."[14] A sizable population of Catholics in British North America would be "fit instruments in the hands of power, to reduce the ancient free Protestant colonies to the same scale of slavery with themselves."[15]

Independence and the advent of the constitutional republic did not remove the Protestant self-conception of the now independent North American Union. Providentialist Protestant commitments governed much of the diplomacy of the new United States during and after the military phase of American Revolution, and continued to do so after the states formally achieved separation from Great Britain in 1783. Even King George III (1738–1820) understood that independence had not changed the fundamental socio-religious commitments of the United States. When John Adams met the British sovereign in 1785, the latter seemed hopeful that some sort of diplomatic rapprochement would be possible. Great Britain and the United States, said the King, could be friendly if the "circumstances of language, religion, and blood"—an allusion to the United States' British Protestant origins—could have their "natural and full effect."[16]

The treaties John Adams concluded in the aftermath of the American Revolution treated Protestant European powers differently than Roman Catholic ones. His treaty

---

14. Walter Nugent, *Habits of Empire: A History of American Expansion* (New York: Alfred A. Knopf, 2008), 8–9.

15. See also Kody W. Cooper and Justin Buckley Dyer, *The Classical and Christian Origins of American Politics: Political Theology, Natural Law, and the American Founding* (Cambridge: Cambridge University Press, 2022), 151.

16. William Henry Trescott, *The Diplomatic History of the Administrations of Washington and Adams, 1789–1801* (Boston: Little, Brown, 1857), 58.

with the Netherlands included provisions regarding rights of conscience that were nowhere to be found in treaties with France or Spain. In 1828 Theodore Lyman II (1792–1849)—a writer, philanthropist, and mayor of Boston from 1834 to 1836—remarked on the diplomacy of the United States in the 1780s. Articles respecting right of conscience, he believed, were "peculiar to the treaties made by the U. States with the protestant nations of the continent of Europe."[17] Similar provisions, he noticed, were found in the American republic's treaties with the Kingdom of Prussia and Sweden.[18]

Protestant diplomatic identity in the Early Republic should not surprise us. Ministers from 1800 to 1865 enjoined Americans to understand that God signally favored the United States, and that divine favor meant that the American republic had to keep faith politically not just in its domestic actions, but in its interactions with the broader world. God kept the United States out of the Napoleonic Wars, argued Congregationalist minster Timothy Alden (1771–1839), specifically in order for the United States to protect liberty and Christianity. The "hand of heaven, in a most eminent degree," thwarted the machinations of America's enemies, "at home, and…abroad," and preserved the United States from that "awful war, which…lost its primary object" and "burned with the unhallowed lust of universal domination" as it "drenched Europe in the blood of millions,

---

17. Theodore Lyman, *The Diplomacy of the United States: Being an Account of the Foreign Relations of the Country from the First Treaty with France, in 1778, to the Present Time*, vol. 1 (Boston: Wells and Lilly, 1828), 78.

18. See also Henry P. Bowditch, "Theodore Lyman," *Proceedings of the American Academy of Arts and Sciences* 34, no. 23 (1899): 656–63.

and even tinged the Nile with the stain of her guilt."[19] Alden, like other New Englanders in particular, saw the United States as an American Israel playing a part in "Christian history."[20] The United States Navy, he extolled, had "already checked the daring presumption of the marauding sons of Europe."[21] American internal resources, rapid population growth, and enterprising spirit gave it a privileged place among the nations. "One might venture to predict, that the period is advancing, when the wooden walls of America will be able to bid defiance to the world." Religion in the United States, "the religion of Jesus, 'the noblest gift of God to man,' prevails and triumphs, in this distant land, to the joy of angels and the happiness of millions. The desert has been made to rejoice and blossom like the rose."

Adulation of the United States characterized sermons like Alden's. David Humphreys (1752–1818), the United States minister to Spain at the beginning of the nineteenth century, shared Alden's triumphalism but also warned readers against moral and religious apathy in a series of poems written while in Madrid. Humphreys, like many Connecticut gentry of the era, attended Yale in the years that preceded the American Revolution. In New Haven he befriended future Yale president Timothy Dwight IV and shared Dwight's Federalist political views in the years that followed the American Revolution.[22] Humphreys served as an *aide*

---

19. Timothy Alden, *The Glory of America: A Century Sermon, Delivered at the South Church, in Portsmouth, New Hampshire* (Portsmouth: William Treadwell, 1801), 23-24.

20. Alden, *The Glory of America*, 40.

21. Alden, *The Glory of America*, 45.

22. Frank Landon Humphreys, *The Life and Times of David Humphreys: Soldier—Statesman—Poet*, vol. 1 (New York: G.P. Putnam's

de camp to George Washington during the Revolutionary War and saw the maintenance of federal power as a primary means of preserving American liberty in the Early National Era. His nationalist vision also included commercial and economic independence for the United States. It was Humphreys who introduced merino sheep into the United States in order to create a domestic wool industry.[23]

When John Adams sent Humphreys to Spain in 1797, barely two dozen ships of various sizes composed the United States Navy. Incensed by what the French Directory—the revolutionary junta who ruled between the Terror and the rise of Napoleon—saw as the United States' perfidy by signing the Jay Treaty with Britain, France regularly attacked American shipping between 1797 and 1799 in what became known as the Quasi War. Humphreys spent six years in Portugal before his posting in Spain and saw firsthand in both Iberian kingdoms what he perceived to be an innate socio-moral weakness in Roman Catholic societies. The United States' weaknesses, thought Humphrey, were by contrast material and military. And yet this gave Humphreys caution. The new republic had too few ships and needed military strengthening, certainly—but there was no guarantee that the American republic would not also slip into the sort of moral and religious decadence that sapped Spain and Portugal of their social vitality.[24]

Sons, 1917), 29–36, 101–25.

23. Mark Sturges, "Fleecing Connecticut: David Humphreys and the Poetics of Sheep Farming," *New England Quarterly* 87, no. 3 (2014): 464–89.

24. See Gregory E. Fehlings, "America's First Limited War," *Naval War College Review* 53, no. 3 (2000): 101–43; Martha Elena Rojas, "'Insults Unpunished': Barbary Captives, American Slaves, and the Negotiation of Liberty" *Early American Studies* 1, no. 2 (2003): 159–86.

Warnings about moral apathy and decadence pervaded Humphreys' poetry. The stanza below is representative for both its anti-Catholic language and for the priority placed on moral action.

> Not thus enervate nations tempt the seas,
> By luxury lull'd in soft voluptuous ease;
> Thence sloth begets servility of soul,
> Degrades each part, contaminates the whole;
> And taints intorpid veins the thickening blood,
> Like the green mantle on a mire of mud.
> Where convents deal the poor their daily broth,
> See charity herself encourage sloth!
> Though helpless some, more lazy join the troop,
> And healthful beggars swell the shameless groupe.
> Will heav'n benignant on those nations smile,
> Where sloth and vice are less disgrace than toil?
> With opiates drunk, in indolence reclin'd,
> Unbrac'd their sinews, and debauch'd their mind,
> Can crowds, turn'd cowards, self-esteem retain,
> Or long unspoil'd of freedom's gifts remain?
> 'Tis by the lofty purpose, desperate deed,
> Of men who dare for liberty to bleed,
> By long endurance, fields with crimson stain'd,
> That independence won, must be maintain'd.

Humphreys' conception of maintaining independence was not simply a commitment to constitutional and creedal freedoms. There were specific moral hallmarks that separated the United States from supposedly weak Roman Catholic kingdoms, and those moral hallmarks had their foundation in Protestant social distinctives.[25]

---

25. David Humphreys, *The Miscellaneous Works of David Humphreys:*

The particular reading of history received by Humphreys and his fellow Yale alumnus turned diplomat, Joel Barlow (1754–1812), found enthusiastic expression in Protestant ministers in the North throughout the last half of the eighteenth century, and those ideas made their way into the writings of diplomatic actors in the direct employ of the American republic after 1789. Religious influences were not seen as merely "spiritual" in the era, and American diplomats would not have tried to separate their religious and political identities. Ezra Stiles (1727–1795), a Congregationalist minister, posited that the United States was to be the political culmination of "civil and religious" liberty. The rise and decline of empires, Stiles told the gathered legislature of the state of Connecticut, was determined by their moral state. If the United States acted morally and in accordance with the divine will, God would elevate it "high above all nations."[26] David Humphreys' understanding of the United States' place in the world mirrored Stiles'. The former conceded that there were "new doctrines" like rationalism being taught in the United States in the new nineteenth century.[27] He admitted the importance of "the proper use of human means," but declared that "our highest help and last reliance is on the GOD of BATTLES." In the Christian deity, explained Humphreys, "our forefathers, when few in numbers, and feeble in resources, trusted, and were not deceived. What can be more glorious than heroic achievements in a just cause?" The American Revolution was waged, he extoled, under the auspices of heaven: "The

---

Late Minister Plenipotentiary from the United States of America to the Court of Madrid (New York: T & J Swords, 1804), 101.

26. Cherry, *God's New Israel*, 83.

27. Humphreys, *The Miscellaneous Works of David Humphreys*, 372.

Holy One, who inhabits Eternity, has not disdained to style himself the Lord of Hosts, or to go forth to battle with the armies of his people." Americans could rightly invoke "his name," confide in "his strength," and march "under the banners of independence." Humphreys insisted that "In the day of difficulty will we resort to his Sanctuary." Returning to his theme of societal action to keep the United States righteous and in God's favor, Humphreys confessed he was "afraid we have not been grateful enough to that Almighty Protector who has caused us to dwell in tranquility, while so many nations have been grievously afflicted with the calamities of war." "A nation without religion and morals," he warned, "is always ripening fast for that state of corruption which often precedes decay, and terminates in ruin." "Under a due conviction of our relations, dependencies, and duties," the American republic should "never neglect to avail ourselves of all those means which the experience of mankind and our own reason point out as best calculated for the preservation of our inestimable civil and religious privileges!"

The single most influential diplomat of the era, John Quincy Adams (1767–1848), attended three church services on Sundays and saw public morality and religion—particularly Christianity—as vital to the maintenance of republican virtue. The French Republic's rejection of Christianity and the cavalier way in which the French Republic's diplomats treated their American counterparts enraged Adams. Still a relatively young man in 1793, he wrote a series of attacks on the French Revolution and the French Republic even as he urged the United States to stay officially neutral in the wars of Europe. Adams's writings represented the views of the Federalist administration of George Washington closely enough that the Secretary of State, Edmund Randolph (1753–1813), tapped Adams to serve as the United States resident minister to the Netherlands. He later filled diplomatic posts in Prussia, Russia, and the United Kingdom.[28]

Adams's letters, published in the Spring of 1793 under the pseudonym Marcellus, revealed his vision for an American diplomatic regime explicitly and fundamentally underpinned by Christian moral teaching and historically Protestant socio-political considerations. "The rights of nations," Adams said, "are nothing more than an extension of the rights of individuals to the great societies, into which the different portions of mankind have been combined."[29] National rights were "all mediately or immediately derived from the fundamental position which the author of Christianity has taught us as an article of religion." Adams denounced the French Revolution for replacing Christian conceptions of liberty with licentiousness and libertinism. French liberty fundamentally was nothing more than the individual's ability to do whatever he wanted so long as the action did not cause harm to fellow citizens. Adams spurned French liberty entirely in favor of historically Christian concepts: "'Whatsoever,' says the Saviour of mankind, 'you would that men should do to you, do ye even so to them.'" The United States, therefore, needed to be diplomatically cautious and "do nothing contrary to the rights of others" so that that the American Union could "continue to enjoy and to deserve the blessings of freedom. Let us do as we should choose others might do to us, and we shall deserve the favors of Heaven." The United States respected the desires of

---

28. James Traub, *John Quincy Adams: Militant Spirit* (New York: Basic, 2016), 64; Samuel Flagg Bemis, "John Quincy Adams and George Washington," *Proceedings of the Massachusetts Historical Society* 67 (1941): 365–84.

29. Worthington Chauncey Forbes, *The Writings of John Quincy Adams*, vol. 1, *1779-1796* (New York: Macmillan, 1913), 139.

other nations, even if it might not ideologically agree with them. Adams's Marcellus writings posited a Christian articulation of national self-determination, and the American republic followed Adams's scheme for half a century. When he assumed his duties in the Fall of 1794 Adams launched one of the most notable careers in American political history and put his uniquely religious stamp on the Early Republic's diplomatic establishment.[30]

The legacy of Adams and others provided a Protestant intellectual framework for American diplomacy, but the question of Christianity's relationship to the government of the United States has typically been litigated by historians and laypeople asking if the United States was an officially Christian government. The answer is more ambiguous than secularists or theocrats want with regard to American diplomacy. Among the first major treaties the United States signed that addressed the question of the religion of the state was the 1797 Treaty of Tripoli, which the United States signed with the Bey—a type of minor ruling prince—of Tripoli (which corresponds roughly with the northern parts of modern day Tripoli) to protect American shipping from Tripolitan and later Tunisian and Algerian marauders. So-called Barbary pirates—they operated in collusion with the North African princes who technically owed allegiance to the Ottoman Empire but were *de facto* independent—plagued American merchantmen throughout the late eighteenth century. Negotiators sent by President John Adams signed a treaty that, among other things stated in its

---

30. See Daniel G. Laron and Greg Russell, "The Ethics of Power in American Diplomacy: The Statecraft of John Quincy Adams," *The Review of Politics* 52, no. 1 (1990): 3–31.

eleventh article that the United States government was *not* founded in the Christian religion.[31]

On its face then, the 1797 treaty seems clear. Brooke Allen thinks it affirms the secularist thesis she puts forth in *Moral Minority*.[32] The treaty of Tripoli was, she says, a triumph of Madisonian separationism. John Adams and Timothy Pickering (1745–1829)—an establishmentarian high Federalist—she reminds the reader, both approved the treaty. Even that evidence, however, is hardly proof that the United States meaningfully rejected its Christian commitments in the treaty. In fact, Adams and Pickering wanted the treaty signed quickly, and appear to have been willing to let the provision remain if it convinced the Muslim privateers to leave American ships alone. The reality of Christianity's place in American diplomacy was nonetheless very different. John Fea posits that if the treaty was correct and the United States government was not founded on the Christian religion, "someone forgot to tell the American people."[33] Early National Americans who followed the rudimentary press coverage of the Quasi War with the Barbary states viewed the conflict as a sort of "holy war." The treaty's sentiment that the United States was not founded on the Christian religion, Fea explains, "can hardly be reconciled with the way that politicians, historians, clergy, educators, and other writers perceived the United States in the first one hundred years of its existence."

---

31. Michael Kitzen, "Money Bags or Cannon Balls: The Origins of the Tripolitan War, 1795–1801," *Journal of the Early Republic* 16, no. 4 (1996): 601–24; Frank Lambert, *The Barbary Wars: American Independence in the Atlantic World* (New York: Hill and Wang, 2005), 8.

32. Allen, *Moral Minority*, 142.

33. Fea, *Was America Founded as a Christian Nation?*, 4.

Theodore Lyman II thought the Treaty of Tripoli's statement on Christianity and the United States was an invalid superfluity, that the negotiating consul had exceeded his authority, and that that provision—like the entire treaty—was abrogated so quickly by the Muslims it never went into force. Lyman castigated the negotiator and said it would have been more "reasonable and judicious" if the United States' agent "had satisfied himself with providing freedom of worship for the consul and his family."[34] Declaring the United States a non-Christian country, Lyman complained, was unnecessary and inaccurate. There was, he declared "perhaps, not a civilized state in the world where so large a portion of the inhabitants are Christians" as in the United States. There were so few Jews, he stated, that it was nearly impossible to consider them a significant population. Lyman understood the meaning of the eleventh article of the treaty, but not its object: "A Jew, Turk or Hindoo, Atheist or the Heathen may hold any office of trust, honour or profit under the federal Constitution. But if the government of this country is not founded on the Christian religion, on what religion is it founded?" "With the same justice," he continued, "it might be said, that our civil institutions are not founded on good morals and good education, not more important, surely, than religion." In the hands of the American people, religion was "not an instrument, employed for sectarian purposes, nor is our republican form of government made an instrument for the political conversion of other people." Despite the fact that Christianity was not a political weapon in of the United States' regime, Americans were "a Christian people, and that religion, though not a political instrument, is, nevertheless, a necessary and principal element in our society." Lyman did not stipulate

---

34. Lyman, *Diplomacy of the United States*, 2:382.

whether the United States was Protestant or not, but that
seemed to matter little to Americans and to Europeans in
1797 or later in 1804 when Stephen Decatur (1779–1820)
and a contingent of Marines assaulted the bey's fortress and
forced him to a peace with the United States. Even Pope
Pius VII (r.1800–1823) celebrated the American action and
announced that "the American commander, with a small
force, in a short space of time, has done more for the cause
of Christianity than the most powerful nations of Christendom have done for ages!"[35] Charles Sumner (1811–1874),
future senator from Massachusetts, wrote in 1847 that the
United States' conflict with and final victory over the Barbary Pirates was the final chapter of a war between Muslims
and Christianity that stretched back to the medieval era.[36]

American self-conception as divinely favored over and
against the powers of the world did not need to be churchly
to be motivational. Andrew Jackson (1767–1845), a ferocious disestablishmentarian, nonetheless regularly and publicly said that God was on America's side, because America
was particularly righteous and because America was particularly free. In the War of 1812, this led Jackson to see even
other ostensibly Christian powers as the enemies of God.
Righteous indignation toward Britain littered Jackson's
letters to his officers, to government officials in Nashville
and Washington, and also to his wife Rachel. If she ever
forgot the horrors that compelled him to leave her for the
difficulties of battle, he urged her to recall British depravity.
Jackson urged Rachel to "recollect...that the god of battle

35. Joseph Wheelan, *Jefferson›s War: America›s First War on Terror
1801–1805* (New York: Carroll & Graf, 2003), 195.

36. Charles Sumner, *White Slavery in the Barbary States: A Lecture Before the Boston Mercantile Library Association, Feb. 17, 1847* (Boston:
William D. Ticknor, 1847), 34.

cries aloud for vengeance."[37] His army was "the means in [God's] hands to punish the infamous Britons for their sacrilegious deeds." Jackson affirmed this poetical and religious ideal by declaring it "the only true and noble principle on which the energies of the nation should be brought into action."[38] Britain's perceived tyranny made necessary the response of "a free people compelled to reclaim by the power of their arms the right which God has bestowed on them." Failure to fight tyranny represented a moral, poetical, and religious failure in Jackson's mind. An American, he wrote, "must feel grateful to the Ruler of the Universe for placing his condition in a country where wealth and happiness can flow in a thousand channels."[39] When the republic's citizens understood and contemplated the "almost unlimited extent of our territory—The magnitude of our rivers—The Great fertility of our soils and the mild institutions of our government," they could let their "prophetic imaginations take a range, and contemplate our importance two centuries hence!" God, according to Jackson, preserved the long-term durability of the republic. More importantly, the republic's civil institutions needed to be founded on natural law in the same way the natural special foundations of the United States were: "Ought we not to believe that the God of Nature, intended our civil institutions to be formed on a large scale of empire, to be in uniformity with his mighty works of nature?"

---

37. Andrew Jackson to Rachel Jackson, January 1813, *The Correspondence of Andrew Jackson*, vol. 1, *To April 30 1814,* ed. John Spencer Bassett (Washington, DC: Carnegie Institute, 1926), 272.

38. Division Orders, 7 March 1812, in *The Correspondence of Andrew Jackson*, 1:220–21

39. "'The Departure From Nashville', A Journal of the Trip Down the Mississippi," in *The Correspondence of Andrew Jackson*, 1:263.

Jackson's wartime presence at religious observances helped keep morale up among the soldiers. Jackson studiously attended divine services of all types. He carefully sponsored Christian devotion in camp while rejecting any sectarian sponsorship of a particular confessional or denominational background. His army eventually included Baptists, Episcopalians, Methodists, Presbyterians, and Roman Catholics. So long as ministers kept their messages devoted to saving souls—and supporting the military cause of the United States—Jackson attended and lent his dignity to religious proceedings. When flatboats transported Jackson's army on the Cumberland River in the winter of 1812/13, he allowed a Methodist itinerant, Lerner Blackman (1781–1815), to construct a platform to serve as a pulpit on one of the vessels. The army assembled on other boats, Jackson and his officers included, and listened as the minister preached: "Thirteen companies of infantry with officers, a general, his staff and, suite, were formed on the tops of a number of boats floating together. A minister of the Christian religion, stood upon a pulpit in the midst of them."[40] A member of Jackson's force seemed awed that the "gospel morality of Christ was heard to resound upon the bosom of a river and upon the spot, where, within the memory of several present, the buffalo had come to drink." More impressive to the soldier, Blackman preached in a place where "Indians ambushed solitary travelers," and where "the enterprising whiteman had cautiously crept along, in continual peril of his life."

Jackson's belief in separation of church and state never led him to support removing religion from the civil or social sphere. He had no problem, for example, with min-

---

40. Andrew Jackson Edmondson, *Journal When a Volunteer under General Andrew Jackson in 1812–1813*, 3–4.

isters telling soldiers that God was on their side—hardly an *apolitical* message. Jackson allowed ministers of various denominations to address troops with minimal supervision. Reverend Blackman's sermon received not only permission but support from Jackson. He called Blackman's remarks "very appropriate" and sensible, and identified Blackman as chaplain to the army—a title at once unofficial but still formal.[41] As long as a Christian minister remained committed to a non-sectarian message, he enjoyed General Jackson's patronage. In the case of Jackson's army, Blackman apparently enjoyed the support of the officers, men, and general. Blackman informed Jackson that as a minister of God, the former's duty called him to minister the Word of God on Sunday and to "admonish those around him." Blackman concluded his sermon with what Jackson called "a very affecting prayer for the success of the expedition, and for the individual happiness of the general, officers and men engaged in carrying it on."

The victory of Jackson's forces over the British army at the Battle of New Orleans in January, 1815 gave Jackson another opportunity to illustrate his sense of the American republic's providential destiny. Jackson believed that his victory "proved fatal" to British success in Louisiana: "Their loss on that day, was prodigious—exceeding according to their own accounts as well as to ours, 2600."[42] Jackson acknowledged that among the dead lay the British commander, an almost symbolic marker of divine judgment in favor of the United States' forces. Jackson saw the hand of God in

---

41. "Departure from Nashville," *Correspondence of Andrew Jackson*, 1:257.

42. Andrew Jackson to David Holmes, Head Quarters 7. M. District, 18 Jan 1815 in *The Papers of Andrew Jackson*, ed. Harold D. Moser, vol. 3, *1814-1815* (Knoxville: University of Tennessee Press, 1991), 249.

his success and praised the Almighty loudly: "If ever there was an occasion on which providence interfered, immediately, in the affairs of men it seems to have been on this." Jackson claimed that credit for the victory lay with divine providence: "What but such an interposition could have saved this country?" A grateful and perhaps even prayerful Jackson admonished those under his command to "mingle our joys & our thanksgiving together."[43]

The general's retroactive homage to divine favor appeared out of place to those who knew him, but Jackson's supporters immediately celebrated his words as an indication of an increasingly pious mind. A book published just after Jackson's death posited that there was "not in our language a more beautiful form of prayer and thanksgiving than is contained in a portion of his congratulatory and farewell address to his soldiers at New Orleans."[44] Jackson, the author argued, meekly gave "all the glory of the victory to the God of battles, in whom he had put his trust." The general seemed aware of the risk he ran, and how close he came to failing by offering "up sincere thanksgiving for the remarkable interposition of Heaven on our behalf."[45] The city of New Orleans held a lavish service of thanksgiving attended by Jackson and other state officials. The then-apostolic administrator of the Roman Catholic Diocese of Louisiana and the Two Floridas, Louis William Valentine DuBourg (1766–1833), presided over the ceremony and reminded

---

43. Andrew Jackson to David Holmes, 18 Jan 1815, *Papers of Andrew Jackson*, 3:249-50.

44. John Frost, *Pictorial Life of Andrew Jackson*, vol. 3, *1814-1815* (Hartford, CT: Belknap & Hamersly, 1847), 542.

45. Andrew Jackson to James Winchester 31 January 1815, *Papers of Andrew Jackson*, 3:262.

Jackson "how easy had it been for you, general, to forget the prime Mover of your wonderful successes."[46] The Bishop warned Jackson not to "assume to yourself a praise which must essentially return to that exalted source whence every sort of merit is derived." Jackson had issued a religiously worded proclamation, however, that convinced New Orleans that the culturally Calvinist Tennessean was now "better acquainted with the nature of true glory" because he "justly placing the summit of your ambitions in approving yourself the worthy instrument of Heaven's merciful designs." The first impulse of Jackson's religious heart, believed the priest "was to acknowledge the signal interposition of Providence your first step is a solemn display of your humble sense of His favors."

Once the United States achieved peace with Great Britain, the republic stood on a more solid footing from which to exert itself diplomatically on the North American continent and in Europe. Between 1815 and 1860, Andrew Preston notes, Americans became more willing to exert power abroad.[47] The American Union's intellectuals also increasingly made a case for why the United States should be a force for good, at least in the Western Hemisphere. The establishment of the domestic "Benevolent Empire" comprising Protestant reform societies picked up pace in the 1830s. The Benevolent Empire's energy came from Northern Whig evangelicals. Support for the Benevolent Empire was not universal; Southern slaveholders, particularly high church Episcopalians and Presbyterians, feared the reformist energies of evangelicals would very soon be turned against slav-

---

46. Louis William Valentine DuBourg, "Victory and Peace," *Poughkeepsie Herald*, Wednesday, February 22, 1815.

47. Preston, *Sword of the Spirit, Shield of Faith*, 123.

ery. Roman Catholics also balked at the overwhelmingly Protestant tone of American reformist ideologies domestically and in foreign policy. Both southern slaveholders and Roman Catholics supported Jacksonian Democrats because of their antiformalist and autonomous treatment of public religion. Still, Preston proposes, both parties supported activist foreign policy, and did so "largely under the banner of Christ." Protestant reformers of all stripes "included the application of Christian love to foreign policy as well as domestic policy."[48]

The United States' relatively sparse institutional diplomatic apparatus—the state department itself employed only a couple dozen clerks throughout the first half of the nineteenth century—meant that creative use of non-diplomats to further foreign policy became a norm for the United States. No group filled that niche more regularly or more willingly than Protestant missionaries, who often formed the first American diplomatic interests in geographies that American commerce had yet to penetrate. In the case of the Early Republic, changes in domestic economies and the United States' relationship with the British Empire led to missionaries replacing merchants, particularly in South Asia and Indochina. In some cases, the only reason the United States posted consuls to a given locale was because of the arrival of missionaries. In 1833, Joseph Balestier (1788–1858) arrived as consul in Singapore just before a group of missionaries did. It was the arrival of the United States diplomatic presence that convinced missionaries the area was appropriate for mission work. Often, the United States' diplomacy worked in tandem to further missionary and merchant interests. As the United States merchant class became more evangelical, the perceived tensions between doing the

48. Preston, *Sword of the Spirit, Shield of Faith*, 125.

work of God and the work of mammon disappeared in the minds of many Americans.[49]

Native Americans and the conditions of the republic's western frontier in general defined major aspects of the United States foreign policy throughout the nineteenth century. The American Southwest generally became a priority in the diplomatic aftermath of the Adams-Onís Treaty of 1819, in which Spain ceded Florida to the U.S. and in which the boundary between the U.S. and Mexico was defined. After 1820 the administration of James Monroe (1758–1831) prioritized diplomacy with independent Latin American nations, particularly newly independent Mexico.

Unfortunately not all of the president's choices for ambassadorial work matched John Quincy Adams's excellence as a diplomat. Monroe and Adams chose Joel R. Poinsett (1779–1851), a Charleston aristocrat of Huguenot stock, to go on a secret mission to Mexico in 1822. Poinsett served as a congressman and never wavered in his commitment to American-style liberties. Monroe and Adams picked Poinsett precisely because the latter could be trusted to endorse and hopefully inspire Latin America's revolutionary movements to replicate the United States constitutional settlement. Poinsett's well-intentioned but hardly subtle favoritism of Mexico's liberals against conservatives earned him a reputation for intrigue; Poinsett saw the supposed intrigue

---

49. See George C. Herring, *Years of Peril and Ambition: U.S. Foreign Relations, 1776–1921* (New York: Oxford University Press, 2008), 201–2; Michael A. Verney, "An Eye for Prices, an Eye for Souls: Americans in the Indian Subcontinent, 1784–1838," *Journal of the Early Republic* 33, no. 3 (2013): 397–431; Preston, *Sword of the Spirit, Shield of Faith*, 124–25; Conroy-Krutz, *Christian Imperialism*, 185.

as principled loyalty to constitutionalists over Mexico's Catholic militarists.[50]

Poinsett conceived of himself as an agent of a Protestant country, and he bore out the association of Protestantism with religious liberty and representative government that U.S. diplomats cultivated in post-independence Latin America.[51] He criticized the Mexican constitution for establishing the Roman Catholic church and for its prohibition of Protestant worship. Poinsett also hoped that Mexico would not send a diplomatic mission to the Papal States. When he published his memoir of his time in Mexico, he noted how foreign and even profane Mexico's cultural, political, and social practices sounded to "our Protestant ears."[52] Poinsett additionally theorized that Anglophone Protestant settlement in Mexico's northern states, particularly Texas, would civilize Mexicans. He hoped "that with the progress of the settlements being brought into nearer contact with us, they may be civilized."[53] Civilizing Mexico *via* acculturating Mexicans to American cultural norms—including Protestantism—would help Mexicans to eventually "adopt

---

50. See Light T. Cummins, "John Quincy Adams and Latin American Nationalism," *Revista de Historia de América*, no. 86 (1978): 221–31; Dorothy M. Parton, "The Diplomatic Career of Joel Roberts Poinsett" (PhD diss., Catholic University of America, 1934), 50–15; Ralph E. Weber and Joel R. Poinsett, "Joel R. Poinsett's Secret Mexican Dispatch Twenty," *South Carolina Historical Magazine* 75, no. 2 (1974): 67–76.

51. Fred Rippy, *Joel R. Poinsett: Versatile American* (Berkeley: University of California Press, 1968), 125.

52. Joel R. Poinsett, *Notes on Mexico, Made in the Autumn of 1822: Accompanied by an Historical Sketch of the Revolution, and Translations of Official Reports on the Present State of That Country with a Map* (Philadelphia: Carey and Lea, 1825), 25.

53. Poinsett, *Notes on Mexico*, 315.

a more tranquil kind of life," and enjoy "advantages held out by religion and society."[54] Poinsett also saw annexation of Mexican territory as an inevitable culmination of American religious and social influence. Americanized Mexicans, he said, would "become useful members of our nation."[55] The very history of the continent, he argued in 1841, was a story of the blessings of civil and religious liberty" marching across North America from the moment the Pilgrims landed in 1620.[56]

Hugh S. Legare (1797–1843), another Charlestonian who served as the United States' first *chargé d'affaires* or resident minister to Belgium between 1832 and 1836, likewise couched the American republic's constitutional freedoms in religious terms. He chided British parliamentarians and lords for their sometimes sneering treatment of the United States and impressed on the Britons and Europeans he met that the United States supported order, liberty, and Christianity without resorting to monarchy or establishmentarianism. In response to a book by a British traveler in North America who claimed the 1789 American constitutional settlement created anarchy, Legare parroted Milton's adulation of "the free government which we have so dearly purchased." Americans enjoyed a "free commonwealth, held by the wisest men in all ages, the noblest, the manliest, the equallest, the justest government." The American republic fulfilled Milton's hopes for a government "most agreeable to all due liberty and proportioned equality, both human,

---

54. Poinsett, *Notes on Mexico*, 315-316.

55. Poinsett, *Notes on Mexico*, 316.

56. Joel R. Poinsett, *Discourse, on the Objects and Importance of the National Institution for the Promotion of Science* (Washington, DC: P. Force, 1840), 42.

civil and Christian, most cherishing to virtue and true religion."[57]

United States diplomacy changed dramatically in the 1840s as liberal nationalist movements gained momentum in Europe. The rise of the Young America movement, particularly within the Democratic Party, made engagement with Europe and the exportation of American-style democracy a priority.[58] Members of the Young America movement like Episcopal clergymen Caleb S. Henry (1804–1884) saw Protestant ethics as the ultimate standard for truth and human liberty, and they elevated them above numerical majorities. Young America brought a renewed sense of revolutionary fervor to American politics and to some Protestant churchmen. That fervor, however, ran against the nativism of old stock Protestants, particularly those who favored the Whig Party and who feared the rise of *en masse* immigration and its effect on republican practice in the United States. Former Vice President and former Secretary of State John C. Calhoun's (1782–1850) patronage remained a force in the state department to the degree that the American republic's response to liberal democracy in Europe, however sympathetic, was more muted than European revolutionaries and their numerically small but passionate sympathizers in the United States hoped for.[59] Joseph R. Underwood

---

57. Hugh Swinton Legare, *Writings of Hugh Swinton Legaré, Late Attorney General and Acting Secretary of State of the United States* (Charleston: Burges and Hughes, 1845), 265.

58. See Mark Power Smith, *Young America: The Transformation of Nationalism before the Civil War* (Charlottesville: University of Virginia Press, 2022); Yonatan Eyal, *The Young America Movement and the Transformation of the Democratic Party, 1828–1861* (Cambridge: Cambridge University Press, 2007), 68.

59. Charles M. Wiltse, "A Critical Southerner: John C. Calhoun on

(1791–1876), U.S. Senator from Kentucky and married to one of that Commonwealth's most prominent Presbyterian families, warned his colleagues that while Americans might cheer the overthrow of monarchy in Paris, France's other revolutions had all ended in disaster.[60]

Popular revolts in Paris, Vienna, Rome, and in other capitals precipitated a series of liberal revolutions in Europe in 1848–1849 that affected all the great powers save Britain and Russia. True to form, Americans showed initial enthusiasm for the revolutions. James Buchanan (1791–1868), a churchgoing Presbyterian and Secretary of State in the Polk administration, wrote excitedly about the February 1848 Revolution in France, which overthrew the liberal constitutionalist king, Louis Phillipe I (1773–1850), calling the deposition a "glorious revolution in favor of liberty and republican government."[61] U.S. diplomats across Europe recognized the new governments as thrones toppled. However, conservatism soon typified the responses of Protestant divines even more than it had in the years following the American Revolution. Major Protestant thinkers, such as James Henley Thornwell, and John Williamson Nevin (1803–1886), all viewed the liberal revolutionaries with suspicion. Lajos Kossuth (1802–1894), an attorney from Hungary's Calvinist minor gentry who led an eventually un-

---

the Revolutions of 1848," *Journal of Southern History* 15, no. 3 (1949): 299–310.

60. "Hon. Joseph R. Underwood," *The American Review: A Whig Journal Devoted to Politics and Literature*, vol. 7 (New York: 1848), 614; Richard C. Rohrs, "American Critics of the French Revolution of 1848," *Journal of the Early Republic* 14, no. 3 (1994): 359–77.

61. Merle Curti, "The Impact of the Revolutions of 1848 on American Thought." *Proceedings of the American Philosophical Society* 93, no. 3 (1949), 209.

successful rebellion against Hungary's Habsburg monarchs, enjoyed a rapturous welcome when he visited American cities. Nevin called Kossuth a "veritable antichrist of the age" and worried that Kossuth wanted to important European style social egalitarianism into the United States.[62] James Henley Thornwell thought foreigners—be they Protestant or Roman Catholics—more often than not irreligious radicals who would corrupt pure American republicanism and transform it into an atheist social democracy. Both men, along with Congregationalist Edward Norris Kirk and others, saw little in the liberal revolutions to recommend them to Americans.[63]

The United States' crucible, and the event that guaranteed its powerful place in world history for the next century, came in the form of the Civil War. The Civil War stamped out southern and slaveholding priorities in United States diplomacy, but it did not revolutionize American self-conception of its place in the world religiously. In the midst of the Civil War, a rogue U.S. Navy captain, Charles Wilkes (1798–1877), stopped a British packet ship named the Trent carrying two southern diplomats to Great Britain.[64] British opinion was outraged and demanded Lord Palmerston's government make an example to the United States. Cooler heads prevailed, but not before a minor war scare in northern American cities. John Russell, 1st Earl Russell

---

62. Timothy Mason Roberts, *Distant Revolutions: 1848 and the Challenge to American Exceptionalism* (Charlottesville: University of Virginia Press, 2009), 114.

63. Curti, "The Impact of the Revolutions of 1848 on American Thought," 209–15.

64. See Thomas Le Grand Harris, *The Trent Affair: Including a Review of English and American Relations at the Beginning of the Civil War* (Indianapolis: Bowen-Merrill, 1896), 97–116.

(1792–1878), the British foreign secretary and later Prime Minister, sent word through intermediaries that the British government would not act belligerently if the United States government returned the two southern commissioners. Lincoln's government agreed. William H. Seward, the American Secretary of State, told his agents he was "disposed to confer and act with earnestness" if Britain wanted a peaceful resolution to the Trent Affair.[65] "If so," Seward wrote, "we are disposed to meet them in the same spirit, as a nation chiefly of British lineage, sentiments, and sympathies—a civilized and humane nation—a Christian people."

---

65. William Henry Seward, Mr. Seward to Mr. Adams, November 30, 1861, in *The Diplomatic History of the War For the Union*, ed. George E. Baker, vol. 5 (Boston: Houghton, Mifflin, 1884), 294.

CHAPTER VII

INDIANS

In October 1825, the Reverend Moody Hall sat at his log house in western Georgia. He lived in a place that white settlers saw as either pristine uninhabited territory or as a wilderness inhabited by benighted Indian savages. Neither presumption was true. Western Georgia formed part of the Cherokee nation's historic territory, and the Cherokees were hardly savages.

A generation earlier Christian missionaries from North Carolina had arrived in the Cherokee territory. A decade or so later Congregationalists and Presbyterians from New England made homes among the Cherokees, who were seen as eager to receive the civilizational benefits of Christianity. Methodists and Baptists came after the War of 1812.[1]

---

1. Emmet Starr, *History of the Cherokee Indians and Their Legends and Folk Lore* (Oklahoma City: Warren, 1921), 252–53; Linton McGeb Collins, "The Activities of the Missionaries Among the Cherokees," *Georgia Historical Quarterly* 6, no. 4 (1922): 285–322; Theda Perdue and Michael C. Green, *The Cherokee Nation and the Trail of Tears* (New York: Viking, 2007), 32.

The uneven effect of Protestant missionary work in the Cherokee nation mean that by 1825 two populations of Cherokees existed. Some Cherokees saw Christianity as a way of maintaining the Cherokee nation against the on-slaught of white society. Buck Watie (1802–1839)[2] and his cousin John Ridge (c.1802–1839), members of prominent Cherokee families with mixed European heritage, for exam-ple, were educated locally by Moravians and later traveled to New England for education in a mission school.[3] They met and married white women, but eventually saw white soci-ety as not delivering on the promises of Christianity. Ridge and Watie, however, saw this fault as that of white society and not Christianity itself. Other Cherokees, however, did see Christianity as necessarily destructive of Indian society; whatever benefits might come from Christianization and modernization weren't worth the loss of traditional Cher-okee identity.

It was one of those Cherokees—unreconciled to Chris-tianity, modernity, and the American republic's sovereign-ty—that approached the home of Moody Hall on a crisp evening in October 1825. The Indian—armed and appar-ently intoxicated—approached Hall's home and threatened him. Hall, convinced the Cherokee had set out to kill him, warned other whites about the danger from the Indians whom they were ostensibly supposed to convert. Hall, how-

---

2. Buck Watie was also known as Elias Boudinot. His full Cherokee name at birth was *Gallegina Uwati*. When his father converted to Chris-tianity, Buck took the name "David". When he came to Burlington, New Jersey as a teenager, he met Elias Boudinot (1740–1821), Presi-dent of the American Bible Society and one of the Founding Fathers. Watie asked Boudinot for permission to use his name, and did so for the rest of his life.

3. Daniel Blake Smith, *American Betrayal: Cherokee Patriots and the Trail of Tears* (New York: Henry Holt, 2011), 26–42.

ever, did not only appeal to God for safety. He, and most missionaries to Native Americans, saw the United States government as a chief guarantor of sustained missionary work among those groups. American missionaries, he cautioned, "will not be safe in this land until the United States government interferes."[4]

Protestant missionary interaction with Native Americans in the Early Republic required and made use of state interventions by the United States to provide for the physical safety of Protestant missionaries. The United States also saw itself as the civilizational custodian of missionary work. The aims of the federal republic, and the aims of Protestant missionaries, dovetailed not only inferentially but explicitly as well. Francis Paul Pucha wrote in his book *The Great Father: The United States Government and the American Indians* that "it was quietly understood, by government as well as church leaders, that the American civilization offered to Indians was Christian civilization, that Christianity was a component of civilization and could not and should not be separated from it."[5] Ultimately, missionaries united with the courts and the federal legislature to stem the tide of white democratic settlement, particularly in the South. An alliance between missionaries, Native Peoples, and the Supreme Court unsuccessfully fought state governments looking to dispossess Indians of their rightful lands. Whatever failings missionaries might have had in their state-supported dealings with Native Americans, the Jacksonian removal

4. William G. McLoughlin, *Cherokees and Missionaries, 1789–1839* (Norman: University of Oklahoma Press, 1995), 202.

5. Francis Paul Paucha, *The Great Father: The United States Government and the American Indians,* vol. 1 (Lincoln: University of Nebraska Press, 1984), 146.

of federally sponsored missionaries paved the way for the eventual brutalities of Indian removal.

Although the idea of explicit missionary involvement with the federal government sounds unpalatable to latter-day evangelicals fearful of the church entangling itself with the state and forfeiting its spiritual commission, the cooperation between the federal government and missionaries formed in the Federalist era from 1789 to 1801 actually proved to be more beneficial to Native Americans than the Jeffersonian policy that followed it.[6] Jefferson did not withhold material provisions from the Indians, but his innate secularism and dislike of institutional religiosity meant that he did not prioritize missionary cooperation to the same degree that Washington and Adams did. Missionaries, for example, were among the most ardent believers in the idea that Indian assimilation was preferable to conflict between whites and Indians, and they also had more direct experience of the terms and limitation of assimilation. Jefferson's secularism led him to abandon the Federalist Indian policies that included material assistance, religious education, and proselytization in favor of a policy of so-called "benevolence" undertaken in a hodgepodge fashion by state governments far less interested in Indian assimilation and far more interested in Indian lands. It was Jefferson, Christian Keller rightly reminds us, who first proposed Indian Removal as federal policy.[7]

---

6. Mary Young, "Review: Indian Policy in the Age of Jefferson" in *Journal of the Early Republic* 20, no. 2 (2000): 297–307.

7. Christian B. Keller, "Philanthropy Betrayed: Thomas Jefferson, the Louisiana Purchase, and the Origins of Federal Indian Removal Policy" *Proceedings of the American Philosophical Society* 144, no. 1 (2000): 39–66.

Jefferson's policy of separation of religion and government passed to his Jacksonian successors; so too did his commitment to Indian removal. The best evidence of this is that Indian removal was enacted by Jackson's separationist Democratic Party expressly against the joint commitments of the federal judiciary and missionaries, and over against two generations of United States treaty commitments to Native Americans.

The paradox of Indian removal is that John Marshall's defense of Indians and the right of missionaries to work undisturbed by state government was predicated on his belief that because Indians had been essentially conquered, the United States owed a measure of federally supported benevolence to them. For Marshall, benevolence, civilization, and Christianity all went together, and the United States owed the Indians all three. Marshall's view, which he shared with his fellow Federalists who created the United States' initial and more missionary-friendly Indian policy, was undoubtedly paternalistic, with all the unfortunate side effects that came with white paternalism, but it was a Christian paternalism that ultimately sided with native peoples, against the indifferent and ultimately unsympathetic paternalism of Jefferson, Jackson, and Democratic-leaning white Southern settlers that ultimately led to mass Indian deaths on what became known to Indians as the Trail of Tears.[8]

Missionary aims, according to Francis Paul Pucha, dovetailed with Christianity's place in the federal government's civilizational mission in the Early Republic: "The

---

8. See Kathleen Sands, "Territory, Wilderness, Property and Reservation: Land and Religion in Native American Supreme Court Cases," *American Indian Law Review* 36, no. 2 (2011): 253–320; Robert Remini, *Andrew Jackson: The Course of American Freedom, 1822–1832* (Baltimore: Johns Hopkins University Press, 1981), 276.

missionary goal, seen in this light, differed little from the goal of Washington, Jefferson, and other public statesmen."[9] Federalist policy makers of the Washington and Adams administrations made no efforts to hide the cooperation between the state and missionaries. Henry Knox (1750–1806), Washington's Secretary of War, proposed a program of integration for Native Peoples within the borders of the United States that revolved around providing farming implements and other basic material needs for Indians and paying Protestant missionaries to live among respective indigenous groups.[10] The policy convinced some missionaries to take the federal government up on the offer. Missionaries like Presbyterian Gideon Blackburn (1772–1838) in the Southeast and Roman Catholics like Gabriel Richard (1767–1832) in the Great Lakes region showed the United States commitment to broad national Christianization of native peoples.[11]

This Federalist policy for Indians included more aggressive Christianization for Native Americans but also treated them as equals worthy of the trust and goodwill of the American republic. It also recognized that religion necessarily had to accompany material benefits if the social conditions that Federalist policymakers hoped to achieve for Indians were going to be attained. Thomas L. McKenney (1785–1859) served as Superintendent of Indian Affairs through the presidencies of James Monroe and John Quincy Adams and largely continued the Federalist Indian

---

9. Pucha, *The Great Father,* 146.

10. Bernard W. Sheehan, *Seeds of Extinction: Jeffersonian Philanthropy and the American Indian* (Chapel Hill: University of North Carolina Press, 1973), 120-21.

11. Sheehan, *Seeds of Extinction,* 122.

program until he was replaced by Andrew Jackson because the latter viewed him as too sympathetic to Native Peoples' fight against relocation. McKenney summed up the United States' approach to Indians up to that point by noting that "religious observances, and the ceremonies of the church, are all excellent, and should form part of every system for the conversion of the savage into the civilized man and Christian," but he maintained that religious practices "were not sufficient, of themselves, to accomplish this great end."[12]

Civilization, both material and religious, stood as a shared state and missionary goal that paired the aims of the American republic and missionaries. Protestant missionaries to Native Peoples in the Early Republic stated unashamedly that their goals were civilization as much as they were spiritual. In fact they saw the two goals as largely synonymous. The United Foreign Missionary Society, a non-sectarian entity founded in 1817 to proselytize western states, incorporated Congregationalist, Presbyterian, and other Protestant efforts. Their board stated in 1823 that missionary institutions should be established to convey to Indians "the benefits of civilization and the blessings of Christianity."[13] The board looked with "cheering hope" forward to "the period when the savage shall be converted into the citizen" and when the "hunter shall be transformed into the mechanic."[14] Middle class Protestant society was the aspiration of the Indian missionaries. Farms, workshops, schoolhouses, and church, exclaimed the missionaries, "shall adorn ev-

---

12. Sheehan, *Seeds of Extinction*, 126.

13. Robert F. Berkhofer Jr., *Salvation and the Savage: An Analysis of Protestant Missions and American Indian Response, 1787–1862* (Lexington: University Press of Kentucky, 2021), 10.

14. Berkhofer, *Salvation and the Savage*, 11.

ery Indian village," and the "fruits of industry, good order, and sound morals shall bless every Indian dwelling." Across the continent "from the Mississippi to the Pacific, the red man and the white man shall everywhere be found, mingling with the same benevolent and friendly feelings, fellow citizens of the same civil and religious community." Membership in the same civil and religious community, for the missionaries, was a chief evidence that native peoples and whites were "fellow heirs to a glorious inheritance in the kingdom of Immanuel."[15]

The union of missionary goals and state policy marked a distinct change from the relationship between missionaries and the imperial state during the colonial era. Eighteenth century missionaries, Ned Blackhawk maintains in his work on Native Americans, "had been the first to ally with Indian peoples over land, rights, and protection."[16] One Indian leader emphasized that Protestant missionaries in British North America "treated native peoples better than colonists and other imperial officials." Indians alleged that while colonists and imperial state actors mistreated them and engaged in corruption for material gain, missionaries' interactions with indigenous peoples routinely made respect and love priorities without regard to economic and or social benefits that might be accrued from engaging Indians. Some missionaries gained venerable reputations among Native American peoples that lasted for several generations.

15. See also Clifford M. Drury, "The Western Missionary Society, 1802–1836," *Journal of the Presbyterian Historical Society* 28, no. 4 (1950): 233–48.

16. Ned Blackhawk, *The Rediscovery of America: Native Peoples and the Unmaking of U.S. History* (New Haven: Yale University Press, 2023), 150.

Missionaries in the Early Republic enjoyed a much cozier relationship with the American empire than colonial missionaries had with the British Empire, but that did not mean that they traded a good relationship with Native Peoples for a good relationship with the American republic. The change began with the advent of the American republic but became more obvious after the War of 1812. Missionary work, particularly before 1830, centered around New England. Missionaries assumed their way of bringing Christianity to the worldwide masses was particularly blessed by God, but their ambitions sometimes fell afoul of the United States government. The American republic of the era employed missionaries as Indian agents, and Christianity formed an important part of the Union's civilizational demands on Native American groups. Government missionaries sometimes clashed with independent ones in aims and political commitments. The War of 1812, for example, interrupted missionary efforts in what is now the modern Midwest, infuriating New Englanders who faulted James Madison for stopping the march of the gospel.[17] As head of state, Madison implored Native Americans to heed the American civilizational program.[18] White articulations of thrift and industry remained foreign to Native American groups in the Early Republic. Anglo-American agriculture and white sedentary lifestyles were, according to Madison, what indigenous peoples had been created for. Even as head of state, Madison felt no compunction about speaking in Christian language. God created Native Americans

---

17. Sam Haselby, *The Origins of American Religious Nationalism* (New York: Oxford University Press, 2015), 221.

18. Gastón Espinosa, ed., *Religion and the American Presidency: George Washington to George W. Bush with Commentary and Primary Sources* (New York: Columbia University Press, 2009), 132–33.

to be happy, Madison declared, and obediently heeding the United States program of civilization (and Christianization) would make Indians spiritually and materially secure.

Native groups varied in their reception of missionary efforts in the Early Republic, but by the 1820s missionaries in the Midwest and in Southern states believed Indians needed protection from settler populations. The reasons, Sam Haselby notes, lay in the missionaries' increasingly firm conviction that frontier populations—uniformly less religious than Americans who lived in major cities and along the eastern seaboard—cared little for the souls of Indians and only wanted their lands.[19] The American Bible Society continued to conflate major aspects of white civilization with Christianization and vice versa, but by 1818 they wanted to let Indians retain a significant measure of traditional Indian culture and societal practice. Indian languages, for example, were to be prioritized in Bible translation instead of assuming that Indians would need to learn English in order to receive spiritual instruction. More controversial, particularly for white settlers in the South, was the extent to which missionaries hoped that Indians would have a secure claim to their own lands in order to achieve what white missionaries believed was civilization. Andrew Jackson saw missionary support for Indian land claims as little more than religious sentimentalism.[20] Convinced that he was a tribune defending the republican rights and privileges of the common man, and encultured by experiences and narratives of white conflicts with Indians, Jackson ignored the pleas of

---

19. Haselby, *The Origins of American Religious Nationalism*, 297; Andrew Burstein, *The Passions of Andrew Jackson* (New York: Alfred A. Knopf, 2003), 67.

20. Andrew Burstein, *The Passions of Andrew Jackson* (New York: Alfred A. Knopf, 2003), 67.

missionaries and sided exclusively with settlers against the missionaries and against federally appointed Indian agents.

Jackson's war against missionaries largely represented a conflict within Protestantism regarding the nature and role of churchly institutions on the frontier. Beginning in 1800, settler religiosity, fueled by the spiritualist revivals at places like Cane Ridge, Kentucky, threw off institutional Protestantism and its historic commitments (both in establishmentarian and disestablishmentarian traditions) to working with government and other social institutions to enact the social and moral order in society in favor of religion marked by subjective emotional enthusiasm largely devoid of hard ethical, intellectual, or political commitments. In 1811 Presbyterian minister Samuel Porter (1760–1825) complained that in western Pennsylvania "a spirit of innovation, hostile to all existing systems, has gone forth into the world, and is to be found in operation within the precincts of the Christian church."[21] Revivalist Christianity, warned Porter, risked moving from the extremes into the center, turning Christianity from an institutional and by proxy ritualistic religion into one devoid of any institutional commitments, which Porter feared devolved into unhinged licentiousness. "Human nature, in avoiding one extreme, tends to the other."[22] The candid and well-informed would grant "that if a bigoted attachment to human system prevailed in some periods that have passed, the present tendency is to a lawless catholicism." Revivalist frontier religion favored "a liberality in sentiment, which affects to look down on systems and confessions of faith as old-fashioned, musty, useless lum-

---

21. Joseph Smith, *Old Redstone; Or, Historical Sketches of Western Presbyterianism, Its Earliest Minister, Its Perilous Times, and Its First Records* (Philadelphia: Lippincott, Grambo, 1854), 371–72.

22. Smith, *Old Redstone*, 372.

ber, not calculated for this enlightened, refined philosophic age." Frontier religion—if it could be called that—combined near-total disdain for meaningful institutional religion with an embrace of early folk racism, *à la* Jeffersonian enlightenment, that posited the impossibility of whites and Indians living together in harmony. That it was supposedly childlike, supposedly naïve, and supposedly socially primitive Indians that needed to be moved nonetheless told the tale that race and land, and not religion or philosophy, was the primary motivator for white settlers ravenous for Indian territory.[23]

The frontier, before or after revivals, never passed muster as a paragon of orthodoxy or orthopraxy among Protestant intellectuals and ministers. Church attendance and churchly practice of any type waned as white populations moved from the Atlantic states into the frontier.[24] Ministers, not settlers, brought civilization, and Protestant clerics often encountered opposition to their ministries from prominent white settlers more than from Native Peoples to whom they ministered. Under the Plan of Union that united the Congregationalist and Presbyterian churches in western states for the sake of missionary work, missionaries like Connecticut's Ezekiel Chapman (1757–1843) faced off with local grandees in northern Ohio who "unmercifully and indecently" slandered missionaries to Indians.[25] Local whites routinely and publicly flouted Christian morality,

---

23. Merrill D. Peterson, *Thomas Jefferson and the New Nation: A Biography* (Oxford: Oxford University Press, 1970), 776.

24. James MacGregor Burns, *The American Experiment: The Vineyard of Liberty, 1787–1863* (New York: Alfred A. Knopf, 1981), 493.

25. Amy DeRogatis, "Models of Piety: Plan of Union Missionaries on the Western Reserve, 1800—1806," *Journal of Presbyterian History* 79, no. 4 (2001), 263.

and they, according to Chapman, cursed the Congregationalists and Presbyterians for even sending missionaries into western states. Another Plan of Union missionary, Joseph Badger (1757–1846), dealt with a local man the former claimed was a "violent deist," who was insulted at having missionaries live among settlers. White settlement, in the eyes of Protestant clerics, was neither necessarily Christian, nor civilized.[26]

Philander Chase (1775–1852), first Episcopal bishop of Ohio, published a pamphlet arguing that the American frontier was a region in danger of not only becoming less Protestant, but of becoming downright uncivilized, even as Americans settled the frontier regions of Ohio and the new states being carved out of the Northwest Territory. Chase founded Kenyon College in 1824 in order to civilize white society in Ohio. Frontier settlement, far from being an *en masse* civilizing force, risked creating a society that exceeded its parent society's institutional means of civil, cultural, and civil catechesis. "It is well known," warned Chase, "that the progress of settlement at the west has hitherto far outstripped the means of religion and learning."[27] He observed that a "few years ago Ohio was a wilderness; no trace of civilized man was seen in all her extended forests. That state is now inhabited by a million of immortal souls." Settlement had not brought order in the abstract; it brought an uncontrollable demographic force that overwhelmed not only the pristine western forests but that also overwhelmed previous generations of settlers: "As with a mighty stream, collecting itself from all quarters of the world, the western country has

26. DeRogatis, "Models of Piety," 264.

27. Philander Chase, *A Plea for the West* (Boston: Samuel Parker, 1827), 3.

been overspread ere those who were left behind were aware that the settlement had commenced." Ohio and the states of the Northwest Territory made "this sudden transition from an old to a new world; a transition which for its extent and celerity is unexampled in the history of man." While some attempts at schooling and churching were attempted in the initial waves of settlement, "impossibilities could not be effected."

Chase lamented that "the means of perpetuating the science and piety of his forefathers could not be obtained, nor continued, while every man had, not only to pay into the treasury of the United States, frequently his last dollar for the soil under his feet," and subsequently "to contend with the manifold difficulties of subduing the forest; difficulties which undermine and destroy the natural constitution of more than one generation before they are entirely overcome."[28] It was, said the bishop, "literally impossible" to "institute schools, build colleges and churches, and maintain ministers of the gospel, in any degree adequate to the great necessity" during the initial period of settlement. Lack of education and religion was not a benign accident. The still relatively short experience of the American republic's frontier, he worried, had "witnessed the sad consequences. The son, save in very few instances, knows not, nor, unless something more is speedily done, is he ever like to know what his father knew. A deterioration both in knowledge and religion takes place, too painful to describe." The citizenry of the American republic—and the sovereign republican union they formed—were not to be moral or religious bystanders regarding the Christianization of the frontier. "Placed by the providence of God over a portion of the Christian community in Ohio, and feeling for their

28. Chase, *Plea for the West*, 3.

welfare," the bishop "deemed himself in duty bound to do something in his humble sphere for the common good, in trying to remedy and prevent these dreadful evils, ignorance and irreligion."

The bishop made good on his word throughout his ministry. In the Fall of 1825, Chase encountered Native Peoples in Ohio—Oneidas and Mohawks—who showed an interest in Anglican liturgies, and he celebrated them as models of piety. Indians, Chase wrote, were "decent and dignified in their manners they received me with great respect."[29] When Chase relayed that he "came among them to do them good and not harm—to pray with them—and to preach the Gospel in the name of Jesus Christ our common Saviour—they fully comprehended my meaning and gave me a hearty welcome." The Indians even had a Book of Common Prayer, and they knew how to use it. They sang together "the metre Psalms & Hymns, their version being the same measure with the English, I could join with them in this also." The bishop recalled that their voices were "uncommonly sweet and full they sang tunes with which, most happily." Chase stated that he had never witnessed "more order" in worship than among the Indians, a far cry from the wild revivalism of frontier whites. The Native Peoples gave what he happily called "plain...indications of true devotion." Although some of the Oneidas and Mohawks "could speak a little English," "the Sermon was interpreted to them in their own language." He took pride in the Indians' desire to regularize their ecclesiology too: "They have used Lay Baptism, they say, out of imperious necessity, yet would be much rejoiced to quit that great irregularity if they could have an authorized ministry." Chase pronounced

29. Philander Chase, "Excerpt of Letter Dated October 10th, 1825," *Philander Chase Letters*, 541.

himself "most favorably impressed towards these poor people, and my attachment to our primitive Liturgy mightily strengthened by this instance of its great utility."

Protestant leaders, particularly those from churches not yet influenced by the revivals, saw settler interactions with Indians for what they were and proclaimed flatly that irreligious white settlers were harming Indian populations that had achieved relative social stability in the first three decades of the nineteenth century. Jackson Kemper (1789–1870), a missionary bishop of the Episcopal Church to the Great Lakes region, believed that degraded frontier whites introduced vice among the Indians who in turn reverted to an analogous level of degradation. A few years before his 1838 trip through Wisconsin, Kemper recorded in his journal that Winnebago Indians had formerly been industrious and "raised enough corn for themselves and to sell to the forts."[30] The advent of whites settlers, however, had made Wisconsin's Native Peoples "degenerated and lazy," and he bewailed what he perceived as drunkenness and constant starvation. Kemper, however, did not resort to removal as the natural or necessary policy to reconcile whites and Indians. He believed that fuller inclusion into white Protestant religious bodies would resolve whatever cultural tensions existed. Schools administered by Episcopal rectors and supported by the Foreign Missionary Society rescued, said Kemper, several hundred Indian children "from degradation and vice and ignorance and death" and taught them "the arts and feelings of civilized life and the principles of the Gospel."[31] Kemper saw education and white enculturation as sufficient

---

30. Jackson Kemper. "A Trip through Wisconsin in 1838," *Wisconsin Magazine of History* 8, no. 4 (1925), 426.

31. Howard Morris Stuckert, "Jackson Kemper, Presbyter," *Historical Magazine of the Protestant Episcopal Church* 4, no. 3 (1935), 143.

evidence of Indian advancement. These were enough for Indians to live comfortably beside whites. Indian children, he extolled, "exhibit by their conduct and writing evidence of the Gospel on their souls." Dismantling mission schools in favor of a policy of Indian removal west would be to "abandon the only post we have among the heathen." Kemper worked to place the church among Indians. While he still exhibited paternalistic white attitudes, his conviction that Indians could indeed learn civilization in their own lands set him apart from Jeffersonian secularists who saw removal as the only way of resolving the relationship between white Protestants and Indians.

Protestants who rejected revivalism and the primacy of the desires of white settler democracy denounced politicians and their allies who argued that Indians could not be civilized. The American Bible Society translated the Bible for Indians east and west of the Mississippi River and sent missionaries to as many Native Peoples as possible in the years that followed the War of 1812.[32] The American Bible Society defied settlers—many of whom viewed Jefferson as their ideological north star—and sent missionaries to Indian groups whom white settlers hoped to displace. Bible Society missionaries shared paternalistic white attitudes with other Americans, but they saw missionary work as focused on Christianizing indigenous populations where they were, not as a preparatory enterprise to eventually remove Indians. Assimilation, not mobilization, is what the American Bible Society hoped for the indigenous populations among whom its missionaries work and for whom they made translations.

---

32. John Fea, *The Bible Cause: A History of the American Bible Society* (New York: Oxford University Press, 2016), 105; Thomas C. Moffett, *The Bible in the Life of the Indians of the United States* (New York: American Bible Society, 1916), 7–8.

The American Bible Society's second annual report made clear the group's commitment to Indian territorial claims when they rebuked figures in public life who made statements about Indians being by nature uncivilized. The "doctrine" that Indians could not be "civilized" was the "slander of men who covet their lands."[33]

Covetous whites, particularly in Southern states, stood to gain Indian lands if they could displace the missionary allies of Native Peoples first. The Jacksonian coalition that came into office in 1828 made Indian Removal a priority. Compared to the white tenants of Georgia and Alabama, Andrew Jackson tended towards moderation on the question of removal. However, his secretary of war, John Eaton (1790–1856), influenced the president to take a firmer line with the Indians. The president inferentially threw his support behind a series of laws passed by the Georgia state legislature that ignored numerous treaties signed with Native Peoples, particularly the five so-called Civilized Tribes, or Southeastern peoples, since 1789. Those nations—the Choctaws, Chickasaws, Creeks or Muscogee, Seminoles, and the Cherokees—lived across traditional Indian territories stretching from southwestern Virginia to southern Mississippi. Andrew Jackson made it plain to them that they needed to submit to the raft of state laws functionally dispossessing them of their own lands and also making their very right to live in or near their traditional territories subject to the caprice of land-hungry whites. If the Indians did not submit, they would have to move or be destroyed. Jackson clothed his removal push in the language of a caring father. His red children and his white children lived too close to each other for the good of either. But beyond the Missis-

---

33. American Bible Society, *Second Annual Report* (New York, 1818), 16–17.

sippi, "your father has provided a country large enough for all of you, and he advises you to remove to it."[34] That way the Indians' "white brothers" would no longer trouble them because whites had no claim to the lands in the West Jackson pledged to provide to Native Peoples. As long as "the grass grows or the water runs," Jackson promised, Indians would live on their lands unmolested in "peace and plenty."

Promises from Andrew Jackson seemed less convincing than promises from previous presidents. None of Jackson's predecessors acted as forcefully to bring about the removal of indigenous peoples from their lands, and none of them willingly abrogated the tacit alliance between missionaries and federal Indian agents as Jackson sought to do. It is important to note that the Indian Removal Act passed by Congress in 1830 did not allow the federal government to ignore federal treaties signed with Native Americans nor did it empower the government to implement forced relocations of Native Peoples. Historian Alfred A. Cave helpfully reminds us that Congress—through the 1830 Indian Removal Act—did not authorize Andrew Jackson to "remove Indians from their homelands at the point of a bayonet," even if that is how the act was widely perceived in 1830 and still is today.[35]

In the 1820s federal Indian policy could have been called a relative success by policymakers who favored some sort of assimilation into the life of the American republic for Native Americans. Proud Christian converts like David Brown (c.1806–1829) told the Superintendent of Indian Affairs that his fellow Cherokees made strides towards re-

---

34. Jon Meacham, *American Lion: Andrew Jackson in the White House* (New York: Random House, 2009), 92.

35. Alfred A. Cave, "Abuse of Power: Andrew Jackson and the Indian Removal Act of 1830," *The Historian* 65, no. 6 (2003): 1330–53.

ligion and civilization, and by most measures they had.[36] James Monroe commissioned Rev. Jedediah Morse to conduct a survey of the Southeastern Peoples for the federal government. Morse reported back that the Indians made good progress materially, religiously, and politically, and that removal was unnecessary for at least four of so-called the Five Civilized tribes. A Christian party existed in the political councils of each of the major Indian nations.[37]

Land-obsessed whites, however, saw what partisans in the government and among missionaries saw as progress as problematic. The state of Georgia in particular worked to establish from the 1790s forward a legal precedent for removing Indians, particularly the Cherokees, from traditional tribal lands. A successful Indian policy spearheaded by the federal government in conjunction with federally sustained missionaries presented an obstacle to getting Indians off the land. In fact, the more like white Americans the Indians became, the more enraged Georgia's politicians were. The Cherokee nation working as a constitutionally governed and increasingly Christian subject nation under the protection of the federal government would be almost impossible to dislodge. Andrew Jackson was more sympathetic to white settlers than any president yet, and Georgia saw his presidency as the moment to force Indians out of the state. The Indian Removal Act didn't demand that Indians move, but Georgia was going to remove them whether the federal government had mandated removal or not. The "principle acts of harassment" Anthony F.C. Wallace notes, "were car-

---

36. Anthony F. C Wallace, *The Long Bitter Trail: Andrew Jackson and the Indians* (New York: Hill and Wang, 1993), 59.

37. Wallace, *The Long Bitter Trail*, 60-62.

ried out by the governments and citizens of southern states" against Indians, federal agents, and missionaries.[38]

No figure represented the alliance of the federal government and missionaries better than Samuel Worcester (1798–1859). A Congregationalist minister originally from Vermont, Worcester attended the University of Vermont and Andover Theological Seminary. He, like many other young seminarians in the era, pursued a missionary vocation and affiliated with the American Board of Commissioners for Foreign Missions. While not officially affiliated with any denomination, the ABCFM largely consisted of clerics from Calvinist denominations, particularly the Congregationalists, German Reformed, and Presbyterian churches. Although Worcester originally wanted to serve overseas, he accepted a position to serve among the Cherokees in Georgia. Worcester and his wife Ann assumed the stewardship of a mission in Brainerd, Georgia, in September of 1825. The Worcesters brought to Georgia typical white Christian assumptions about missionary work. They wanted to make the Cherokees "English in their language, civilized in their habits, and Christian in their religion."[39] Samuel gained fluency in Cherokee and began to translate the Christian Scriptures. A few years after his arrival, however, the state of Georgia wasted no time in beginning its attacks on the Cherokees once Andrew Jackson took office in 1829. The legal battle between Georgia and the Cherokees lasted three years, with some decisions bringing legal victories for the state, and others for the Indians. Legal victory was never synonymous with the Cherokees' clear title to their land,

38. Wallace, *The Long Bitter Trail*, 75.

39. A. J. Langguth, *Driven West: Andrew Jackson and the Trail of Tears to the Civil War* (New York: Simon & Schuster, 2010), 74.

however, and the state of Georgia used constitutional trick-ery and outright illegal power grabs to force its will on the Cherokees and missionaries. It was the treatment of mis-sionaries that eventually proved to be the crucible of Indian Removal.

Two major cases defined conflict between the Cher-okees, Georgia, and missionaries.[40] The first was *Cherokee Nation v Georgia* in 1831. In that case the court found against the Indians based not on their claims regarding the unlawfulness of Georgia's actions but on the respective standing of the Indians. The Court found that the Chero-kees as a subject nation did not have the same constitution-al rights as citizens of the United States, but they did not declare Georgia's legal hounding of the Cherokees lawful either. The second case, and in many ways the more influen-tial one, was *Worcester v Georgia* in 1832. By 1831 Georgia had passed a series of laws that can only be described as state-sanctioned harassment of the Cherokees and of their white Protestant allies. Georgia passed laws demanding whites living in the Cherokee nation to have a license from the state of Georgia and to take a special oath drawn up by Georgia governor Wilson Lumpkin (1783–1870) and his cronies. The governor knew that missionaries like Worcester encouraged Cherokees to resist the state of Georgia, so he used the law to prosecute Worcester and a few other mis-sionaries. Worcester refused the oath and declared that it would "greatly impair or destroy his usefulness as a minister of the Gospel." Georgia courts found Worcester guilty and sentenced him to hard labor in the summer of 1831.

Support for the missionaries seemed hard to find in Southern state houses, but federal officers offered what

---

40. See Stephen Breyer, "The Cherokee Indians and the Supreme Court," *Georgia Historical Quarterly* 87, no. 3/4 (2003): 408–26.

support they could. Indian removal may have been hard to stop, but it could be mitigated. The Supreme Court, led by Associate Justice John McLean (1785–1861), ruled against the state of Georgia and declared the oath laws, among others, unconstitutional.[41] Although the Cherokees were a subject nation of the United States, their relationship was directly with the federal government and that superseded any laws that Georgia might make for Indian territory. Cherokees—particularly converts to Christianity—recognized the inevitable and wanted to get as good a treaty as possible from the federal Congress if removal became unavoidable. Justice McLean, a devout Methodist with an obvious soft spot in his heart for missionaries and Cherokees, proposed meeting with the Cherokee delegation and offered whatever support he could for their cause. Theodore Frelinghuysen, a Dutch Reformed senator from New Jersey famous for his eloquence and piety, warned Congress that their treatment of the Cherokees threatened to bring divine judgment on the United States for not living up to its divine purpose to bring light to the nations. The American Republic had been exalted by God "to the very summit of prosperity," said Frelinghuysen, and now it defied God through its immoral treatment of Native Peoples.[42]

Worcester had no illusions about the Cherokees' future. They would have to move, but he would go with them.

---

41.   Edwin A. Miles, "After John Marshall's Decision: Worcester v. Georgia and the Nullification Crisis," *Journal of Southern History* 39, no. 4 (1973): 519–44; Smith, *American Betrayal*, 138; Francis P. Weisenberger, *The Life of John McLean: A Politician on the United States Supreme Court* (New York: Da Capo, 1971), 175.

42.   Bennett Kravitz and Arnon Gutfield, "'Let Us Save Them Now, or We Never Shall': Rhetoric and Recriminations in the Cherokee Removal Debate," *Studies in Popular Culture* 23, no. 2 (2000), 4.

Novelist and historian John Ehle offered the best treatment of the tie between morality, religion, and politics of Indian Removal in his still magisterial work *The Trail of Tears: The Rise and Fall of the Cherokee Nation*. Worcester understood that Indian Removal "was a moral issue, a church matter; but it was a political one too," says Ehle.[43] Churches dealt with matters of the soul and hopes for heaven, "a city not built by hands, a more perfect place ruled by God." The church did not claim "New Testament mandates to change the world's governments." Slavery's endurance, argues Ehle, convinced Worcester that on some level religious actions for political ends were impotent. Nonetheless Worcester "felt a fire burning inside to help" the Cherokees in their cause. "The church must try—political or not, government or not, separation of church and state or not—the church must try."

Although missionaries like Worcester and the agents of the federal government did not see traditional Indian culture as appropriate for assimilation, they offered at least some social and cultural acceptance for Indian ways if they were subjected to a form of white Protestant cultural and religious catechesis. The missionaries were not necessarily more socially "progressive" or even "tolerant"—to use our twenty-first century language—than Andrew Jackson. Nor was Jackson as deeply involved in the intricacies of Indian Removal as he is often accused of being. The seventh president was not particularly an Indian hater.[44] What Jackson lacked that the missionaries had in spades was a deep belief in the efficacy and necessity of the relationship between the federal government, Native Peoples, and missionaries.

---

43. John Ehle, *The Trail of Tears: The Rise and Fall of the Cherokee Nation* (New York: Anchor 1988), 233.

44. Bradley J. Birzer, *In Defense of Andrew Jackson* (Washington, DC: Regnery History, 2018), 112–14.

Worcester and other missionaries throughout the Southeast believed that the church must try, and try they did so with the understanding that they would be supported by church and state in an enterprise that undeniably blended the mission of both institutions. "The grand motive," declared *The Missionary Herald* in 1833, that induced Worcester and other missionaries

> to expose themselves to the hardship and ignominious imprisonment which they have endured, was the good of the Cherokees. To the promotion of Christianity and civilization among them they had consecrated their life. It was a sacred work, to which they felt commissioned as missionaries of the Lord Jesus, and they must not hastily retire from it, through fear of what they deemed oppression and violence, when there were laws and tribunals, and magistrates, to whom they could appeal for protection. The apostles, it is believed, appealed in every similar case. Their yielding would have discouraged the Cherokees, by virtually saying to them that the faith of the United States, pledged to them, would be violated; and that the provisions made for their protection in the constitutions, treaties, and laws of this Union would not be enforced; and that the missionaries did not dare trust their own persons on these provisions.[45]

The success of Protestant missionaries always rested on the cooperation between the federal government and missionaries. The missionaries knew that, and they wanted the Indians to know that too.

---

45. *The Missionary Herald* 29 (Boston, 1833), 133.

Although it is impossible to know what would have happened if the Southeastern peoples had never been driven from their lands, it is possible to know what happened on the brutal Trail of Tears. Corrupt merchants contracted to supply Indians with provisions never provided what they were supposed to. At least four thousand Indians died of exposure, disease, or malnourishment. Some research suggests that the number of deaths might be twice that high. A strengthened, rather than reduced, relationship between missionaries and the federal government very likely would have saved lives.

The missionaries never lost faith in federal protection, interestingly enough, and they willingly subjected themselves to Georgia's illegal treatment in order to prove the point that federal law still protected missionaries. "Besides this great motive of doing good to the Cherokees," the missionaries disregarded the law of the state of Georgia because they "had some reference to the securing of their own rights as citizens of the United States and ministers of the gospel."[46] These symbiotic rights were, announced a missionary magazine "invaluable to every man, as an individual." The missionaries as good men also had a duty, "which a good man owes to his country and fellow citizens, to withstand what plainly appears to him to be oppression, and give opportunity for justice to be done by the execution of wholesome laws, even though detriment should come to himself." The missionaries rejected the principle, "that Christian duty requires every good man to retire before a threatened invasion of his rights," because it would be "dangerous in such a government as ours" where federal might could eventu-

---

46. Russell Thornton, "Cherokee Population Losses during the Trail of Tears: A New Perspective and a New Estimate," *Ethnohistory* 31, no. 4 (1984): 289–300; *The Missionary Herald* 29, 133.

ally protect missionaries. "Suitable regard to the authority of the United States, under whose patronage and sanction they had been sent forth, and had labored, required them not hastily to abandon the work intrusted to them." The great tragedy of the relationship between government and missionaries was not, therefore, that the federal government had not protected Indians and missionaries. It was that the new, more secular Jacksonian regime was indifferent to the protection of the relationship between Christian missionaries, Indians, and the United States in the face of land-hungry whites.

CHAPTER VIII

EDUCATION

John Lathrop (1799–1866) knew what he had to say. As the newly appointed president of a new college in a new state on the United States' Old Northwestern frontier, he needed to set the standard of what was expected for his college's faculty. Born to pious Calvinist parents in Upstate New York in the last year of the eighteenth century, Lathrop's own educational and religious preparation had been done "in orthodox fashion, under a clergyman's guidance."[1] He matriculated at Hamilton College in New York, a Presbyterian school best known for training ministers and missionaries. The college Lathrop had been called to lead was also Christian, and it needed masculine Christian patriots to shape the minds of the young men who composed its student body. The ideal professor, Lathrop announced, "should be a man of native vigor, of sound scholarship, of varied attainment, of devotion his especial department, of aptitude to impart instruction, of fidelity to his associates and to the common cause,

---

1. Joseph Schafer, "Chancellor John Hiram Lathrop," *Wisconsin Magazine of History* 23, no. 2 (1939), 207.

of strength of purpose united with a conciliating demeanor."[2] The ideal professor for the college also needed "physical ability and the will to labor. He should know men and things, as well as books. He should be a man of the world, in an unexceptionable sense of the term." Finally and most importantly, "as a subject of God's moral government, his life should be regulated by the Christian ethics, he should be unshaken in the Christian faith, should drink deep of the Christian spirit," and "be animated by the Christian hope." In this way a college professor would help to carry forth the progress of American civilization, for this Christian professor would also be a patriot. "An American heart should beat high in his bosom, and yet his patriotism should ever be chastened by a controlling philanthropy." Lathrop's description of a Christian patriot professor echoed across a land accustomed to denominational liberal arts colleges training a generation of ministers, but Lathrop's college wasn't mean to train ministers. In fact, it wasn't even a denominational college. It was the state-funded University of Wisconsin.

The American Revolution did not create a secular educational realm, nor could the universities of the Early Republic, private or public/state, be called anything other than Christian. The transformation of American education toward any form of secularism lay several generations in the future. George Marsden chronologically places the change in the American educational regime in the generation between 1880 and 1950. Only then were leading American schools "transformed almost beyond recognition."[3] Mars-

---

2. John H. Lathrop, *Inauguration of Hon. John H. Lathrop: LL.D. Chancellor of the University of Wisconsin, at the Capitol, Madison January 16, 1850* (Milwaukee: Sentinel and Gazette, 1850), 49.

3. George Marsden, *The Soul of the American University: From Protestant Establishment to Established Nonbelief* (New York: Oxford Univer-

den's excellent work on American universities, *The Soul of the American University*, rightly notes that church and state created American universities in the Early Republic when traditional Protestants like Anglicans and Presbyterians gave up their opposition to state universities.[4] They did so because it became apparent that traditional Protestants—again generally Anglicans and Presbyterians—could in fact take over state university leadership. Marsden suggests it was evident that the religious foundations of nineteenth-century American education "would have to be some sort of awkward blend of Christian and Enlightenment views. Traditionalist Protestants would have to demonstrate that they were just as enlightened and nonsectarian as the Jeffersonians claimed to be. To do so they would have to borrow from the Jeffersonian book."[5] Marsden is not substantially wrong but he overstates the degree to which the Enlightenment—or Thomas Jefferson—infiltrated the state university regime in the United States in the generations between 1789 and 1861. As we shall see, even Protestant supporters of disestablishment and the ostensibly non-sectarian University of Virginia were not willing to borrow from the so-called Jeffersonian book when it became clear what that book included. Non-sectarian Protestant state schools were still nothing less than Protestant, and nothing less than state institutions. Like John Lathrop's ideal Christian professor for his university in Wisconsin, state universities in the United States were "too profoundly Christian" to be "sectarian" and "too intensely American, to be partizan."[6]

sity Press, 1994), 31.

4. Marsden, *The Soul of the American University*, 69-70.

5. Marsden, *The Soul of the American University*, 75.

6. Lathrop, *Inauguration of Hon. John H. Lathrop*, 49.

The innate religiosity of state institutions of higher education remained constant until after the American Civil War. A representative example in the Early Republic was Delaware's charter of Newark College—now the University of Delaware—in 1833. Newark College from the outset claimed to be a state university whose mission was to bring "the richest blessings to this State, and confer pure joys upon a multitude of immortal minds."[7] John Holmes Agnew (1804–1865), a Presbyterian minister and professor of languages at Newark, told its inaugural class that their university's success was tied to its students' and faculty's fidelity to Christianity. Newark College might whither "in the bud by the frosts of neglect," or wilt in "scorching heat of passionate excitement."[8] If college leadership wasn't careful, there might be "thrust within its precincts, to guide its sons, those who shall imbue their minds with prejudices against Christianity, and political principles subversive of our happy Union." Agnew hoped however that the college "may ever call to its aid, those who love the *Bible* , and will delight to infuse its vivifying and elevating principles of action into the youthful mind." Only by relying on respecters of the Christian Scriptures could the college train up "a generation of moral and useful citizens, an honor to their Alma Mater, and a rich gift to their government."

Agnew left no ambiguity where the foundations of the college's administration lay. "In the foundation of a College, where there are yet no bad precedents established, and much may be left to the discretion of a judicious Faculty," college statutes needed to "embrace a few fixed principles of

---

7. John Holmes Agnew, *Inaugural Address Delivered at the Opening of Newark College by Professor John Holmes Agnew; Newark, Delaware, May 8, 1834* (Philadelphia: William F. Geddes, 1834), 3.

8. Agnew, *Inaugural Address*, 4.

immutable rectitude, derived from the best code of moral law the world ever saw, the Bible, and let these be unalterable, not only as the laws of the Medes and Persians, but as the righteous government of God himself."[9] Because the Bible's moral laws were "unerring, universally applicable," and defined the "eternal rule of right, they never need, and never ought to be changed." Agnew made clear to his listeners that government, education, and the Bible all existed in a necessary symbiosis. College-bound young men needed to understand that the faculty and administration at Newark intended to govern them as moral agents, possessing "intellect and, conscience, and will." Students needed to be reminded that they were "responsible to God, to the community, and to their own persons, for the right and useful exercise of these powers." It was necessary for the college community to see that the administrators recognized in their charges "an ability to distinguish between right and wrong, and a high moral sense." That moral sense, argued Agnew, was "enlightened by the Christian principles of this Christian people," and deterred college age males "in ordinary circumstances, from the commission of indecorous and disorderly acts, and induce the cultivation of *whatever so things are just, true, honest, lovely, and of good report.*"[10] Every curricular decision and every policy governing Newark College, Agnew declared, should "be founded on that evangelical sense of morality, which in his calmer moments, at least, will speak powerfully in the bosom of every student, in its favor."[11]

---

9. Agnew, *Inaugural Address*, 6.

10. Agnew, *Inaugural Address*, 6-7.

11. Agnew, *Inaugural Address*, 7.

The earliest state universities in the American republic were those founded in the South. The University of Georgia (1785), the University of North Carolina (1789), and South Carolina College (1800) each represented their state's wish to educate its elite young men in the precepts that state legislatures believed important for a healthy republican society. In the case of North Carolina, Presbyterians led the way in its founding in the hopes of educating their sons in the Calvinist tradition.[12] In Georgia, transplanted New England Congregationalists dreamed a religious institution into existence as a state university. Clergymen headed each of these institutions, and of the major southern universities only the University of Virginia—founded much later than its three sister colleges—made any pretense to being meaningfully non-sectarian.[13] States carved out of the Northwest Territory followed their Southern sisters in creating state universities. They also sought clerics to serve as college presidents, principles, and preceptors. The first state college founded west of the Appalachian mountains, Ohio University, began its life in the newly chartered town of Athens with a newly minted Princeton graduate and Presbyterian minister, Jacob Lindley (1774–1857), as its leader.[14]

Much has been made of the Founding Era being essentially Classical and Deist, and ostensibly not particularly Christian. This analysis has made its way into works on education well. In her work on collegiate life in the Early

---

12. William D. Snider, *Light on the Hill: A History of the University of North Carolina at Chapel Hill* (Chapel Hill: University of North Carolina Press, 1992), 2–23.

13. Thomas G. Dyer, *The University of Georgia: A Bicentennial History, 1785–1985* (Athens: University of Georgia Press, 1985), 1–22.

14. Betty Hollow, *Ohio University, 1804–2004: The Spirit of a Singular Place* (Athens: Ohio University Press, 2003), 10–12.

Republic, Margaret Sumner posits that after 1800 and the advent of the Second Great Awakening "waves of evangelical revivalism transformed and expanded the definition of education" and the definition of an ideal society.[15] This supposedly more Christian understanding of education was "merging an intellectual world governed by classicism, masculinized reason and virtue and 'common sense,' with one that invoked the authority of biblical revelation" and "feminized emotion and virtues." Although it is outside the scope of this work to address the question of whether Christianity actuated feminine values instead of masculine classical ones, it is clear that the collegiate institutions founded at the end of the eighteenth century in the United States were no less Christian than ones founded in the supposedly more evangelical Early Republic.

Christianity's relationship to education in a disestablishmentarian context and the subsequent relationship of church and populace to disestablishment was hardly uniform or even clear to citizens of the American republic in 1800. What is obvious is that almost no one wanted education to actually have a secular foundation. Even Presbyterian partisans of Thomas Jefferson realized that their vision of education was very different than that of the third president. Presbyterians discovered unforeseen, and in their minds unwanted, consequences of disestablishment and *en masse* religious freedom when Jefferson moved to make Thomas Cooper (1759–1839) the first professor of natural science and law at the University of Virginia.[16] The appointment enraged Virginia Presbyterians, who knew the freethinking

---

15. Margaret Sumner, *Collegiate Republic: Cultivating an Ideal Society in Early America* (Charlottesville and London: University of Virginia Press, 2014), 3.

16. Peterson, *Thomas Jefferson*, 978.

Cooper was publicly open about his rejection of traditional Christian beliefs. John Holt Rice, a well-regarded minister in Richmond and the intellectual leader of Calvinists in the state, wrote an article in the magazine he edited denouncing Jefferson and Cooper's potential employment. Merrill Peterson noted that Holt "did not call for a Calvinistic university but for one where religion had a respectable place in the curriculum, in the faculty, in divine worship."[17] Holt considered a university without religion an aberration. Peterson explained Holt's position: "a university conducted without preference as to religious sect was one thing, a university without religion, or indeed motivated by rationalistic zeal against orthodoxy, quite another."[18]

Rice and his partisans undeniably believed their position was consistent. Rice sought to influence the workings of a state institution, having previously argued that the "religion of the meek and benevolent Savior, was not designed to be an engine of state; an instrument of erecting a despotism to control the consciences of men" or to "crush every manly independent feeling of the soul, and extinguish every spark of liberty."[19] Presbyterians, Rice said, were "not a society of Jesuits: we have no secret articles of faith, to be executed, when some deep, subtle contrivance shall have enabled us to procure an establishment of Presbyterianism." The disconnect between Jefferson and his former Presbyterian partisans over what constituted religious freedom in the political order became almost comical during Rice and Jefferson's dispute over Cooper. Rice pleaded that he was not a Jesuit,

---

17. John Holt Rice, *The Duties of a Gospel Minister* (Madison: Log College Press, 2018), Kindle Locations 208–210, 211–12.

18. Rice, *Duties of a Gospel Minister*, Kindle Locations 211-12.

19. Rice, *Duties of a Gospel Minister*, Kindle Locations 211-12.

while Jefferson accused him and his fellow Presbyterians of being exactly that. The most "restive" opposition, Jefferson bewailed, was from Presbyterian "priests" who dreaded "the advance of science as witches do the approach of day-light; and scowl on the fatal harbinger announcing the subversion of the duperies on which they live."[20] In this opposition, he sneered, "Presbyterian clergy take the lead. The tocsin is sounded in all their pulpits, and the first alarm denounced is against the particular creed of Doctor Cooper; and as impudently denounced as if they really knew what it is."

If Rice and Virginia's Presbyterians actually believed in total disestablishment, complete separation of church from the state's educational apparatus, and absolute freedom of religion—like James Iredell, Jefferson, and the latter's Baptist partisans—he had no constitutional, intellectual, or legal foundation from which to argue against Jefferson appointing whoever he wanted to teach at the state's university. And so it is clear he did not actually believe in Jeffersonian disestablishmentarianism in the context of state universities, and neither did most Presbyterians in the Early Republic. Like many Christians in the historical record, they adopted popular and innovative contemporaneous political and social rhetoric. Their assumptions about the consequences of disestablishment, however, were neither well-considered or even consistent with their own tradition. That a freedom of religion might include a freedom to not practice religion at all, or to be agnostic, seems never to have occurred to Presbyterians in the Early Republic. It did, however occur to Jefferson. In his work on Jefferson and education in Virginia, Alan Taylor noted that "Jefferson dedicated the University

---

20. Thomas Jefferson to José Corrêa da Serra, Monticello, 11 April 1820, *Founders Online*, National Archives, https://founders.archives. gov/?q=11%20April%201820&s=1211311111&sa=&r=38&sr=.

to 'the illimitable freedom of the human mind,'" but the third president "assumed that the free pursuit of truth always led to his conclusions."[21] Presbyterians served as useful allies in Jefferson's war against the Church of England, but they refused to admit the actual consequences of what that support meant in regard to their own highly valued educational priorities. Like Jefferson, they assumed that freedom of religion always led to their conclusions. The experience of religion at the University of Virginia proved how wrong that assumption was.

Virginia's Jeffersonian separationism in the context of state universities was never the national norm in the Early Republic. Ideological commitment not only to Christianity's place in education, but also to state education as an instrument to enact a Christian republic, was common among educators at U.S. state institutions in the nineteenth century. The leading intellectual founder of the University of North Carolina, Samuel McCorkle (1746–1811), made clear that his mission was to create a Christian republic and that a state university was his chosen instrument to do so. In the 1790s, the creation of a Christian republic *via* a Christian state university seemed more urgent than ever. The board of the college wanted Christianity to be a constituent and foundational part of a broader curriculum, while McCorkle wanted what was in effect a state-funded Presbyterian seminary. "The most leading members of the board," McCorkle complained, "have not the same views I have of that education, morality, and religion which should be at the bottom of the institution."[22] McCorkle "reprobate[d] the modern

---

21. Alan Taylor, *Thomas Jefferson's Education* (New York: Norton, 2019), 238.

22. Thomas T. Taylor, "Samuel E. McCorkle and a Christian Republic, 1792–1802," *American Presbyterians* 63, no. 4 (1985), 378.

French system of education which would govern wholly by reason" without the discipline of institutional Christianity, what McCorkle termed "the rod of correction."

McCorkle did not get his vision of a university enacted exactly to his liking, but the University of North Caroline didn't miss its visionaries mark by much. McCorkle's hope that Chapel Hill, the site of the university, would be "for religion as the ancient hill of Zion" was in many ways fulfilled by the first president of the University of North Carolina, Joseph Caldwell (1773–1835).[23] Local primary academies, almost of all of them headed by Presbyterian ministers, fed Chapel Hill's college in the last decade of the eighteenth century and the first two decades after 1800. Henry Alexander White (1861–1926), one of the nineteenth century's best chroniclers of Presbyterian intellectual life, noted that these small primary schools "trained the people of North Carolina to believe that Christianity must fill the atmosphere even of a state school."[24] The innate religiosity of the state's populace and the customary institutional place of Christianity meant that "Joseph Caldwell preached the gospel every Sunday in the chapel at the university, had the Bible taught in the school itself and opened the work of each day with public prayer in presence of all the students." Like the other heads of state universities in the antebellum era, "Caldwell upheld the Christian religion as a necessary element in the training given by a university."[25]

State universities filled a public role in the Early Republic. The activities of the classroom formed just one

23. Henry Alexander White, *Southern Presbyterian Leaders* (New York: Neale, 1911), 203–204.

24. White, *Southern Presbyterian Leaders*, 204.

25. White, *Southern Presbyterian Leaders*, 204–205.

aspect of the mission of state universities. Chapel services became a crucial gathering point where collegiate communities mixed with the wider public. Chapel services occurred at every major state university—even the supposedly secular University of Virginia eventually caved and held chapel services—and townspeople routinely attended because more often than not the university chaplain was the only or one of the only ordained clergymen in a respective locale.[26] Chapel services exemplified the institutional commitment to—usually Protestant—Christianity within the disestablished constitutional order. At his 1850 inauguration as chancellor of the University of Wisconsin, John Lathrop discouraged the idea of enforcing a religious test in the state's university, but he confidently could tell the board of trustees several years later that the University of Wisconsin's "students are assembled at prayers daily in the chapel of the university, at the morning hour for commencing study and recitation."[27] In the case of the University of North Carolina, William Mercer Green (1798–1887), an ordained Episcopal priest and eventually the first Episcopalian bishop of Mississippi taught logic and rhetoric and served as the college chaplain.[28] He taught during the week, ran the college's chapel services, and preached every other Sunday in the local parish church when it was erected in 1844. Green's chapel

---

26. See Chapters 3 and 4 in Henry Y. Gamble, *God on the Grounds: A History of Religion at Thomas Jefferson's University* (Charlottesville: University of Virginia Press, 2020).

27. John H. Lathrop, *Inauguration of Hon. John H. Lathrop*, 49; *Annual Report of the Board of Regents of the University of Wisconsin, for the Year 1855* (Madison: Calkins & Proudfit, 1856), 53.

28. Kemp P. Battle, *History of the University of North Carolina: From Its Beginning to the Death of President Swain, 1789-1868*, vol. 1 (Raleigh: Edwards & Broughton), 546-47.

services dovetailed with the addresses that he gave to the various literary societies on campus.

The public popularity and relative celebrity of college professors generally led to eventual publication of chapel messages from divines and lay professors who taught religious subjects. Publishers in New York successfully sought to bring James Henley Thornwell's chapel addresses to the public while he was still serving as president of South Carolina College in 1855.[29] John Holmes Agnew, then professor at the University of Michigan, granted permission to a women's benevolence society when they asked to publish a speech he gave to the Monroe, Michigan, Female Seminary in the summer of 1851.[30]

Evidence for the thorough Christianization of public colleges lies not only in the public addresses and presence of figures like Agnew, Green, and Thornwell on campuses, but also in the content of their public lectures. In 1823 Rev. Robert Henry, professor of logic and moral philosophy at South Carolina College and its future president, used an on-campus chapel address to argue for why nations need to submit to the Christian deity. "It shall be my endeavour in the further prosecution of this discourse, in humble reliance on divine assistance, to impress your minds with a feeling conviction of this truth."[31] Henry argued:

---

29. James Henley Thornwell, *Discourses on Truth: Delivered in the Chapel of the South Carolina College* (New York: Robert Carter & Brothers, 1855).

30. John Holmes Agnew, *Woman's Office and Influence: An Address before the Monroe Female Seminary* (New York: John F. Trow, 1851).

31. Robert Henry, *Religion Productive of National Prosperity: A Sermon, Delivered on Thanksgiving Day, February 5th, 1823; in the Chapel of the So. Ca. College* (Columbia: D. & J. M. Faust, 1823), 4.

I. That God is, in a peculiar sense, more the Ruler of some Nations than of others.

II. To point out the prosperity, which flows from this peculiar care of the Supreme Being.

III. To indicate the means, by which a nation may preserve its title to this peculiar adoption.[32]

Henry conceived of the relationship between the American republic and Christianity in a way that was thoroughly consistent with what twenty-first century Americans breathlessly praise or anathemize as "Christian Nationalism," but there were important differences. Henry rejected the idea that the law could create a religious establishment or legally name Christianity as the religion of the state, and he rejected the idea that the state could in any way be sacralized.

Nonetheless, the thrust of his argument was clear: some countries bow the knee to God, and some do not, and the American people had better be sure their republic was among the former. Law, argued Henry, had to have some foundation other than mere temporal power and there must, he declared, "be some other principle, by which the evil passions of men may be kept in order, not only, when immediately under the inspection of the Magistrate, but at all times, and in all circumstances."[33] That other principle did not exist "except in Religion," which was the "moral instrument of sufficient energy for such comprehensive purposes." Religion alone "can restrain the wicked by punishments as certain and as weighty as their crimes: she alone enables the good to become fellow workers with the divinity

---

32. Henry, *Religion Productive of National Prosperity*, 4-5.

33. Henry, *Religion Productive of National Prosperity*, 9.

himself, by imitating his benevolence and rejoicing in the universal diffusion of happiness." Only religion enabled humans "to submit cheerfully to all those individual privations, which are necessary for the attainment of the public good." In all parts of life, Henry told the gathered undergraduates and the public, "in every posture of our affairs,' religion's command was the same... 'Hold fast thine integrity,' for all must soon appear at the bar of God to answer for the deeds done in the body, whether they have been good or evil." If the apprehension of God's presence could be rendered constant to the students and to citizens of the American republic, "it is scarcely conceivable that we should deliberately wander from His commandments." "A nation fearing God," said Henry, "will not only have peace at home; it will also command respect abroad."[34] The benefits of Christianity to the American republic were such that it was unimaginable that the United States should not aspire to the "peculiar adoption and favour of God."[35] Amusingly, when Henry delivered this address at South Carolina College in 1823, Thomas Cooper, having resigned under pressure from his role at the University of Virginia, was the college president. When he later resigned in 1833 due to public pressure over his religious views, Henry would be his temporary successor.

Publicly funded universities in the United States imbued their students with the belief that Christianity was necessary for the success of the American republic and that it was synonymous with civilization. William Mercer Green used a lecture at the University of North Carolina to extol what he argued was the near total effect of public Christianity on the development of Western social progress. For

---

34. Henry, *Religion Productive of National Prosperity*, 10-11.

35. Henry, *Religion Productive of National Prosperity*, 12.

Green, Christianity was less the culmination of a Western intellectual, religious, or social tradition and more a revolutionary conqueror that subdued the Greeks and Romans. He stated flatly that the "religion of the Bible is the highest ornament and the surest safeguard of national prosperity."[36] Green noted that personal piety was essential to the body politic of the American republic and all nations. He also believed that the social effects of Christianity represented a conquest of paganism that elevated the human condition. "Involuntary proofs of the beneficial effects of Christianity on individual character, are abundantly supported by similar testimony to its benign influence on society generally."[37] No sooner did "the mild religion of the Son of God obtained a footing in the world, than its benevolent spirit became a bond of union between independent nations. The middle wall of partition, which had so long divided the Jewish and Gentile world, crumbled at its touch." Pagan virtues that fed "pride and revenge, those fertile sources of war and bloodshed, were supplanted by humility and forgiveness. Into every family it came a messenger of love, a dispenser of peace." Christianity gave women a better life as it "took by the hand the softer sex," and eased "their shoulders of the onerous burdens that barbarous superstition had put upon them." Christians lifted women "from a degraded and servile state, and gave to them that equal rank in refined society to which they are justly entitled." The religion of Christ "abolished polygamy, and restricted the power of divorce. Unnatural crime has fled at its approach. The harshness of parental authority has been tempered by the mild precepts

---

36. William Mercer Green, *The Influence of Christianity upon the Welfare of the Nations* (Hillsborough: Dennis Heart, 1831), 6.

37. Green, *Influence of Christianity*, 16.

of the gospel." Instead of the pagan practice of "putting to death the old and the decrepit, and weak and deformed children, as was sanctioned by the laws of many heathen states," Christianity's benevolent genius "spread over these hapless members of the human family the ample aegis of the law, and erected asylums for their preservation and relief." Marital relationships and the relationships between parents and children, "which formerly differed but little from that of master and slave, are now stripped of all unnecessary power. The poor and the ignorant have been taken under the patronage of the rich and enlightened." Prosperous Christians allowed themselves to be "taxed to feed the hungry, clothe the naked, and heal the afflicted."[38] No matter what form or degree human misery took, "the spirit of Christianity opens to its relief the hand of private benevolence and munificent storehouses of public charity."[39]

Christianity, argued Green, also "erected houses of refuge for every grade and species of human suffering. It has established schools for the gratuitous instruction of the poor."[40] Green shared his theme of education and religion as the primary vehicles for the alleviation of poverty with the mass of the United States' citizenry in the Early Republic. In the case of publicly funded colleges like the University of Georgia, the populations who pushed for its establishment had neither wealth nor education. For this reason the agrarian citizenry of Southern and Western states relied on the hope that the religion of Christ "penetrated into the noxious dungeon, and not only lighted its darkness with the lamp of eternal life but placed within the reach of its

---

38. Green, *Influence of Christianity*, 16-17.

39. Green, *Influence of Christianity*, 17.

40. Green, *Influence of Christianity*, 17.

wretched tenant every comfort that the strict claims of justice will allow." The expansive course of Christian benevolence had even "descended to the care of inferior animals by discountenancing every exercise of cruelty towards them and by making their ease and security a subject of legal enactment." Human individuals, human societies, and even animals experienced the benevolent reign of Christendom. "Instead then, of asking, 'what has Christianity done?' we may demand 'What has it not done toward meliorating the condition of man?'"

Henry Tappan (1805–1881), chancellor of the University of Michigan, often gave public addresses on Sundays as a sort of *de facto* Bible study. He also spoke on the state of religious life at the college. Tappan rejected the idea that the University of Michigan could implement a system wherein all denominations in the United States could be represented in its faculty. Even if he could give denominations equal representation, he saw it as immaterial to the condition of Christianity on campus precisely because the university was not a church. Episcopalians and Congregationalists, among other groups, had been represented in the university faculty, and Tappan saw no reason why an institution that was neither state nor church should worry about a faculty member's confessional identity. Even that principle, however, proved to be less than absolute. After Tappan hired a certain Dr. Brunnow he felt led to inquire whether the man was a Catholic or a Protestant. Brunnow turned out to be a Lutheran (to Tappan's relief, one imagines). Michigan like many other institutions, retained the Early Republic anti-Catholicism to the point that it hired almost every sort of Protestant, but still displayed residual fear of the Roman Church. The Sunday afternoon lectures that Tappan gave, "either on natural theology, or the evidences of Christianity, or morals, or on some point of practical Christianity," were not static mere Christian lectures but deeply informed by Tappan's Presbyterianism.[41] His claim in 1858 that "denominationalism and proselytism have not appeared among us, and yet much healthful religions influence has been exerted" was undoubtedly true because the University of Michigan, while understandably disclaiming sectarianism, was like its sister universities without a doubt already thoroughly Protestant.

Modernization of curriculum in state colleges occurred throughout the Early Republic, even in conservative South Carolina. In 1835, the state legislature of South Carolina decided to overhaul the curriculum and faculty at South Carolina college. Every professor then teaching lost his position, and the state moved to enact a curriculum that included German methods of inquiry and didacticism. Formerly, the college followed a more classical mode of collegiate study that hewed relatively close to the seminary-style Protestant colleges founded in seventeenth-century North America. Before 1835 memorization of the Hebrew and Christian Scriptures accompanied memorization of classical Greek and Roman texts to form the minds of the Early Republic's elite.[42]

Yet curriculum modernization and adoption of more contemporary intellectual trends like German criticism did not represent secularization, dechristianization, or anti-clericalism. Ordained Protestant ministers held three of the

41. Henry P. Tappan, *The University: Its Constitution, and Its Relations, Political and Religious: A Discourse Delivered June 22d, 1858, at the Request of the Christian Library Association* (Ann Arbor: S. B. McCracken, 1858), 33.

42. Wayne K. Durrill, "The Power of Ancient Words: Classical Teaching and Social Change at South Carolina College, 1804–1860," *Journal of Southern History* 65, no. 3 (1999): 469–98.

seven professorships at South Carolina College in 1844.[43] The aforementioned Rev. Robert Henry, an Episcopalian, served as the college's president from 1842 to 1845. William Hooper (1792–1876), an ordained Episcopalian of pronounced evangelical persuasions who eventually became a Baptist, taught Greek and Roman literature. Most famous of all was James Henley Thornwell, a Presbyterian minister who headed the department of Sacred Literature and Evidences of Christianity. While it may surprise twenty-first century readers to discover that a state university subsidized the teaching of Christian moral and religious precepts, most state legislatures believed such professors and classes were necessary to give an appropriate education to their respective elite young men. State colleges in the North and South wove Christianity into their curricula, sometimes through explicitly programmatic apologetics classes as in the case of South Carolina College and the University of North Carolina, and in overwhelmingly Christian moral philosophy or moral science classes taught at colleges in free states like the University of Michigan, the University of Indiana, and the University of Vermont and in slave states like the University of Alabama and the University of Mississippi. Invariably eminent divines taught moral philosophy or moral science classes.[44] At Alabama, Basil Manly (1798–1868), the col-

---

43. Edwin L. Green, *A History of South Carolina College* (Columbia: State Company, 1916), 37, 44–55; William S. Powell, ed., *The Dictionary of North Carolina Biography*, vol. 3 (Chapel Hill: University of North Carolina Press, 1988), 202–3; *Catalogue of the Trustees, Faculty and Students of South Carolina College* (Columbia: Morgan's Press, 1844), 4

44. *University of Michigan. Catalogue of the Officers and Students in the Department of the Arts and Sciences 1843–4* (Ann Arbor: Michigan Argus Office. 1843), 5; *Annual Report of the Indiana University Including the Catalogue for the Academic Year, MDCCCLVI–VII. Bloomington*

lege's president and one of the era's best known Baptist ministers, taught moral science.[45] Publicly supported Cincinnati College in Ohio—later the University of Cincinnati—made Presbyterian cleric William H. McGuffey (1800–1873), the creator of the McGuffey primers used widely in secondary education in the nineteenth century, Professor of Evidences for Christianity.[46]

Christian and more specifically Protestant commitments informed more than curricula and classes in antebellum state universities. Miami University of Ohio—a state-founded and funded institution that traced its roots to Ohio's statehood charters—was essentially a *de facto* Presbyterian college before 1873. In 1825 Robert Hamilton Bishop, a convinced anti-revivalist Presbyterian from Scotland, assumed the presidency. At his installation a fellow Presbyterian minister, John Thompson (1772–1859), declared that Miami's mission to its students was to "imbue their minds, as far as human exertions can effect, with the meliorating

(Indianapolis: Joseph J. Bingham, 1856); *Catalogue of the Officers and Students of the University of Vermont. October....1839* (Burlington: University Press, 1839); *Catalogue of the Officers and Students of the University of Alabama of the State of Alabama: 1844* (Tuscaloosa: M.D.J. Slade, 1844); *Catalogue of the Alumni, Officers, and Students of the University of Mississippi at Oxford, Mississippi, 1857–'58* (Oxford: Mississippian Steam Book and Job Office,1858), 52–53.

45. Jonathan A. Lindsay, "Basil Manly: Nineteenth Century Protean Man," *Baptist History and Heritage* 8, no. 3 (July 1973): 130–43.

46. *The Ohio Gazetteer, and Traveler's Guide: Containing a Description of the Several Towns, Townships and Counties, with Their Water Courses, Roads, Improvements, Mineral Productions, etc. etc.*, ed. Warren Jenkins (Columbus: Isaac M. Whiting, 1837), 537; Gerry Bohning, "The McGuffey Eclectic Readers: 1836–1986," *The Reading Teacher* 40, no. 3 (1986): 263–69.

influence of our holy religion."[47] President Bishop told students that the "Bible is the source of all intellectual as well as moral strength."[48] For that reason, the study of the Bible "shall be connected in the Miami University, with the study of all other systems of religion, morals, and jurisprudence." Miami was so entangled in Presbyterian politics that in 1840 Bishop—an Old School Presbyterian who disliked the moral liberal New School Presbyterian denomination that has formed in 1837—was forced to resign as president for not being ecumenical with the New School. This did not mean that Bishop was as sectarian as his resignation might imply. He saw himself as a modernizer who blended the liberalism of the Enlightenment with conservative Presbyterianism.[49] In South Carolina, Ohio, and elsewhere, Christianity and Protestantism in particular remained a foundational institutional commitment of state universities. Modernization in the years between 1830 and 1840 did not change that in the North or South.

Some Early Republic Protestant divines worried that modernization and a subsequent rise in secularity would break up the Early Republic consensus on the cooperation of church and state in the United States' educational order. Charles Hodge, principle of Princeton Seminary and perhaps the most prestigious Protestant intellectual in the United States in at this point, addressed what he called in the education question in a short work in 1850. Hodge did

---

47. Dale Robb, "Miami University 1809–2002: From Presbyterian Enterprise to Public Institution," *Journal of Presbyterian History* 81, no. 1 (2003), 37.

48. Robb, "Miami University 1809-2002," 38.

49. Thomas D. Matijasic, "The African Colonization Movement and Ohio's Protestant Community," *Phylon* 46, no. 1 (1985): 16–24.

not neatly divide religious and secular education, because the Presbyterians in the era did not admit a binary between the two concepts where education was concerned. There had been at the founding of the republic and the years that followed, Charles Hodge wrote, "substantial agreement among religious men, as to the most essential points involved in the education question."[50] Hodge was "aware that the difference between the religious community and those who, in many instances, control the action of our legislative bodies in, relation to this subject, is radical and irreconcilable." He also lamented the extent to which "many religious men, from different motives, have been led to throw their influence in favour of this latter party, who advocate the exclusion of religious instruction from our public schools." Still, Hodge hoped and believed that as a body the "religious community" was "united and determined in their opposition to any such destructive course."

The destructive course Hodge identified was the secularization of secondary education. Presbyterians, he stated, were united on their educational vision. The evidence was "abundant and conclusive that the great mass of our members, ministers and laymen" were "convinced of the absolute necessity of universal popular education." Protestant ministers were, Hodge argued, united in their belief that "education should be religious." Hodge defined religious education as the proposition "not only that religion ought to be in some way inculcated, but that it should be made a regular part of the course of instruction in all our non-professional educational institutions." Parents, the state, and the church had an "obligation to secure for the young this combined secular and religious training." State, family, and

---

50. Charles Hodge, *The Education Question* (Philadelphia: C. Sherman, 1850), 1.

the church symbiotically worked to educate the republic's young people. The educational enterprise did not "rest on one of these parties to the exclusion of the others, but, as the care of the poor, it rests equally on all, and the efforts and resources of all are requisite for the accomplishment of the object." Obligation "presses all these parties as to the whole work of education. One portion of the work does not belong exclusively to one of them, and another portion exclusively to the others, but each is in its sphere responsible for the whole." Parents were bound "to provide not only for the religious but also for the secular education of [their] children," and "the same is true with regard to the State and to the Church." Because of the "existing state of our country, the Church can no more resign the work of education exclusively to the State, than the State can leave it exclusively to parents or to the Church."

Hodge, like most Protestant clerics of the first half of the nineteenth century, saw public education not as the exclusive province of the state, but as a cooperative effort between the state, the church, and parents. True public education included religion and that could not "be accomplished in the way in which [the church] is bound to see it accomplished, without her efficient co-operation."[51] Churches necessarily were bound, "without interfering either with the State or with voluntary institutions, to provide the means of thorough secular and religious training, wherever they are not otherwise secured."[52] In the performance of this "great duty, the Church cannot rely on the separate agency of her members, but is bound to act collectively, or in her organized capacity."

51. Hodge, *The Education Question*, 1-2.

52. Hodge, *The Education Question*, 2.

Other Protestant clerics shared Hodge's vision of church, state, and family cooperating to implement a public education regime in the United States during the years between the War of 1812 and the Civil War. Strange as it might seem to early twenty-first century readers, the religion was seen not just as a non-negotiable aspect of state education but as the underwriting reason for education in general. In this sense Early Republic Episcopalians, for example, like New Jersey Bishop George Washington Doane, argued that Christianity was the only authority on which education rested. Doane was a controversial presence in the Episcopal Church from 1830 to his death in 1859. An autodidact and rabid high churchman who wrote poetry and inserted himself into the Tractarian controversy in the Church of England, Doane nonetheless worked tirelessly to promote the idea of the patriot-Christian within the still largely Protestant framework of American collegiate education, and he believed colleges served the primary role in molding young men to wed the two.[53] This was not seen as syncretic or even particularly controversial in the nineteenth century. What else, American Protestants might have asked, was a young Baptist, Episcopalian, Presbyterian, or Congregationalist supposed to be if not a patriot and a Christian? "We blend," Doane, confidently asserted at a July fourth celebration in 1853, "in one, the twofold character of the Christian and the Patriot."[54] The bishop's education would

---

53. See Kenneth Walter Cameron, "Wordsworth, Bishop Doane and the Sonnets on the American Church," *Historical Magazine of the Protestant Episcopal Church* 11, no. 1 (1942): 83–91; Lawrence N. Crumb, G W. Doane, John H. Hopkins, H. Potter, and H. B Whipple, "Some American Bishops' Letters to E. B. Pusey," *Anglican and Episcopal History* 69, no. 4 (2000): 504–23.

54. George Washington Doane, *The Young American, His Dangers, His*

"bring up Christian freemen, to be 'a bulwark of our Church and State.'" Colleges, "by precept and example, instilled into our minds the ennobling principles of true Christian patriotism."

Colleges in the United States had to create Christian patriots, argued Doane, because a state that was both irreligious and successful was a metaphysical impossibility: "*The men, to make a State, must be religious men.* States are from God. States are dependent upon God. States are accountable to God. To leave God out of States, is to be Atheist."[55] Doane rejected the notion that Christian scholar-statesmen led to hypocrisy: "I do not mean, that men must cant. I do not mean, that men must wear long faces. I do not mean, that men must talk of conscience, while they take your spoons." Instead, Doane spoke of men "who feel, and own, a God." He precluded a merely theistic construction on his idealized Christian scholar-statesmen by applying Protestant conceptions of sin and respect for the Bible. He hoped for "men, who feel, and own, their sins. I speak of men, who know there is a hell." Leaders of the state who were educated in and acquainted with Protestant conceptions of sin would naturally also know Protestant conceptions of atonement. Doane envisioned men "who think the Cross no shame. I speak of men, who have it in their heart, as well as on their brow. The men that own no future, the men that trample on the Bible, the men that never pray, are not the men to make a State."[56]

Duties, & His Destinies (Philadelphia: Inquirer Press, 1853), 4.

55. George Washington Doane, "The Men to Make a State: Their Making and Their Marks," in *Life and Writings*, 4:239.

56. Doane, "The Men to Make a State", *Life and Writings*, 4:239-40.

In 1850 Doane publicly expanded on the ties between education and the divine. "Education," he told a public gathering in Burlington, New Jersey, "is a divine thing. It is the rescue and restoration of an immortal, fallen, nature. It contemplates its redemption, first; then, its renewal, in the divine image; then, its re-union with God. Its standpoint is the Cross."[57] The channel of education's influence, said the Bishop, was the Church and its "agent is the Holy Spirit." Education was "a divine thing. It is from GOD. It is through GOD. It is for GOD." Even the "*authority*, to educate a human soul," Doane declared, "must come, *from* God." He warned that men reasoned too loosely on the subject of who had the authority to educate in antebellum American society: "They take, for granted, a dominion over human thought, human desire, and human will, which in no other realm of the Creation, is assumed."[58] Even worse than assuming human dominion over the human intellect was the fact that "seduction of the Devil has so won, with human hearts, as to divorce the soul, from God."[59] In so doing, the Devil had caused men to leave God "out of that most gracious work, for which He gave His blessed Son, and sends His Holy Spirit."[60]

The establishment and application of those three above propositions—that that the means, motive, and authority of education come from God—occupied Doane's thoughts on the divine foundations of education. "On them, as on an arch of living rock, this College has been founded. In them,

---

57. George Washington Doane, "Education a Divine Thing," in *Life and Writings*, 4:47.

58. Doane, "Education a Divine Thing," *Life and Writings*, 4:48.

59. Doane, "Education a Divine Thing," *Life and Writings*, 4:54-55.

60. Doane, "Education a Divine Thing," *Life and Writings*, 4:55.

alone, do we desire that it should stand."[61] Through those same propositions, Doane hoped, "these young men…will be its glory and its crown. That, such, they may approve themselves, we ask the charity of your prayers."

Doane gave a summative indictment of what a non-religious education amounted to:

> Education, without the Church; education, without the ministry; education, without the sacraments; education, without prayer; education, without the Bible: in one word, godless education, is the order of the day. And the physical powers of men are educated, and their intellectual faculties, and their social nature, just as a monkey or a parrot might be trained; and all, that God cares most for, and all that is immortal, in its essence, left, to run its own wild way, and do its own wild will. Against all this, we set ourselves, immovably. We have been taught, of holy Paul, as he had learned, from Jesus Christ, our Lord: "beware lest any man spoil you through philosophy and vain deceit, after the tradition of men, after the rudiments of the world, and not after Christ: for, in Him, dwelleth all the fulness of the Godhead, bodily; and ye are complete, in Him." The education, which we undertake, is Christian education.[62]

Doane made clear he was not totally denigrating all modern notions in education. He meant "no disparagement of physical development" and "no disparagement of intellectual training" or "of social cultivation." But the fullest

---

61. Doane, "Education a Divine Thing", *Life and Writings*, 4:48.

62. Doane, "Education a Divine Thing", *Life and Writings*, 4:55.

education that led to the furtherance "of them all, in that, which God designed, should comprehend them all, and give them value, beauty, glory, power and immortality," was "the nurture and the culture of the heart; that, so, the child of God, redeemed, regenerated and renewed, in Jesus Christ, may be 'complete, in Him.'"

Doane's views on education and Christianity never led him to a post at a state university but they were shared widely by divines who did labor in state universities. Robert Hamilton Bishop at Miami University in Ohio did not see Christianity's influence as merely civilizational. Bishop had no qualms about drawing a state supported salary and telling a group of alumni that the "first and most important matter to be attended to by every individual, is, to make sure his own eternal salvation. This is the great and the chief work."[63] Unless salvation was secured, "all our other labors will be only busy idleness, and all our other attainments will be only vanity and vexation of spirit." Denominational identity was, "comparatively speaking, a very small matter…but it is essentially necessary that you should be personally connected with the living Head of the everlasting covenant." No one "living in a Christian land" could "give satisfactory evidence" that he was truly "connected with the only Savior, and a partaker of the only salvation, unless he is visibly connected with some department of the one visible body, and under the influence of the Holy Spirit of promise, endeavoring to walk in all the commandments of the Lord, blameless." The second class of subjects to which Miami's alumni's attention "ought to be daily directed, comprehends all the privileges and duties of the particular situation in

---

63. Robert Hamilton Bishop, *Addresses: No. 1—To the Alumni of Miami University: No.2—To the Farmers of Hamilton County* (Cincinnati: R. P. Brooks, 1845), 1–2.

which every individual of you may be placed." The God "who made you, and who made all things, and who preserves you in the enjoyment of all you possess, has bestowed upon you as a body, an infinite variety of talents, both natural and acquired, and hath given to each of you an infinite variety of opportunities for the full and daily use of each of these; and to each he has said, 'Occupy, till I come.'"

Bishop's 1845 encouragement to the alumni of Miami to occupy until the return of Jesus Christ was not substantively different from Episcopalian Robert Henry's admonition to the students of South Carolina College in 1845 to ensure their nation's obedience to God. Both men assumed the relationship between religion, education, and the civil order was a symbiotic one wherein all three were ultimately inseparable. The reason alumni needed to care about their college was because they needed to care about future generations. Those generations needed to be taught the great truths of the Christian faith. Students at Miami needed to use their time there not merely to educate themselves but to ensure that they were fulfilling their role in bringing about God's kingdom on earth.

> It is in the nature of things utterly impossible that the intellectual and moral and religious improvement of the rising generation, should ever be unconnected with the private and the daily action and enjoyments of any member of the community. Hence it must be the daily duty of every man in every department, to take a deep interest in the welfare of those who are younger than himself…the nearer he approaches towards his three score or four score years, this dependance will be increasing in a greater ratio and with a greater rapidity. Has he been, some thirty or forty years a father? He has children and

grandchildren, just commencing life, who are only multiplied portions of himself. Has he been in business to any extent? The number of youth and their descendants, who have had their characters and their destinies, both for time and eternity, formed by him, has been increasing and is increasing, and will continue to increase long after he himself shall be forgotten. Is he a patriot, and does he put an infinite value upon the fathers and the achievements of the American Revolution? All his hopes or his fears, for good or for ill, so far as his country is concerned, are produced and cherished by the state and character of the rising generation. *Is he a member of that great and growing community, of whose Head it is said that "of the increase of his government and peace there shall be no end?" All his hopes for the fulfilment of promise and prophecy rest upon the fulfilment of one declaration, viz: that ultimately the youth of this community shall be as the dew of the morning.*[64]

The public colleges and universities of the Early Republic served as a chief institutional vehicle for the implementation of Christian theology and Christian practice in the respective states. Christianity was not only a constituent aspect of the intellectual development that state universities gave their students; it was the beating heart of education in state colleges. Much is made of Presbyterians' reactions to the potential employment of Thomas Cooper as a professor of natural science and law at the University of Virginia, and it is often noted—as evidence of some sort of expansive religious liberty milieu—that Cooper later served as president of South Carolina College. Cooper's tenure at

---

64. Bishop, *Addresses: No. 1*, 6–7.

South Carolina proved to be a contentious one, however. The faculty found him meddlesome and invasive. All that might have been borne, however, had he not intruded on Christianity. Maximillian La Borde (1804–1873), a physics professor, recounted in 1859 that "there is an interest dearer than political interest, dear as that is; and this was not safe from his intrusion. I mean the religious. He had his own opinions. He had drunk deep at the fountain of infidelity."[65] Cooper's infidelity created sympathies he shared "with the sneering *savans* of Paris, and sat at the feet of the most skeptical philosophers of England." If there was "any feeling of his nature stronger than all the rest, it was the feeling of opposition to the Christian religion."[66] Cooper, La Borde recounted, believed Christianity "to be a fraud and imposture; an artful contrivance to cheat fools, and scare little children and old women." In his capacity as president of a state university he came "among a people where the universal faith was the faith of Christianity, and he proposed to subvert their altars, and to interfere with their worship." Cooper's infidelity harmed not only the state's college but also the students' trust in their education, particularly in the state mandated chapel services Cooper led: "What must the students think of the man? Not only must such services be a mockery, but all respect for the authority of one, who would lead in such a hypocritical ceremony, must of necessity pass away." Cooper "read the Bible, whose authority he openly denied, and prayed to a God in whom he did not believe, with less of reverence than he would discuss

---

65. Maximilian La Borde, *History of the South Carolina College: From Its Incorporation December 19, 1801 to Nov. 25, 1857, Including Sketches of its Presidents and Professors with an Appendix* (Columbia: Peter B. Glass, 1859), 175.

66. La Borde, *History of the South Carolina*, 176.

the theory of phlogiston, or the hypothesis of the igneous formation of the earth."[67] La Borde, the faculty of South Carolina, and the people of South Carolina, like the people of Indiana, Vermont, Michigan, North Carolina, Ohio, and other states with publicly funded universities, preferred to protect state-funded defenses of Christianity in their universities rather than state-funded secularism.

67. La Borde, *History of South Carolina*, 176-77.

CHAPTER IX

CONCLUSION

In the Preface of this volume, I laid out my main historical contention: that the early United States was a republic of Christians committed to what I have termed "Christian institutionalism"—that is, they wanted to maintain Christian precepts in their nation's various social and political institutions without sacralizing those principles or subordinating the American republic to a church.

The relatively brief survey we have undertaken since then has, I believe, made the case for my contention. We have seen that from the founding of the American Republic until the Civil War, Christians in the United States saw their country as deeply committed to the maintenance of Christian institutionalism in state legislatures, the courts, Sabbath laws, diplomacy, missionary enterprises, and relationships with Native Americans, and in state colleges and universities. This commitment to Christian institutions transcended questions of state churches and establishment or disestablishment. As long as Christians remained committed to upholding Christian institutions in the civil, political, and social structures of the American republic, the United States would be a Christian nation. This Christian nation was not a churchly construction or a popular political one. Rather was built on the backs of Christian institutionalism, maintained and sustained by Americans in government, religion, and broader society, from the American Revolution to the conclusion of the American Civil War.

This Christian institutionalism affected civic, social, and political structures. Constitutional disestablishment was not understood by early Republican politicians to mean that religion and politics were separate. In fact, none of the states who wrote constitutions between 1789 and 1865 used the federal First Amendment in the American Constitution as the model for their states religious provisions, constitutional or statutory. State churches endured until the 1830s, and even the final disestablishment of the state church in New England was not understood to be a concession to the separationist ideology of Thomas Jefferson. Massachusetts, for example, declared even after it disestablished its congregational state church in 1833 that religion was a necessity for the security of the American republic.

The American court system continued to be deeply influenced by Christian, and more specifically Protestant, understandings of civil law. Judges saw Christianity as an immutable part of the American judicial system. Protestantism formed an essential component of English common law. Likewise, judges did not see themselves as bound to rule in ways that affirmed a secular judicial order. American judges saw themselves as perpetuating Christian commitments within the judicial institutions of the American states.

Sabbath laws continued to operate without any major interruption throughout the first half of the nineteenth century, and states committed themselves to upholding it. That the Sabbath was a natural institution did not make it any less Christian or political, particularly to the Protestant majorities who passed laws maintaining commercial and civil restrictions on Sundays.

Internationally, the United States operated institutionally and self-consciously as a Protestant republic committed to expanding liberties that were downstream from Protestant sociopolitical developments. American diplomacy was not the work of a secular republic, trying to imprint secularism as a value worldwide. Non-white nations closer to home in North America understood that the American union was Christian and even Protestant. Native Americans interacted with American missionaries who saw their religious mission as a simultaneously American one. That association was also supported by the federal government, who went to great lengths to support and protect missionaries, and to use missionaries to further the political and social aims of the political American republic. Government-funded missionary work illustrated the degree to which religious and political institutions in the Early Republic were intertwined. Indigenous peoples in the United States understood the tie between missionaries and the American Republic. And they interacted with missionaries and the republic both on terms that should be understood as conceding explicitly Christian identities to both.

State colleges and universities were regularly headed and staffed by Protestant ministers. The same colleges and universities had explicitly Christian commitments worked into their curricula. Although churches did not run state colleges and universities, Protestant churchmen did. Like the courts, state, legislatures, and missionary enterprises of the Early Republic, education was not an example of separating Christianity out from an important and influential civil institution. It was just another example of Christian institutionalism continuing from the colonial era to the Civil War Era.

The focus of this book has been limited to the Early Republic era—that is, the era between the American Founding and the Civil War. The Civil War, of course, changed the United States profoundly in ways that still affect us today, and so it marks a sensible historical cutoff point for the early years of the American nation. Our survey so far has evinced clearly that the Early Republic was, undoubtedly, a Christian nation, and a Protestant one at that. Yet it is worth briefly looking into and beyond the Civil War era to see if this continued to hold true.

In the fall of 1860 the tumultuous election season drew to a close. The election of Abraham Lincoln convinced Southern radicals that the time for political action had arrived. The slaveholding South would not be safe in a Union governed by a man who, many Southerners believed, was allied with violent abolitionists like the recently executed John Brown, who had led an uprising at a federal arsenal at Harper's Ferry in what is now West Virginia.

Lincoln's election triggered the secession in the third week of December, and over the next two months the Deep South states, from South Carolina to Texas, left the Union. In Boston, John Wingate Thornton (1818–1878) watched events carefully, but even as the Union fell apart he put the finishing touches on a work of history entitled *The Pulpit of the American Revolution: Or, The Political Sermons of the of Period of 1776*. Americans, he believed, had forgotten the importance of their Protestant identity, and American unity could survive only if it was predicated on remembering that Protestantism provided the civil, political, and religious cords that unified the American nation. "The Union of the colonies was a condition precedent to American Nationality. One nationality, and that of a Protestant people, was essential to constitutional liberty in America."[1] If the future American states "had become separate independencies at different times, America would have but repeated the history of European divisions and wars."[2] The victory of "the red cross of St. George" over France in the French and Indian War (1754–1763) meant that Great Britain "shielded the brotherhood of English Protestants from the extermination meditated by Papal France, whose military cordon reached along our northern and western frontiers, and thus insured to England the fealty of her Atlantic colonies, till, 'in the fulness of time,' France, by the treaty of 1763, relinquished Canada."[3] Thornton knew that North America's eighteenth-century history culminated not with the creation of a deistic Lockean republic shorn of its religious or even churchly commitments, but with a united Protestant republic that protected all Protestant churches from an overweening civil hierarchy.

The American republic affected what Thornton called "THE true alliance between Politics and Religion" and he hoped his book would teach that "lesson."[4] This true American cooperation between politics and religion came from "the voice of the Fathers of the Republic," and was "enforced by their example." The Founding Fathers "invoked God in their civil assemblies, called upon their chosen teachers of religion for counsel from the Bible, and recognized its precepts as the law of their public conduct." America's revolu-

---

1. John Wingate Thornton, *The Pulpit of the American Revolution: Or, The Political Sermons of the of Period of 1776* (Boston: Gould and Lincoln, 1860), iii.

2. Thornton, *The Pulpit of the American Revolution*, iii-iv.

3. Thornton, *The Pulpit of the American Revolution*, iv.

4. Thornton, *The Pulpit of the American Revolution*, iii.

tionary Fathers "did not divorce politics and religion, but they denounced the separation as ungodly. They prepared for the struggle, and went into battle, not as soldiers of fortune, but, like Cromwell and the soldiers of the Commonwealth, with the Word of God in their hearts, and trusting in him." The Protestant religion "was the secret of that moral energy which sustained the Republic in its material weakness against superior numbers, and discipline, and all the power of England." Thorton believed that to "these sermons—the responses from the Pulpit" the American state "affixed its imprimatur, and thus they were handed down to future generations with a two-fold claim to respect."

Beginning in 1776, a loud majority of American Protestants, particularly those who identified with the Patriot cause, declared to the world that their faith was synonymous with the political precepts of the American founding. Civil liberties, religious liberty, and the freedoms of the American founding were treated as a sort of culmination of the Protestant intellectual and political traditions. This meant for many Americans that instead of America being subsumed into a broader Protestant Christendom, Protestantism, and more broadly Christianity, was subsumed into the American order.

Charles Wadsworth (1814–1882), a prominent Philadelphia minister known today primarily for being a friend and correspondent of the poet Emily Dickinson, told his congregants in 1855 that God had "raised up the United States as a great instrument of Civil and Religious benefit to the world" and that God "raised up this American Nation as a great instrument of civil and spiritual salvation to a world."[5] Wadsworth painted a picture of the development

---

5. Charles Wadsworth, "America's Mission: A Sermon Preached in the Arch Street Presbyterian Church, Philadelphia, on Thanksgiving Day,

of the modern world and the history of Christianity that led to the United States' special place in world history. The great "march and movement of God's providence" created a direct line of providential causation, from "the German reformer, braving, in behalf of that world and that race, the one the tempests of the material, the other the tempests of the moral world," to the "simultaneous rise of English literature and English intolerance, the one producing the English Bible, the Magna Charta of the American Church, the other driving forth that Church with this precious birth-right blessing, to set up the pillar of its Bethel on Plymouth rock."[6] Those historical events were "stormy conflicts that rooted colonial religion like the oak tree, deep amid the foundations of the everlasting hills."[7] The Protestant "great central truth of human equality, has set it above all other political systems as gloriously as the living man of to-day is above the dead fossils of the old geologic races." The "march and magnificence of a subsequent progress" showed "the evolution of far-reaching and Omniscient design," that distinctly marked the United States "as one of God's great instrument [sic] for the world's civil and religious redemption," in the same manner as the "strange call of the Hebrew Patriarch, and the marvelous preservation of the Hebrew law-giver and the magnificent Exodus of the Hebrew people."[8] Protestant Americans stood as "descendants of Abraham" who were "objects of God's special care and divine instrument

Nov. 22, 1855" (Philadelphia: T. B. Peterson, 1855), 5-6.

6. Wadsworth, "America's Mission," 8-9.

7. Wadsworth, "America's Mission," 9.

8. Wadsworth, "American's Mission," 9-10.

for the diffusion over the Gentile world of the light and liberty that abide in the oracles of God."[9]

John Wingate Thorton agreed with Wadsworth and spoke for most American Protestants in the nineteenth century who assumed that the Protestant foundations for their republic had not been destroyed or subverted by the American Revolution. The Civil War, far from secularizing Americans, reminded them that their republic had been one of rich association between church and state even as disestablishment made that association less invasive on the state's part. The pastor of Philadelphia's Coates' Street Presbyterian church, George Duffield IV (1794–1868), celebrated the relationship between the president and churches in a sermon in early 1861. Lincoln issued the first call for a day of national fasting to be held on 4 January 1861. Duffield called presidentially prompted fasts a privilege and reminded his congregants to petition God to "remember us as he did our fathers."[10] Disestablishment had not removed the institutional connections between religion and politics, even for Presbyterians. "As Presbyterians," declared Duffield, "we are in no doubt as to the *propriety* of observing this day." Duffield appealed to the Westminster Standards to justify his argument. "'If at any time,' says our excellent Directory for worship, 'the civil power should think it proper to appoint a fast, it is the duty of the ministers and people of our communion, as we live under a Christian government, to pay all due respect to the same.'" Protestants who looked to the Westminster standards were "at no loss as to the *manner* of observing the day. 'There shall be public worship upon all

---

9. Wadsworth, "America's Mission," 10.

10. George Duffield IV, *The God of Our Fathers: An Historical Sermon Preached in the Coates' Street Presbyterian Church, Philadelphia, Fast Day, 1861* (Philadelphia: T. B. Pugh, 1861), 7.

such days, and let the prayers, psalms, portions of Scripture to be read, and sermons, be all in a special manner adapted to the occasion.'" The Westminster standards, said Duffield, were "more explicit still" regarding the "character of the prayers and sermon" involved in fasts and other actions appointed by the magistrate.

> On fast-days let the minister point out the authority and providences calling to the observation thereof; and let him spend a more than usual portion of time, in solemn prayer, particularly confession of sin, especially of the day and place, with their aggravations, which have brought down the judgment of heaven. And let the whole day be spent in deep humiliation and mourning before God.[11]

The American Revolution, Duffield argued, had not fundamentally altered the relationship between magistrates and churches. Both continued to fulfill their separate but allied roles, and not even the 1789 American innovations to the Westminster Confession changed that. "Evidently in the minds of those who framed the Constitution of the American Presbyterian Church (adopted in the same year, and framed by some of the same men who framed our National Constitution, now in such imminent danger)," proper observance such as fast days and other presidentially appointed religious commemorations, "both on the part of minister and people, was considered by them one of the most solemn and important duties that could possibly be discharged on earth."[12]

---

11. Duffield, *The God of Our Fathers*, 7-8.

12. Duffield, *The God of Our Fathers*, 8.

The Civil War forced Southerners as well as Northerners to confront their own beliefs about the relationship between the church and the state. When Georgia's secession became an accomplished fact in January 1861, the state's Episcopal bishop Stephen Elliott (1806–1866) convened an ecclesiastical council in Savannah to determine the response of the Episcopal Church in Georgia. The bulk of Elliott's speech was an explanation of why he believed he and his diocese were bound to the state of Georgia and not the United States. In doing so, he argued that the church was tied to the state. "The animus of the Protestant Episcopal Church in the United States," declared Elliott, "clearly is, that the Bishop shall go with his jurisdiction."[13] An episcopal bishop was "a Bishop of the Protestant Episcopal Church in the United States, not because he is a Bishop of the Church Catholic, but because he is the Bishop of Maine, or of New York, or of New Jersey, as the case may be." Elliott noted that while, as a church, the Episcopal Church had no share in producing the political and social "condition of things which exists around her, she is nevertheless involved in that condition, and cannot, by any means, be made independent of it."[14] Every member of the church was also a member of the American commonwealth. "And being members at the same time of the Church and of the Commonwealth, the circumstances and relations of the one must affect the circumstances and relations of the other."

It was true, the bishop explained, that "under dominion of infidels as in the times of the primitive Church, the Church of Christ and their Commonwealth were two so-

---

13. Stephen Elliott, *Address of the Rt. Rev. Stephen Elliott: To the Thirty-ninth Annual Convention of the Protestant Episcopal Church in the Diocese of Georgia* (Savannah: John M. Cooper, 1861) 7.

14. Elliott, *Address of the Rt. Rev. Stephen Elliott*, 4.

cieties independent," but that was only because "a state of antagonism existed between Christianity and Paganism, which absolutely forbad any mutual dependency between them."[15] But since the commonwealth "in our times, is, if not professedly, at least practically, Christian, it is almost impossible to draw any line which can separate the relations of the Church from the relations of the Commonwealth."[16] The actions of the Commonwealth were the actions of the citizens of that Commonwealth, and because the citizens who made up the body of the Church also formed state legislatures, there had to be even in the United States "inevitably, a mutual relationship and dependency. It cannot be got rid of, without abolishing the whole framework of constitutional and canonical law which binds together the Protestant Episcopal Church of this country."

Practically, this meant that the Protestant Episcopal Church in the United States affirmed federal disestablishment of religion, but did not, and canonically and doctrinally could not, affirm the particular articulation of federal disestablishment adopted by Thomas Jefferson and his Baptist and Presbyterian allies in Virginia that institutionally separated the relations of the church from the relations of the state. Episcopalians in the nineteenth century did not view themselves as absolutely bound by religious terms set by Jeffersonian separationism, precisely because even a so-called disestablishmentarian government operated as such only so long as there was mutual affirmation of the duties of the commonwealth and Christianity.[17]

---

15. Elliott, *Address of the Rt. Rev. Stephen Elliott*, 4-5.

16. Elliott, *Address of the Rt. Rev. Stephen Elliott*, 5.

17. *Journal of the Public and Secret Proceedings of the Convention of the People Held in Milledgeville and Savannah, in 1861. Together with the*

Historians of American religion have often identified the Civil War as a breaking point when Protestant America began to visibly transform into a more secular republic. Steven Green in his *The Second Disestablishment* wrote that "the second disestablishment was well under way" after 1870.[18] "The previous seven decades had witnessed a transformation in popular and legal attitudes about the interrelationships among Christianity, the law, and civic institutions." The longstanding "belief in the law as religiously grounded, as having divine origins, and representing superior immutable principles had generally been replaced by a perspective of the law as secular and amoral, as primarily functional and adaptive to changing societal needs." Law and politics derived their "authority from popular will, not from some higher source." During this era of supposed change, Green proposes, "the notion that law incorporated Christian principles had lost its legal currency."

Certainly the relationship between religion and institutions changed in the last quarter of the nineteenth century, but the changes were never as far-reaching or as significant as historians have proposed. Influential churchmen and influential statesmen still believed that a necessary institutional relationship between Christianity, and more specifically Protestant Christianity, lay at the roots of the maintenance of the American order.

In many ways, the United States' Protestant regime reached its apotheosis *after* the era in which historians like Steven Green argued it waned. Protestant America's worries, for example, over Catholic schools potentially gaining pub-

---

Ordinances Adopted (Milledgeville, GA: Boughton, Nisbet, Barnes, 1861), 31.

18. Green, *Second Disestablishment*, 329.

lic funding led to a series of laws proposed in the 1870s, all of which aimed to preclude religious institutions from gaining any such funding.[19] James G. Blaine (1830–1893), a U.S. Representative from Maine, proposed an amendment to the Constitution that would have prohibited any direct federal aid to any educational institution that had an official association with a religious group.[20] However subtle the amendment's drafters might have tried to be, the amendment was obviously aimed at Roman Catholic schools and both Catholics and Protestants knew it. Still, Richard White helpfully notes in his *The Republic For Which it Stands* that by 1870 "Protestants largely agreed there was to be no sectarian teaching in public schools, but nonsectarian Protestantism in the form of Bible reading would be central to the curriculum."[21] Protestants generally affirmed the public schools' place in society as the chief catechetical institution for citizenship and felt comfortable with the public schools as an expression of nonsectarian but still Protestant education.

In 1891 the United States Supreme Court classified the United States as a Christian nation. The classification was not binding on Congress or the President, but it still indicated the degree to which Christianity was seen to have

---

19. Tyler Anbinder, *Nativism and Slavery: The Northern Know Nothings and the Politics of the 1850s* (New York: Oxford University Press, 1992), 271–72.

20. McCarley Elizabeth Maddock, "Blaine in the Joints: The History of the Blaine Amendment and the Modern Supreme Court Religious Liberty Doctrine on Education," *Duke Journal of Constitutional Law & Public Policy* 18 (2023): 195–223.

21. Richard White, *The Republic for Which it Stands: The United States During Reconstruction and the Gilded Age, 1865–1896* (Oxford: Oxford University Press, 2017), 316–17.

important status in American institutions. David Josiah Brewer (1837–1910), Associate Justice of the United States Supreme Court, a son of Congregationalist missionaries to Turkey, noted in 1905 that while the United States government affirmed "the separation of church and state...there is nowhere a repudiation of Christianity as one of the institutions as well as benedictions of society. In short, there is no charter or constitution that is either infidel, agnostic or anti-Christian."[22] Wherever there was a civil or political "declaration in favor of any religion it is of the Christian." Numerous political and civil "expressions in [Christianity's] favor," along with "the avowed separation between church and state" was "a most satisfactory testimonial" that Christianity was "the religion of this country." Christianity had "been so wrought into the history of this republic, so identified with its growth and prosperity, has been and is so dear to the hearts of the great body of our citizens, that it ought not to be spoken of contemptuously or treated with ridicule."[23] American citizens recognized "the identification of Christianity with its life, the general belief that Christianity is the best of all religions, that it passed into the lives of our fathers and is taken into the lives of our brethren as something of sacred power-ought, even if not agreeing with all that is claimed for it, to at least accord to it respect."[24]

Conservative Protestants in the twentieth century understood that some cooperative institutional relationship between religion and the state remained a practical necessity for human societies. Presbyterian luminary J. Gresham

---

22. David Josiah Brewer, *The United States a Christian Nation* (Philadelphia: John C. Winston, 1905), 32.

23. Brewer, *The United States a Christian Nation*, 49.

24. Brewer, *The United States a Christian Nation*, 49-50.

Machen (1881–1937) was convinced that Christianity is not a privatized relationship between man and God simply about the salvation of the soul. There is also, he argued, "the social element in Christianity" that is "found not only in communion between man and God, but also in communion between man and man. Such communion appears even in institutions which are not specifically Christian."[25] Christianity, in short, necessarily underpins institutions that are not by definition "Christian." Machen used the example of the family and education to prove his point about Christian institutionalism. "Modern life," he warned, tends "more and more toward the contraction of the sphere of parental control and parental influence. The choice of schools is being placed under the power of the state." The central failing of modern life was that the state no longer cooperated with the family; rather, it tried to replace the family. Machen's solution was not however to call for the state's destruction, but to call for increased Christian presence in institutions. "A revival of the Christian religion would unquestionably bring a reversal of the process; the family, as over against all other social institutions, would come to its rights again." The state itself, argued Machen, "even when reduced to its proper limits, has a large place in human life, and in the possession of that place it is supported by Christianity." Machen, like his antebellum Protestant forbearers, understood that "Christianity assumes no negative attitude, therefore, toward the state, but recognizes, under existing conditions, the necessity of government." Machen and other Protestants in the United States rightly understood that they did not need a churchly or sacralized or even Christian state to maintain Christian institutions in the American re-

---

25. J. Gresham Machen, *Christianity and Liberalism* (New York: Macmillan, 1923), 154.

public, even as they knew the American populace ignored the Christian foundations of American social and civil life at their own peril.

At the outset of this book, we made note of contemporary debates about the ongoing or future status of America as a Christian nation. At both ends of the spectrum in such debates, the historical realities of America's actual religious character in the Early Republic seem often to fall by the wayside. Of course, there is no necessary need for this character to be the same in the future—polities can and do change. And yet history teaches us that attempts by elite minorities to re-narrate and reconfigure the distinctive and historic character of a nation along the lines of a desired polity that is totally alien to that nation's never end well.

American Protestants in particular—for it is nothing less than their history that we have laid out here—do a disservice to both past and present by calling for secularism, by trying to replicate an ahistorical theocracy, or even by treating the social and religious milieu of the republic as adiaphora. Americans are still a religious people, and modern Protestant ministers and intellectuals have to reckon with that fact whether they like it or not. Peter Leithart notes that "modernization was supposed to bring secularization everywhere. In the United States it never happened."[26]

Modern Protestants would do well to understand that while they can't dial back the clock to the Early Republic, they can engage their neighbors by being healthy and responsible stewards of healthy and responsible Christian institutions at the local, municipal, and state levels, and in the arts and sciences as well as in politics—because this is what America's character as a Christian nation has always meant.

---

26. Peter J. Leithart, *The End of Protestantism: Pursuing Unity in a Fragmented Church* (Grand Rapids: Brazos, 2016), 65.

Too often evangelicals in the twentieth century prioritized the individual or an idealized nation, with no thought whatsoever for the life of intermediate institutions—civil, political, and religious—that sustain human civilization. In order to protect Christianity, evangelical Protestants in the twenty-first century can start by taking institutions seriously, and they don't have start with a historical *tabula rasa*. Protestants in the Early Republic believed in the importance of maintaining Christianity in civil and social institutions. For that reason alone, they deserve our attention, if not our respect.

WORKS CITED

Adams, Henry. *John Randolph*. Boston: Houghton, Mifflin, 1889.

Agnew, John Holmes. *Woman's Office and Influence: An Address before the Monroe Female Seminary*. New York: John F. Trow, 1851.

Alden, Timothy. *The Glory of America: A Century Sermon, Delivered at the South Church, in Portsmouth, New Hampshire*. Portsmouth, NH: William Treadwell, 1801.

Allen, Brooke. *Moral Minority: Our Skeptical Founding Fathers*. Chicago, IL: Ivan R. Dee, 2009.

Allitt, Patrick. *The Conservatives: Ideas and Personalities Throughout American History*. New Haven, CN: Yale University Press, 2009.

Alvarez, David J. "American Recognition of the Papal States: A Reconsideration." *Records of the American Catholic Historical Society of Philadelphia* 91, no. 1/4 (1980): 49–57.

American Bible Society. *Second Annual Report*. New York: American Bible Society, 1818.

American Quarterly Review 8. Sept. & Dec., 1830.

Annual Report of the Board of Regents of the University of Wisconsin, for the Year 1855. Madison, WI: Calkins & Proudfit, 1856.

An Appeal to Common Sense and the Constitution, in Behalf of the Unlimited Public Discussion: Occasioned by the Late Trial of Rev. Abner Kneeland for Blasphemy. Boston, 1834.

Anbinder, Tyler. *Nativism and Slavery: The Northern Know Nothings and the Politics of the 1850's.* New York: Oxford University Press, 1992.

Annual Report of the Indiana University Including the Catalogue for the Academic Year, MDCCCLVI–VII. Bloomington. Indianapolis: Joseph J. Bingham, 1856.

Ariens, Michael S. "Church and State in Ohio, 1785–1833." In *Disestablishment and Religious Dissent: Church-State Relations in the New American States, 1776–1833*, edited by Carl D. Esbeck and Jonathan Den Hartog, 249-272 Columbia, MO: University of Missouri Press, 2019.

Aron, Daniel. *Cincinnati: Queen City of the West.* Columbus, OH: Ohio State University Press, 1992.

Bailyn, Bernard. *The Ideological Origins of the American Revolution* . Cambridge, MA: Harvard University Press, 1967.

Baird, Robert. *Religion in America: Religion in America: Or an Account of the Origin, Relation to the State, and Present Condition of the Evangelical Churches in the United States.* New York: Harper & Bros., 1844.

―――. "United States of America: Progress and Prospects of Christianity in the United States of America." In *The Religious Condition of Christendom Exhibited in a Series of Papers Prepared at the Instance of the British Organization of the Evangelical Alliance as Read at its Fifth Annual Conference Held in Freemason's Hall, London, August 20 to September 3, 1851*, edited by Edward Steane. London: James Nesbit, 1852.

Bangs, Nathan. *The Present State, Prospects and Responsibilities of the Methodist Episcopal Church, With an Appendix of Ecclesiastical Statistics*. New York: Lane & Scott, 1850.

Banner, Stuart. "When Christianity Was Part of the Common Law," *Law and History Review* 16, no. 1 (1998): 27–62.

Barany, George. "A Note on the Prehistory of American Diplomatic Relations with the Papal States." *Catholic Historical Review* 47, no. 4 (1962): 508–13.

Barnes, Albert. "The Supremacy of the Laws." *American National Preacher* 12 (Aug 1838): 113-128.

Bassett, John Spencer, ed. *The Correspondence of Andrew Jackson*. 6 vols. Washington, DC: Carnegie Institute, 1926.

Battle, Kemp P. *History of the University of North Carolina: From its Beginning to the death of President Swain, 1789–1868*. Vol. 1. Raleigh, NC: Edwards & Broughton, 1907.

Beach, Rex. "Spencer Roane and the Richmond Junto." *William and Mary Quarterly* 22, no. 1 (1942): 1–17.

Bebbington, David W. *Evangelicalism in Modern Britain: A History from the 1730s to the 1980s.* London: Unwin Hyman, 1989.

Beecher, Catherine E. *A Treatise on Domestic Economy: For the Use of Young Ladies at Home, and at School.* Boston, MA: Thomas H. Webb, 1843.

Beecher, Lyman. "The Preeminent Importance of the Christian Sabbath." In *The American National Preacher: Or, Original Monthly Sermons from Living Ministers of the United States*, vols. 3–4, edited by Austin Dickinson, 159–60. New York: J.&J. Harper, 1828.

Bemis, Samuel Flagg. "John Quincy Adams and George Washington." *Proceedings of the Massachusetts Historical Society* 67 (1941): 365–84.

Bennett, Daniel *Defending Faith: The Politics of the Christian Conservative Legal Movement.* Lawrence, KS: University Press of Kansas, 2017.

Berkhofer, Robert F., Jr. *Salvation and the Savage: An Analysis of Protestant Missions and American Indian Response, 1787–1862.* Lexington: University Press of Kentucky, 2021.

Binney, Horace. *An Eulogy on the Life and Character of John Marshall: Chief Justice of the United States.* Philadelphia, PA: J. Crissy and G. Goodman, 1835.

Birzer, Bradley J. *In Defense of Andrew Jackson*. Washington, DC: RegneryHistory, 2018.

Bishop, Robert Hamilton. *Addresses: No. 1—To the Alumni of Miami University; No. 2—To the Farmers of Hamilton County*. Cincinnati, OH: R. P. Brooks, 1845.

————. "The Man That Gathered Sticks on the Sabbath." *The National Preacher* 9 (Sept 1834): 49–51.

Blackhawk, Ned. *The Rediscovery of America: Native Peoples and the Unmaking of U.S. History* (New Haven, CN: Yale University Press, 2023.

Bohnin, Gerry. "The McGuffey Eclectic Readers: 1836–1986." *The Reading Teacher* 40, no. 3 (1986): 263–69.

Bolt, Robert. "Vice President Richard M. Johnson of Kentucky: Hero of the Thames—Or the Great Amalgamator?" *The Register of the Kentucky Historical Society* 75, no. 3 (1977): 191–203.

Boston, Robert. *Why the Religious Right Is Wrong About Separation of Church and State*. Amherst, NY: Prometheus, 2003.

Bowditch, Henry P. "Theodore Lyman." *Proceedings of the American Academy of Arts and Sciences* 34, no. 23 (1899): 656–63.

Boydston, Jeanne. *The Limits of Sisterhood: The Beecher Sisters on Women's Rights and Woman's Sphere*. Chapel Hill, NC: University of North Carolina, 1993.

Breckinridge, Robert Jefferson. *The Immorality of the Traffic, Manufacture, and Use, of Ardent Spirits as a Drink; and the Duty of Christians to the Temperance Cause.* Baltimore, MD: Sands & Neilson, 1834.

Bremer, Francis J. "Faith and Society: The Making of a Christian America." *Reviews in American History* 32, no. 1 (2004): 7–13.

Brewer, David Josiah. *The United States a Christian Nation.* Philadelphia, PA: John C. Winston, 1905.

Breyer, Stephen. "The Cherokee Indians and the Supreme Court." *The Georgia Historical Quarterly* 87, no. 3/4 (2003): 408–26.

Broers, Michael. *Napoleon: The Spirit of the Age, 1805–1810.* New York: Pegasus, 2018.

Brownson, Orestes. *The American Republic: Its Constitution, Tendencies, and Destiny.* New York: P. O'Shea, 1866.

Bulthuis, Kyle T. *Four Steeples Over the City Streets: Religion and Society in New York's Early Republic Congregations.* New York: New York University Press, 2014.

———. "Religious Disestablishment in the State of New York." In *Disestablishment and Religious Dissent: Church-State Relations in the New American States, 1776–1833*, edited by Carl D. Esbeck and Jonathan Den Hartog, 115-138. Columbia, MO: University of Missouri Press, 2019.

Burns, James MacGregor. *The American Experiment: The Vineyard of Liberty, 1787–1863*. New York: Alfred A. Knopf, 1981.

Burstein, Andrew. *The Passions of Andrew Jackson*. New York: Alfred A. Knopf, 2003.

Cameron, Kenneth Walter. "Wordsworth, Bishop Doane and the Sonnets on the American Church." *Historical Magazine of the Protestant Episcopal Church* 11, no. 1 (1942): 83–91.

Casto, William. "Oliver Ellsworth's Calvinism: A Biographical Essay on Religion and Political Psychology in the Early Republic." *Journal of Church and State* 36 no.2, Summer (1994): 507-526.

Catalogue of the Alumni, Officers, and Students of the University of Mississippi at Oxford, Mississippi, 1857-'58. Oxford, MS: Mississippi Steam Book and Job Office, 1858.

Catalogue of the Officers and Students of the University of Alabama of the State of Alabama: 1844. Tuscaloosa, AL: M.D.J. Slade, 1844.

Catalogue of the Officers and Students of the University of Vermont. October....1839. Burlington, VT: University Press, 1839.

Catalogue of the Trustees, Faculty and Students of South Carolina College. Columbia, SC: Morgan's Press, 1844.

Cave, Alfred A. "Abuse of Power: Andrew Jackson and the Indian Removal Act of 1830." *The Historian* 65, no. 6 (2003): 1330–53.

Channing, Edward. A *History of the United States*. Vol. 3, *The American Revolution, 1761*-1789. New York: Macmillan, 1912.

Chase, Philander. "Excerpt of Letter Dated October 10th, 1825." *Philander Chase Letters*. https://digital.kenyon.edu/chase_letters/541/

———. *A Plea for the West*. Boston, MA: Samuel Parker, 1827.

Cherry, Conrad. *God's New Israel: Religious Interpretations of American Destiny*. Chapel Hill, NC: University of North Carolina Press, 1998.

The Christian Index and Columbian Star. Vol. 1. Philadelphia, PA: Marten and Boden, 1829.

Clark, Gregory. "Timothy Dwight's Moral Rhetoric at Yale College, 1795–1817." *Rhetorica: A Journal of the History of Rhetoric* 5, no. 2 (1987): 149–61.

Cogswell, William. *Religious Liberty: A Sermon, Preached on the Day of the Annual Fast in Massachusetts, April 3, 1828*. Boston, MA: Pierce and Williams, 1828.

Coker, Joe L. *Liquor in the Land of the Lost Cause: Southern White Evangelicals and the Prohibition Movement*. Lexington, KY: University Press of Kentucky, 2007.

Collins, Linton McGeb. "The Activities of the Missionaries Among the Cherokees." *The Georgia Historical Quarterly* 6, no. 4 (1922): 285–322.

Commager, Henry Steele. "The Blasphemy of Abner Kneeland." *The New England Quarterly* 8, no. 1 (1935): 29–41.

Conroy-Krutz, Emily. *Christian Imperialism: Converting the World in the Early American Republic.* Ithaca, NY: Cornell University Press, 2015.

Conser, Walter H., Jr. *God and the Natural World: Religion and Science in Antebellum America.* Columbia, SC: University of South Carolina Press, 1993.

Cooley, Thomas M. *A Treatise on the Constitutional Limitations which Rest Upon the Legislative Power of the States of the American Union.* Boston: Little, Brown, 1868.

Cooper, Kody W., and Justin Buckley Dyer. *The Classical and Christian Origins of American Politics: Political Theology, Natural Law, and the American Founding.* Cambridge: Cambridge University Press, 2022.

Cooper-White, Pamela. *The Psychology of Christian Nationalism: Why People Are Drawn In and How to Talk Across the Divide.* Minneapolis, WI: Fortress, 2022.

Coulter, E. Merton. *College Life in the Old South.* Athens, GA: University of Georgia Press, 1981.

Cross, Jack L. "John Marshall on the French Revolution and on American Politics." *William and Mary Quarterly* 12, no. 4 (1955): 631–49.

Cross, Whitney R. *The Burned-over District : The Social and Intellectual History of Enthusiastic Religion in Western New York, 1800–1850.* Ithaca: Cornell University Press, 2015.

Crumb, Lawrence N., G. W. Doane, John H. Hopkins, H. Potter, and H. B. Whipple. "Some American Bishops' Letters to E. B. Pusey." *Anglican and Episcopal History* 69, no. 4 (2000): 504–23.

Cummins, Light T. "John Quincy Adams and Latin American Nationalism." *Revista de Historia de América*, no. 86 (1978): 221–31.

Cunningham, Noble. *The Jeffersonian Republicans: The Formation of Party Organization, 1789–1801.* Chapel Hill: University of North Carolina Press, 1957.

Curti, Merle. "The Impact of the Revolutions of 1848 on American Thought." *Proceedings of the American Philosophical Society* 93, no. 3 (1949): 209–15.

Davis, David Brion, ed. *The Fear of Conspiracy: Images of Un-American Subversion from the Revolution to the Present.* Ithaca, NY: Cornell University Press, 1971.

Davis, Junius, Alfred Moore, and James Iredell. *Revolutionary Patriots and Associate Justices of the Supreme Court of the United States.* Raleigh, NC: North Carolina Society of the Sons of the Revolution, 1899.

DeRogatis, Amy. "Models of Piety: Plan of Union Missionaries on the Western Reserve, 1800–1806." *Journal of Presbyterian History* 79, no. 4 (2001): 257–75.

De Rougemont, Frédéric. *The Individualists in Church and State*. Translated by Colin Wright. 1844; Repr., Alten, The Netherlands: Wordbridge, 2018.

de Tocqueville, Alexis. *Democracy in America*. Vol. 1. London: Longman, Green, Longman and Roberts, 1862.

Doane, George Washington. "Education a Divine Thing." In *The Life and Writings of George Washington Doane*. Vol. 4, *The Educational Writings of George Washington Doane*, edited by William Croswell Doane. New York: D. Appleton, 1861: 47-58.

———. "Influence Without Intervention, The Duty of our Nation to the World." In *The Life and Writings of George Washington Doane*, Vol. 4: 261-272.

———. "The Men to Make a State: Their Making and Their Marks." In *The Life and Writings of George Washington Doane*, Vol. 4: 235-243.

———. *The Young American, His Dangers, His Duties, & His Destinies*. Philadelphia, PA: Inquirer, 1853.

Doane, William Croswell. *The Life and Writings of George Washington Doane*. Vol. 1, *Memoir of the Life of George Washington Doane*, edited by William Croswell Doane. New York: D. Appleton, 1860.

Douthat, Ross. "A Gentler Christendom." *First Things*, June 2022. https://www.firstthings.com/article/2022/06/a-gentler-christendom

Dreisbach, Daniel L. *Religion and Politics in the Early Republic: Jasper Adams and the Church-State Debate.* Lexington, KY: The University Press of Kentucky, 1996.

Dreisbach, Daniel L. "The Meaning of Church and State: Competing Views." In *The Oxford Handbook of Church and State in the United States,* edited by Derek H. Davis, 207-225. New York: Oxford University Press, 2010.

Drury, Clifford M. "The Western Missionary Society, 1802–1836." *Journal of the Presbyterian Historical Society,* 28, no. 4 (1950): 233–48.

DuBourg, Louis William Valentine. "Victory and Peace," *Poughkeepsie Herald,* Wednesday, February 22, 1815.

Duffield, George IV. *The God of Our Fathers: An Historical Sermon Preached in the Coates' Street Presbyterian Church, Philadelphia, Fast Day, 1861.* Philadelphia, PA: T. B. Pugh, 1861.

Durrill, Wayne K. "The Power of Ancient Words: Classical Teaching and Social Change at South Carolina College, 1804–1860." *Journal of Southern History* 65, no. 3 (1999): 469–98.

"Dutch Church of Albany v Bradford, Dec. 1826." In *Reports of Cases Argued and Determined in the Supreme Court, and in the Court for the Trial of Impeachment and Correction of Errors in the State of New York,* edited by Esek Cowen. Vol. 8. Albany, NY: William Gould, 1829.

Dwight, Theodore. *An Oration, Delivered at New-Haven on the 7th of July, A.D. 1801: Before the Society of Cincinnati, for the State of Connecticut Assembled to Celebrate the Anniversary of American Independence.* Hartford, CN: Hudson and Goodwin, 1801.

Dwight, Timothy, IV. *The Conquest of Canaan: A Poem, in Eleven Books.* Hartford: Elisha Babcock, 1785.

———. *Theology: Explained and Defended in a Series of Sermons.* Vol. 1. New York: Harper & Brothers, 1846.

Dyer, Thomas G. *The University of Georgia: A Bicentennial History, 1785–1985.* Athens, GA: University of Georgia Press, 1985.

Edmondson, Andrew Jackson. *Journal When a Volunteer under General Andrew Jackson in 1812–1813.*

Ehle, John. *The Trail of Tears: The Rise and Fall of the Cherokee Nation.* New York: Anchor, 1988.

Elliott, Stephen. *Address of the Rt. Rev. Stephen Elliott: To the Thirty-Ninth Annual Convention of the Protestant Episcopal Church in the Diocese of Georgia.* Savannah, GA: John M. Cooper, 1861.

Esbeck, Carl D., and Jonathan J. Den Hartog, eds. *Disestablishment and Religious Dissent: Church-State Relations in the New American States, 1776–1833.* Columbia, MO: University of Missouri Press, 2019.

Espinosa, Gastón, ed. *Religion and the American Presidency: George Washington to George W. Bush with Commentary and Primary Sources.* New York: Columbia University Press, 2009.

Eyal, Yonatan. *The Young America Movement and the Transformation of the Democratic Party, 1828–1861.* Cambridge: Cambridge University Press, 2007.

Farmer, James O., Jr. *The Metaphysical Confederacy: James Henley Thornwell and the Synthesis of Southern Values.* Macon, GA: Mercer University Press, 1986.

Fea, John. *Believe Me: The Evangelical Road to Donald Trump.* Grand Rapids, MI: Eerdmans, 2018.

———. *The Bible Cause: A History of the American Bible Society.* New York: Oxford University Press, 2016.

———. *Was America Founded as a Christian Nation?* Louisville, KY: Westminster John Knox, 2011.

Fehlings, Gregory E. "America's First Limited War." *Naval War College Review* 53, no. 3 (2000): 101–43.

Fenton, Elizabeth. "Birth of a Protestant Nation: Catholic Canadians, Religious Pluralism, and National Unity in the Early U.S. Republic." *Early American Literature* 41, no. 1 (2006): 29–57.

Ferling, John. *Adams vs. Jefferson: The Tumultuous Election of 1800.* Oxford: Oxford University Press, 2004.

Finn, Nathan A. "1776: The Year That Shaped the Post-Christian West." *The Gospel Coalition*, November 9, 2023.

Finney, Charles G. *Memoirs of Rev. Charles G. Finney*. New York: Fleming H. Revell, 1876.

First Annual Report of the General Union for Promoting the Observance of the Christian Sabbath. New York: J. Collord, 1829.

Fish, Carl Russell. *The Rise of the Common Man*. New York: Macmillan, 1927.

Foner, Eric. *The Fiery Trial: Abraham Lincoln and American Slavery*. New York: Norton, 2010.

Forbes, Worthington Chauncey. *The Writings of John Quincy Adams*. Vol. 1, *1779–1796*. New York, NY: Macmillan, 1913.

Ford, Lacy K. *Origins of Southern Radicalism: The South Carolina Upcountry, 1800–1860*. New York: Oxford University Press, 1988.

Freeman, F. *Religious Liberty: A Discourse Delivered at the Congregational Church at Hanson on the Fourth of July, 1832*. Plymouth, MA: Benjamin Drew Jr., 1832.

French, Rodrick S. "Liberation from Man and God in Boston: Abner Kneeland's Free-Thought Campaign, 1830–1839." *American Quarterly* 32, no. 2 (1980): 202–21.

Fried, Stephen. *Rush: Revolution, Madness, and Benjamin Rush, the Visionary Doctor Who Became a Founding Father*. New York: Broadway Books, 2018.

Frost, John. *Pictorial Life of Andrew Jackson*. Hartford, CT: Belknap & Hamersly, 1847.

Fuller, I. F. R., and M. W. Fuller. "Supreme Court of Illinois. Samuel Chase et al. v. Charles E. Cheney." *The American Law Register* 19, no. 5 (1871): 295–319.

Fuller, Wayne E. *Morality and the Mail in Nineteenth-Century America*. Urbana, IL: University of Illinois Press, 2003.

Gamble, Henry Y. *God on the Grounds: A History of Religion at Thomas Jefferson's University*. Charlottesville: University of Virginia Press, 2020.

Gerber, Scott Douglas. "Introduction: The Supreme Court before John Marshall." In *Seriatim: The Supreme Court Before John Marshall*, edited by Scott Douglas Gerber, 1–25. New York: NYU Press, 1998.

Gibbs, George C., ed. *Reports of Cases Argued and Determined in the Supreme Court of the State of Michigan*. Vol. 3. Detroit, MI: S.D. Elwood, 1856.

Gillett, E. H. *History of the Presbyterian Church in the United States of America*. Vol. 1. Philadelphia, PA: Presbyterian Publishing Committee, 1864.

Glasgow, William M. *History of the Reformed Presbyterian Church in America*. Baltimore, MD: Hill & Harvey, 1888.

Goldman, Samuel. *After Nationalism: Being American in the Age of Division*. Philadelphia, PA: University of Pennsylvania Press, 2021.

Gordon, Sarah Barringer. "Blasphemy and the Law of Religious Liberty in Nineteenth-Century America." *American Quarterly* 52, no. 4 (2000): 682–719.

Gould, Andrew C. *Origins of Liberal Dominance: State, Church, and Party in Nineteenth-Century Europe*. Ann Arbor, MI: University of Michigan Press, 1999.

Grant, J. A. C. "The Natural Law Background of Due Process." *Columbia Law Review* 31, no. 1 (1931): 56–81.

Grasso, Christopher. *Skepticism and American Faith: From the Revolution to the Civil War*. Oxford: Oxford University Press, 2018.

Green, Edwin L. *A History of South Carolina College*. Columbia, SC: State Company, 1916.

Green, Steven K. *Inventing a Christian America: The Myth of the Religious Founding*. Oxford: Oxford University Press, 2015.

———. *The Second Disestablishment: Church and State in Nineteenth-Century America*. New York: Oxford University Press, 2010.

Green, William Mercer. *The Influence of the Christianity Upon the Welfare of the Nations*. Hillsborough, NC: Dennis Heart, 1831.

Greenberg, Amy S. *Manifest Manhood and the Antebellum American Empire*. Cambridge: Cambridge University Press, 2005.

Greene, L.F. *The Writings of the Late Elder John Leland*. New York: G.W. Wood, 1845.

Gushee, David P. *Defending Democracy from its Christian Enemies*. Grand Rapids, MI: Eerdmans, 2023.

Gutjahr, Paul C. *The Book of Mormon: A Biography*. Princeton: Princeton University Press, 2012.

Guyatt, Nicholas. *Providence and the Invention of the United States, 1607–1876*. Cambridge: Cambridge University Press, 2007.

Hall, Mark David. *Did America Have a Christian Founding?: Separating Modern Myth from Historical Truth*. Nashville, TN: Thomas Nelson, 2019.

———. *Proclaim Liberty Throughout the Land: How Christianity Has Advanced Freedom and Equality for All Americans*. New York: Fidelis, 2023.

Harrington, Samuel H., ed. *Reports of Cases Argued and Adjudged in the Superior Court and Court of Errors and Appeals of the State of Delaware Under the Amended Constitution*. Vol. 2. Dover: S. Kimmey, 1841.

Harris, Thomas Le Grand. *The Trent Affair: Including a Review of English and American Relations at the Beginning of the Civil War*. Indianapolis: Bowen-Merrill, 1896.

Haselby, Sam. *The Origins of American Religious Nationalism*. New York: Oxford University Press, 2015.

Hastings, Martin. "United States-Vatican Relations." *Records of the American Catholic Historical Society of Philadelphia* 69, no. 1/2 (1958): 20–55.

Hatch, Nathan O. *The Democratization of American Christianity*. New Haven, CN: Yale University Press, 1989.

Haw, James, F. F. Beirne, and R. S. Jett. *Stormy Patriot: The Life of Samuel Chase*. Baltimore, MD: Maryland Historical Society, 1980.

Henry, Robert. *Religion Productive of National Prosperity: A Sermon, Delivered on Thanksgiving Day, February 5th, 1823; in the Chapel of the So. Ca. College*. Columbia, SC: D. & J.M. Faust, 1823.

Henry, Stuart C. *Unvanquished Puritan: A Portrait of Lyman Beecher*. Grand Rapids, MI: Eerdmans, 1973.

Herring, George C. *From Colony to Superpower: U.S. Foreign Relations Since 1776*. New York, NY: Oxford University Press, 2008.

———. *Years of Peril and Ambition: U.S. Foreign Relations, 1776–1921*. New York, NY: Oxford University Press, 2008.

Heyrman, Christine Leigh. *Southern Cross: The Beginnings of the Bible Belt*. New York: Alfred A. Knopf, 1997.

Hinton, John Howard. *The Test of Experience, Or, The Voluntary Principle in the United States*. London: Albert Cockshaw, 1851.

Hixson, Walter L. *The Myth of American Diplomacy: National Identity and U.S.* Foreign Policy. New Haven, CT: Yale University Press, 2008.

Hodge, A. A. *The Life of Charles Hodge D.D. LL.D. Professor in the Theological Seminary Princeton N.J.* New York: Charles Scribner's Sons, 1880.

Hodge, Charles. *The Education Question.* Philadelphia, PA: C. Sherman, 1850.

————. *Systematic Theology.* Vol. 3, *Soteriology.* Grand Rapids, MI: Eerdmans, 1940.

Hollow, Betty. *Ohio University, 1804–2004: The Spirit of a Singular Place.* Athens, OH: Ohio University Press, 2003.

Holmes, Oliver W. "Sunday Travel and Sunday Mails: A Question Which Troubled Our Forefathers." *New York History* 20, no. 4 (1939): 413–24.

"The Hon. Joseph R. Underwood." In. Vol. 7, *The American Review: A Whig Journal Devoted to Politics and Literature.* New York, NY: 609–614.

Howe, Mark DeWolf. *The Garden and the Wilderness: Religion and Government in American Constitutional History.* Chicago: University of Chicago Books, 1965.

Huebner, Timothy S. "The Consolidation of State Judicial Power: Spencer Roane, Virginia Legal Culture, and the Southern Judicial Tradition." *Virginia Magazine of History and Biography* 102, no. 1 (1994): 47–72.

Hughes, John, and John Breckenridge. *A Discussion of the Question, Is the Roman Catholic Religion, in Any Or in all the Principles of its Doctrines, Inimical to Civil or Religious Liberty? And of the Question, Is the Presbyterian Religion, in Any Or in all the Principles of its Doctrines, Inimical to Civil or Religious Liberty?*. Baltimore, MD: John Murphy, 1836.

Humphreys, David. *The Miscellaneous Works of David Humphreys: Late Minister Plenipotentiary from the United States of America to the Court of Madrid.* New York: T & J Swords, 1804.

Humphreys, Frank Landon. *The Life and Times of David Humphreys: Soldier—Statesman—Poet.* Vol. 1. New York: G.P. Putnam's Sons, 1917.

Imholt, Robert J. "Connecticut: Land of Steady Habits." In *Disestablishment and Religious Dissent: Church-State Relations in the New American States, 1776–1833*, edited by Carl D. Esbeck and Jonathan Den Hartog, 327-350. Columbia, MO: University of Missouri Press, 2019.

———. "Timothy Dwight, Federalist Pope of Connecticut." *New England Quarterly* 73, no. 3 (2000): 386–411.

Irons, Charles F. *The Origins of Proslavery Christianity: White and Black Evangelicals in Colonial and Antebellum Virginia.* Chapel Hill, NC: University of North Carolina Press, 2008.

Jackson, Andrew. Andrew Jackson to David Holmes, Head Quarters 7. M. District, 18 Jan 1815. In *The Papers of Andrew Jackson*. Vol. 3, *1814-1815*, edited by Harold D. Moser. Knoxville, TN: University of Tennessee Press, 1991: 249-250.

———. Andrew Jackson to James Winchester, 31 January 1815. In *The Papers of Andrew Jackson*, Vol. 3: 261-263.

———. Division Orders, 7 March 1812. In *The Correspondence of Andrew Jackson*, Vol. 1, *To April 30 1814*. Edited by John Spencer Bassett. Washington, DC: Carnegie Institute, 1926: 220–21.

———. "'The Departure From Nashville', A Journal of the Trip Down the Mississippi." In *The Correspondence of Andrew Jackson*, Vol. 1: 256-271.

———. Andrew Jackson to Rachel Jackson, January 1813. In Vol. 1 of *The Correspondence of Andrew Jackson*: 271-272.

Jay, John. "Federalist 2." In *The Federalist: A Commentary on the Constitution of the United States*, by Alexander Hamilton, John Jay, James Madison. New York: M. Walter Dunne, 1901.

Jefferson, Thomas. *Notes on the State of Virginia*. Boston: Lilly and Wait, 1832.

———. Thomas Jefferson to Benjamin Rush, Monticello, 23 September 1800, *Founders Online*, National Archives, https://founders.archives.gov/documents/Jefferson/01-32-02-0102.

———. Thomas Jefferson, Thomas Jefferson to Lafayette, 26 December 1820, *Founders Online*, National Archives, https://founders.archives.gov/documents/Jefferson/03-16-02-0400.

———. Thomas Jefferson to José Corrêa da Serra, 11 April 1820. *Founders Online*, National Archives, https://founders.archives.gov/documents/Jefferson/98-01-02-1213.

———. Thomas Jefferson to James Smith, Monticello, 8 December 1822. In *The Papers of Thomas Jefferson, Retirement Series*. Vol. 19, *16 September 1822-30 June 1823*. Edited by Daniel P. Jordan. Princeton: Princeton University Press, 2022: 213-214.

———. Thomas Jefferson to Major John Cartwright, Monticello, 5 June 1824. In *The Writings of Thomas Jefferson*. Vol. 16. Edited by Andrew A. Lipscomb and Albert Ellery Bergh. Washington, D.C.: Thomas Jefferson Memorial Association, 1904: 42-52.

Jenkins, Warren, ed. *The Ohio Gazetteer, and Traveler's Guide: Containing a Description of the Several Towns, Townships and Counties, with Their Water Courses, Roads, Improvements, Mineral Productions, etc. etc.* Columbus: Isaac M. Whiting, 1837.

John, Richard R. "Taking Sabbatarianism Seriously: The Postal System, the Sabbath, and the Transformation of American Political Culture." *Journal of the Early Republic* 10, no. 4 (1990): 517–67.

Johns, John. *A Memoir of the Life of the Right Rev. William Meade, D.D., Bishop of the Protestant Episcopal Church in the Diocese of Virginia*. Baltimore, MD: Innes, 1967.

Johnson, David. *Irreconcilable Founders: Spencer Roane, John Marshall, and the Nature of America's Constitutional Republic.* Baton Rouge, LA: Louisiana State University Press, 2021.

Jordan, Daniel P. *The Papers of Thomas Jefferson, Retirement Series.* Vol. 19. Princeton: Princeton University Press, 2022.

Journal of the Public and Secret Proceedings of the Convention of the People Held in Milledgeville and Savannah, in 1861, Together with the Ordinances Adopted. Milledgeville, GA: Boughton, Nisbet, Barnes State Printers, 1861.

"Judge Spencer Roane of Virginia: Champion of States' Rights Foe of John Marshall." *Harvard Law Review* 66, no. 7 (1953): 1242–59.

Kabala, James A. *Church-State Relations in the Early American Republic, 1787–1846.* London: Routledge, 2016.

Kafer, Peter K. "The Making of Timothy Dwight: A Connecticut Morality Tale." *The William and Mary Quarterly* 47, no. 2 (1990): 189–209.

Keller, Christian B. "Philanthropy Betrayed: Thomas Jefferson, the Louisiana Purchase, and the Origins of Federal Indian Removal Policy." *Proceedings of the American Philosophical Society* 144, no. 1 (2000): 39–66.

Kemper, Jackson. "A Trip through Wisconsin in 1838." *The Wisconsin Magazine of History* 8, no. 4 (1925): 423–45.

Kendall, Willmoore. *The Conservative Affirmation*. Washington, DC: Regnery Gateway, 2022.

Kent, James. *Commentaries on American Law*. Vol. 1. New York: O. Halsted, 1832.

Kidd, Thomas S. *Patrick Henry: First Among Patriots*. New York: Basic Books, 2011.

———. *Thomas Jefferson: A Biography of Spirit and Flesh*. New Haven, CN: Yale University Press, 2022.

———. *Who is An Evangelical? The History of a Movement in Crisis* (New Haven: Yale University Press, 2019.

Kidd, Thomas S., and Barry Hankins. *Baptists in America: A History*. New York: Oxford University Press, 2015.

Kingsbury, Harmon. *The Sabbath: A Brief History of Laws, Petitions, Remonstrances and Reports, with Facts and Arguments, Relating to the Christian Sabbath*. New York: Robert Carter, 1840.

Kirk, Edward Norris. *The Church Essential to the Republic. A Sermon*. New York: American Home Missionary Society, 1848.

Kirk, Russell. *The Conservative Mind: From Burke to Eliot*. Washington DC: Gateway, 2016.

Kitzen, Michael. "Money Bags or Cannon Balls: The Origins of the Tripolitan War, 1795–1801." *Journal of the Early Republic* 16, no. 4 (1996): 601–24.

Klein, Rachel N. *Unification of a Slave State: The Rise of the Planter Class in the South Carolina Backcountry, 1760–1808*. London: University of North Carolina Press, 1990.

Kneeland, Abner. *A Review of the Evidences of Christianity: In a Series of Lectures*. Boston, 1831.

Konkle, Burton Alva. *John Motley Morehead and the Development of North Carolina, 1796–1866*. Philadelphia, PA: William J. Campbell, 1922.

Kravitz, Bennett, and Arnon Gutfield. "'Let Us Save Them Now, or We Never Shall': Rhetoric and Recriminations in the Cherokee Removal Debate." *Studies in Popular Culture* 23, no. 2 (2000): 1–23.

Kurland, Philip B. *Religion and the Law: Of Church and State and the Supreme Court*. Chicago, IL: Aldine, 1961.

La Borde, Maximilian. *History of the South Carolina College: From Its Incorporation December 19, 1801 to Nov. 25, 1857, Including Sketches of Its Presidents and Professors with an Appendix*. Columbia, SC: Peter B. Glass, 1859.

Lambert, Frank. *The Barbary Wars: American Independence in the Atlantic World*. New York: Hill and Wang, 2005.

Langguth, A. J. *Driven West: Andrew Jackson and the Trail of Tears to the Civil War*. New York: Simon & Schuster, 2010.

Laron, Daniel G., and Greg Russell. "The Ethics of Power in American Diplomacy: The Statecraft of John Quincy Adams." *The Review of Politics* 52, no. 1 (1990): 3–31.

Lathrop, John H. *Inauguration of Hon. John H. Lathrop: LL.D. Chancellor of the University of Wisconsin, at the Capitol, Madison January 16, 1850.* Milwaukee, WI: Sentinel and Gazette, 1850.

Lears, Jackson. *Rebirth of a Nation: The Making of Modern America, 1877–1920.* New York: HarperCollins, 2009.

Legare, Hugh Swinton. *Writings of Hugh Swinton Legaré, Late Attorney General and Acting Secretary of State of the United States.* Charleston, SC: Burges and Hughes, 1845.

Leithart, Peter J. *The End of Protestantism: Pursuing Unity in a Fragmented Church.* Grand Rapids, MI: Brazos, 2016.

Levy, Leonard W. "Satan's Last Apostle in Massachusetts." *American Quarterly* 5, no. 1 (1953): 16–30.

———. "Terrett v. Taylor." In *Encyclopedia of the American Constitution,* edited by Leonard W. Levy. New York: Macmillan, 1986.

Lincoln, Abraham. "Second Inaugural Address." In *Abraham Lincoln's Speeches,* edited by L.E. Chittenden, 358–61. New York: Dodd, Mead, 1896.

Lincoln, Charles Z. *The Civil Law and the Church.* New York: Abingdon, 1916.

Lindsay, Jonathan A. "Basil Manly: Nineteenth Century Protean Man." *Baptist History and Heritage* 8, no. 3 (July 1973): 130–43.

Linn, William. *Serious Considerations on the Election of a President: Addressed to the Citizens of the United States.* New York: John Furman, 1800.

Lipscomb, Andrew A., and Albert Ellery Bergh, eds. *The Writings of Thomas Jefferson.* Vol. 16. Washington, DC: Thomas Jefferson Memorial Association, 1904.

Loughery, John. *Dagger John: Archbishop John Hughes and the Making of Irish America.* Ithaca, NY: Cornell University Press, 2018.

Lyman, Theodore. *The Diplomacy of the United States: Being an Account of the Foreign Relations of the Country from the First Treaty with France, in 1778, to the Present Time.* 2 vols. Boston, MA: Wells and Lilly, 1828.

Macaulay, Thomas Babington. *The History of England from the Accession of James II.* Vol. 3. Chicago, IL: Donohue, Henneberry & Co, 1890.

Machen, J. Gresham. *Christianity and Liberalism.* New York: Macmillan, 1923.

Manseau, Peter. *The Jefferson Bible: A Biography.* Princeton: Oxford University Press, 2020.

Marsden, George. *The Soul of the American University: From Protestant Establishment to Established Nonbelief.* New York: Oxford University Press, 1994.

Martin, Lerone. *The Gospel of J. Edgar Hoover: How the FBI Aided and Abetted the Rise of White Christian Nationalism.* Princeton, NJ: Princeton University Press, 2023.

Marty, Martin E. *Righteous Empire: the Protestant Experience in America*. New York: Harper & Row, 1977.

Matijasic, Thomas D. "The African Colonization Movement and Ohio's Protestant Community." *Phylon* 46, no. 1 (1985): 16–24.

Maxcy, Jonathan. "An Oration Delivered at the First Congregational Meeting House, in Providence, on the Fourth of July, 1799." In *The Literary Remains of the Rev. Jonathan Maxcy, D.D.*, edited by Romeo Elton, 381–84. New York: A. V. Blake, 1844.

May, Nicholas. "Holy Rebellion: Religious Assembly Laws in Antebellum South Carolina and Virginia." *American Journal of Legal History* 49, no. 3 (2007): 237–56.

McCarley, Elizabeth Maddock. "Blaine in the Joints: The History of the Blaine Amendment and the Modern Supreme Court Religious Liberty Doctrine on Education." *Duke Journal of Constitutional Law & Public Policy* 18 (2023):195–223.

McCrossen, Alexis. *Holy Day, Holiday: The American Sunday*. Ithaca, NY: Cornell University Press, 2000.

McCullough, David. *The Pioneers: The Heroic Story of the Settlers who Brought the American ideal West*. New York: Simon & Schuster, 2019.

McGivigan, John R. *The War against Proslavery Religion: Abolitionism and the Northern Churches, 1830–1865*. Ithaca, NY: Cornell University Press, 1984.

McKnight, John. *A View of the Present State of the Political and Religious World.* New York: Isaac Collins and Son, 1802.

McLoughlin, William G. *Cherokees and Missionaries, 1789–1839.* Norman, OK: University of Oklahoma Press, 1995.

—. "Isaac Backus and the Separation of Church and State in America." *The American Historical Review* 73, no. 5 (1968): 1392–413.

McRee, Griffith J. *Life and Correspondence of James Iredell: One of the Associate Justices of the Supreme Court of the United States.* Vol. 2. New York: D. Appleton, 1857.

Meacham, Jon. *American Lion: Andrew Jackson in the White House.* New York: Random House, 2009.

Mead, Sidney E. *The Old Religion in the Brave New World: Reflections on the Relation Between Christendom and the Republic.* Berkeley, CA: University of California Press, 1977.

Meade, William. *A Brief Review of the Episcopal Church in Virginia: From Its First Establishment to the Present Time.* Richmond, VA: William McFarland, 1845.

Miles, Edwin A. "After John Marshall's Decision: Worcester v. Georgia and the Nullification Crisis." *Journal of Southern History* 39, no. 4 (1973): 519–44

Moffett, Thomas C. *The Bible in the Life of the Indians of the United States.* New York: American Bible Society, 1916.

Moore, Russell D. *Onward: Engaging the Culture Without Losing the Culture.* Nashville, TN: B&H, 2015.

———. "The State of Evangelical America." *The New York Times,* July 30, 2023.

Morris, Benjamin F. *Christian Life and Character of the Civil Institutions of the United States.* Philadelphia, PA: George W. Childs, 1864.

Morse, Jedediah. "The Present Dangers and Consequent Duties of the Citizens." In *The Fear of Conspiracy: Images of Un-American Subversion from the Revolution to the Present,* edited by David Brion Davis. Ithaca, NY: Cornell University Press, 1971: 45-48.

Neem, Johann N. "The Elusive Common Good: Religion and Civil Society in Massachusetts, 1780–1833." *Journal of the Early Republic* 24, no. 3 (2004): 381–417.

Newmyer, R. Kent. *Supreme Court Justice Joseph Story: Statesman of the Old Republic.* Chapel Hill, NC: University of North Carolina Press, 1985.

Noll, Mark A. *America's God: From Jonathan Edwards to Abraham Lincoln.* Oxford: Oxford University Press, 2002.

———. *The Civil War as a Theological Crisis.* Chapel Hill, NC: University of North Carolina Press, 2006.

Nolt, Steven M. *Foreigners in Their Own Land: Pennsylvania Germans in the Early Republic.* University Park, PA: Pennsylvania State University Press, 2002.

Noonan, John T., Jr. *The Lustre of Our Country: The American Experience of Religious Freedom*. Berkeley, CA: University of California Press, 1998.

Norton, John N. *The Life of the Rt. Rev. William White, D. D., Bishop of Pennsylvania*. New York: Church Book Society, 1856.

Norton, Mary Beth. *Liberty's Daughters: The Revolutionary Experience of American Women, 1750–1800*. Ithaca, NY: Cornell University Press, 1980.

Novak, Michael, and Jane Novak. *Washington's God: Religion, Liberty, and the Father of Our Country*. New York: Basic, 2006.

Nugent, Walter. *Habits of Empire: A History of American Expansion*. New York: Alfred A. Knopf, 2008.

O'Sullivan, John L. "The Great Nation of Futurity." *United States Magazine and Democratic Review* 6, no. 23 (1839): 426–30.

Onishi, Bradley. *Preparing for War: The Extremist History of White Christian Nationalism—and What Comes Next*. Minneapolis, WI: Broadleaf, 2023.

Orth, John V., and Paul Martin Newby. *The North Carolina State Constitution*. Oxford: Oxford University Press, 2013.

Owsley, Frank L., Jr. "The Fort Mims Massacre." *Alabama Review* 24 (1971): 192–204.

Paley, William. *The Works of William Paley: With a Life of the Author*. Vol. 2. London: Thomas Tegg, 1825.

Parton, Dorothy M. "The Diplomatic Career of Joel Roberts Poinsett," PhD diss., Catholic University of America, 1934.

Patterson, Isaac Franklin, ed. *The Constitutions of Ohio: Amendments, and Proposed Amendments*. Cleveland, OH: Arthur H. Clark, 1912.

Paulsen, Michael A. "Religion, Equality, and the Constitution: An Equal Protection Approach to Establishment Clause Adjudication," *Notre Dame Law Review* 61 (1986): 311–17.

Pearl, Cyril. *The Sabbath a Divine Institution. A Reply to Arguments on the Negative of the Question "Ought the Law Requiring the Opening of our Post Offices and the Transportation of Our Mails on the Christian Sabbath be Repealed?" Delivered before the Bangor Forensic Club, January 1831*. Boston, MA: Pierce and Parker, 1831.

Perdue, Theda, and Michael C. Green. *The Cherokee Nation and the Trail of Tears*. New York: Viking, 2007.

Perry, Samuel L. *The Flag and the Cross: White Christian Nationalism and the Threat to American Democracy*. Oxford: Oxford University Press, 2022.

Perry, William Stevens. *The History of the American Episcopal Church, 1587–1883*. Vol. 2. Boston: James R. Osgood, 1885.

Peters, Richard, ed. *Condensed Reports of Cases in the Supreme Court of the United States.* Vol. 3. Philadelphia, PA: John Grigg, 1831.

Peterson, Mark. *The City-State of Boston: The Rise and Fall of an Atlantic Power, 1630–1865.* Princeton: Princeton University Press, 2019.

Peterson, Merrill D. *Thomas Jefferson and the New Nation: A Biography.* Oxford: Oxford University Press, 1970.

Poinsett, Joel R. *Discourse, on the Objects and Importance of the National Institution for the Promotion of Science.* Washington, D.C.: P. Force, 1840.

———. *Notes on Mexico.* Philadelphia, PA: Carey and Lea, 1825.

Powell, J. H., *Richard Rush: Republican Diplomat, 1780–1859.* Philadelphia, PA: University of Pennsylvania Press, 1942.

Powell, William S., ed. *The Dictionary of North Carolina Biography.* Vol. 3. Chapel Hill, NC: University of North Carolina Press, 1988.

Preston, Andrew. *Sword of the Spirit, Shield of faith: Religion in American War and Diplomacy.* New York: Alfred A. Knopf, 2012.

Proceedings in Relation to the Formation of the Auxiliary Union of the City of Boston, for Promoting the Observance of the Christian Sabbath, with the Address of the General Union to the People of the United States. Boston, MA: T. R. Marvin, 1828.

Pucha, Francis Paul. *The Great Father: The United States Government and the American Indians*, vols. 1 and 2. Lincoln, NE: University of Nebraska Press, 1984.

The Religious Monitor, and Evangelical Repository. Vol. 6. Albany, NY: Webster and Wood, 1829–30.

Remini, Robert. *Andrew Jackson: The Course of American Freedom, 1822–1832*. Baltimore: Johns Hopkins University Press, 1981), 276.

Report of the Arguments of the Attorney of the Commonwealth, at the Trials of Abner Kneeland, for Blasphemy, in the Municipal and Supreme Courts in Boston, January and May, 1834. Boston: Beals, Homer, 1834.

Reports of Cases Argued and Determined in the Supreme Court of the State of Missouri. Vol. 20. St. Louis, MO: George Knapp, 1855.

Rice, John Holt. *The Duties of a Gospel Minister*. Madison, MS: Log College Press, 2018.

Rippy, Fred. *Joel R. Poinsett: Versatile American*. Berkeley, CA: University of California Press, 1968.

Rives, Nathan S. "'Is Not This a Paradox?' Public Morality and the Unitarian Defense of State-Supported Religion in Massachusetts, 1806–1833." *New England Quarterly* 86, no. 2 (2013): 232–65.

Robb, Dale. "Miami University 1809–2002: From Presbyterian Enterprise to Public Institution." *Journal of Presbyterian History* 81, no. 1 (2003): 35–54.

Roberts, Timothy Mason. *Distant Revolutions: 1848 and the Challenge to American Exceptionalism.* Charlottesville, VA: University of Virginia Press, 2009.

Rohrer, James R. "Sunday Mails and the Church-State Theme in Jacksonian America." *Journal of the Early Republic* 7, no. 1 (1987): 53–74.

Rohrs, Richard C. "American Critics of the French Revolution of 1848." *Journal of the Early Republic* 14, no. 3 (1994): 359–77.

Rojas, Martha Elena. "'Insults Unpunished': Barbary Captives, American Slaves, and the Negotiation of Liberty." *Early American Studies* 1, no. 2 (2003): 159–86.

Rosenfeld, Richard. *American Aurora, A Democratic Republican Returns: The Suppressed History of Our Nation's Beginnings and the Heroic Newspaper that Tried to Report It.* New York: St Martin's Griffin, 1997.

Rush, Benjamin. Benjamin Rush to Elias Boudinot, 9 July 1788. In *The Sacred Rights of Conscience: Selected Readings on Church-State Relations in the American Founding,* edited by Daniel L. Dreisbach and Mark David Hall, 354. Indianapolis, IN: Liberty Fund, 2009.

Rush, Richard. *Two Letters on Public Subjects from Richard Rush, of Pennsylvania, to William Henry Trescott, of South Carolina.* Philadelphia, PA: L. R. Bailey, 1851.

Ryrie, Alec. *The Protestants: The Faith that Made the Modern World.* New York: Penguin, 2017.

Sands, Kathleen. "Territory, Wilderness, Property and Reservation: Land and Religion in Native American Supreme Court Cases." *American Indian Law Review* 36, no. 2 (2011): 253–320

Schafer, Joseph. "Chancellor John Hiram Lathrop." *The Wisconsin Magazine of History* 23, no. 2 (1939): 207–36.

Schaff, Philip. *America: A Sketch of the Political, Social, and Religious Character of the United States, in Two Lectures.* New York: C. Scribner, 1855.

———. *Church and State in the United States: Or, The American Idea of Religious Liberty and its Practical Effects.* New York: Charles Scribner's Sons, 1888.

Schauinger, J. Herman. *William Gaston, Carolinian.* Milwaukee, WI: Bruce, 1949.

Seidel, Andrew. *The Founding Myth: Why Christian Nationalism Is Un-American.* New York: Union Square, 2019.

Sergeant, Thomas, and Abraham Small. *Reports of Cases Adjudged in the Supreme Court of Pennsylvania: 1824.* Vol. 3. Philadelphia, PA: Abraham Small, 1824.

Seward, William Henry. Mr. Seward to Mr. Adams, November 30, 1861. *The Diplomatic History of the War For the Union.* Vol. 5, edited by George E. Baker. Boston, MA: Houghton, Mifflin, 1884: 293-295.

Sheehan, Bernard W. *Seeds of Extinction: Jeffersonian Philanthropy and the American Indian.* Chapel Hill: University of North Carolina Press, 1973.

Simon, James F. *What Kind of Nation: Thomas Jefferson, John Marshall, and the Epic Struggle to Create a United States*. New York: Simon and Schuster, 2003.

Smith, Daniel Blake. *American Betrayal: Cherokee Patriots and the Trail of Tears*. New York: Henry Holt, 2011.

Smith, Edwin Burritt, and Ernest Hitchock eds. *Reports of Cases Adjudged and Determined in the Supreme Court of Judicature and Court for the Trial of Impeachments and Correction of Errors of the State of New York*. Vol. 4. Newark, NY: Lawyer's Cooperative Publishing, 1883.

Smith, Eric C. *John Leland: A Jeffersonian Baptist in Early America*. New York: Oxford University Press, 2002.

Smith, Joseph. *Old Redstone; Or, Historical Sketches of Western Presbyterianism, Its Earliest Minister, Its Perilous Times, and Its First Records*. Philadelphia: Lippincott, Grambo, 1854.

Smith, Mark Power, *Young America: The Transformation of Nationalism before the Civil War*. Charlottesville: University of Virginia Press, 2022.

Smith, Miles. "'Turning up Their Noses at the Colonel': Eastern Aristocracy, Western Democracy, and Richard Mentor Johnson." *The Register of the Kentucky Historical Society* 111, no. 4 (2013): 525–61.

———. "The Uselessness of 'Christian Nationalism.'" *Mere Orthodoxy*, July 18, 2022.

———. "Would That It Really Were 'Christian Nationalism.'" *The American Conservative*, March 8, 2021.

Smith, Samuel H., and Thomas Lloyd, eds. *Trial of Samuel Chase: An Associate Justice of the Supreme Court of the United States, Impeached by the House of Representatives for High Crimes and Misdemeanors, Before the Senate of the United States.* Vol. 1. Washington, D.C.: Samuel H. Smith, 1805.

Smith, Samuel Stanhope. *The Lectures, Corrected and Improved, Which Have Been Delivered for a Series of Years in the College of New-Jersey; On the Subjects of Moral and Political Philosophy.* Vol. 1. New York: Whiting and Watson, 1812.

Snider, William D. *Light on the Hill: A History of the University of North Carolina at Chapel Hill.* Chapel Hill, NC: University of North Carolina Press, 1992.

Snyder, Christina. *Great Crossings: Indians, Settlers, and Slaves in the Age of Jackson.* Oxford: Oxford University Press, 2017.

The South-Carolina Justice of Peace: Containing All the Duties, Powers, and Authorities of that Office, as Regulated by the Laws Now of Force In this State, And Adapted to the Parish and County Magistrate. New York: T. & J. Swords, 1810.

Stahr, Walter. *Seward: Lincoln's Indispensable Man.* New York: Simon & Schuster, 2012.

Starr, Emmet. *History of the Cherokee Indians and Their Legends and Folk Lore.* Oklahoma City: Warren, 1921.

Stewart, Katherine. *The Power Worshippers: The Dangerous Rise of Religious Nationalism.* New York: Bloomsbury, 2020.

Stone, Geoffrey R. *Sex and the Constitution: Sex, Religion, and Law from America's Origins to the Twenty-First Century.* New York: Liverlight, 2017.

Story, Joseph. *Commentaries on the Constitution of the United States with a Preliminary Review of the Constitutional History of the Colonies and States, before the Adoption of the Constitution.* Vol. 3. Boston, MA: Hilliard, Gray, 1833.

Story, William W., ed. *Life and Letters of Joseph Story.* Vol. 1. London: John Chapman, 1851.

Strange, Alan D. "The Doctrine of the Spirituality of the Church in the Theology of Charles Hodge." *Mid-America Journal of Theology* 25 (2014): 101–16.

Stuckert, Howard Morris. "Jackson Kemper, Presbyter." *Historical Magazine of the Protestant Episcopal Church* 4, no. 3 (1935): 130–51.

Sturges, Mark. "Fleecing Connecticut: David Humphreys and the Poetics of Sheep Farming." *The New England Quarterly* 87, no. 3 (2014): 464–89.

Sumner, Charles. *White Slavery in the Barbary States: A Lecture Before the Boston Mercantile Library Association, Feb. 17, 1847.* Boston, MA: William D. Ticknor, 1847.

Sumner, Margaret. *Collegiate Republic: Cultivating an Ideal Society in Early America.* Charlottesville: University of Virginia Press, 2014.

Tappan, Henry P. *The University: Its Constitution, and its Relations, Political and Religious: A Discourse Delivered June 22d, 1858, at the Request of the Christian Library Association.* Ann Arbor, MI:S. B. McCracken, 1858.

Taylor, Alan. *Thomas Jefferson's Education.* New York: Norton, 2019.

Taylor, Thomas T. "Samuel E. McCorkle and a Christian Republic, 1792–1802." *American Presbyterians* 63, no. 4 (1985): 375–85.

Thornton, Russell. "Cherokee Population Losses During the Trail of Tears: A New Perspective and a New Estimate." *Ethnohistory* 31, no. 4 (1984): 289–300.

Thornwell, James Henley. *Discourses on Truth: Delivered in the Chapel of the South Carolina College.* New York: Robert Carter & Brothers, 1855.

————. "Reasons for Separate Organization," In *The Collected Writings of James Henley Thornwell.* Vol. 4, *Ecclesiastical,* edited by John B. Adger and John L. Girardeau, 439-445. Richmond, VA: Presbyterian Committee on Publication, 1873.

————. "The Christian Doctrine of Slavery," In *The Collected Writings of James Henley Thornwell,* Vol. 4: 398-436.

————. "Slavery and the Religious Education of the Colored Population" in *Southern Presbyterian Review* 4 (1850–1851).

————. *The State of the Country: An Article Republished from The Southern Presbyterian* Review. Columbia, SC: Southern Guardian Steam Power Press, 1861.

Thorpe, Francis Newton. *The Federal and State Constitutions, Colonial Charters, and Other Organic Laws of the States, Territories, and Colonies Now or Heretofore Forming the United States of America.* Vol. 6. Washington, DC: Government Printing Office, 1909.

Thorton, John Wingate. *The Pulpit of the American Revolution, or, The Political Sermons of the Period of 1776.* Boston, MA: Gould and Lincoln, 1860.

Tillman, Seth Barrett. "A Religious Test in America? The 1809 Motion to Vacate Jacob Henry's North Carolina State Legislative Seat—A Reevaluation of the Primary Sources." *North Carolina Historical Review* 98, no. 1 (January 2021): 1–41.

Torba, Andrew, and Andrew Isker. *Christian Nationalism: A Biblical Guide for Taking Dominion and Discipling Nations.* Self-published, 2022.

Toth, Michael C. *Founding Federalist: The Life of Oliver Ellsworth.* Wilmington, DE: ISI Books, 2014.

Traub, James. *John Quincy Adams: Militant Spirit.* New York: Basic, 2016.

Trescott, William Henry, *The Diplomatic History of the Administrations of Washington and Adams, 1789–1801.* Boston, MA: Little, Brown, 1857.

Turner, Kathryn. "The Midnight Judges." *University of Pennsylvania Law Review* 109, no. 4 (1961): 494–523.

Tuveson, Ernest Lee. *Redeemer Nation: The Idea of America's Millennial Role.* Chicago, IL: University of Chicago Press, 1968.

University of Michigan. Catalogue of the Officers and Students in the Department of the Arts and Sciences 1843–4. Ann Arbor, MI: Michigan Argus Office. 1843.

U.S. Congress, Senate, "Report on Stopping the United States Mail, and Closing the Post-offices on Sunday, January 19, 1829, 20th Cong., 2d sess., Senate Doc. 46, 19 Jan. 1829." In *American State Papers, Class VII: Post Office Dept,* edited by Walter Lowrie and Walter S. Franklin, 211–13. Washington, DC: Gales and Seaton, 1834.

Verhoeven, Tim. "The Case for Sunday Mails: Sabbath Laws and the Separation of Church and State in Jacksonian America." *Journal of Church and State* 55, no. 1 (2013): 71–91.

Verney, Michael A. "An Eye for Prices, an Eye for Souls: Americans in the Indian Subcontinent, 1784–1838." *Journal of the Early Republic* 33, no. 3 (2013): 397–431.

Wadsworth, Charles. *America's Mission: A Sermon Preached in the Arch Street Presbyterian Church, Philadelphia, on*

Thanksgiving Day, Nov. 22, 1855. Philadelphia, PA: T. B. Peterson, 1855.

Wald, Kenneth D., and Allison Calhoun-Brown. *Religion and Politics in the United States.* Lanham, MD: Rowman & Littlefield, 2014.

Walker, Andrew T. *Liberty for All: Defending Everyone's Religious Freedom in a Pluralistic Age.* Grand Rapids, MI: Brazos, 2021.

Wallace, Anthony F. C. *The Long Bitter Trail: Andrew Jackson and the Indians.* New York: Hill and Wang, 1993.

Walther, C. F. W. "Fourth of July Address Presented at a Christian Youth Group." In *From Our Master's Table: Sermons and Addresses Already Appearing Since 1847 Partly in Pamphlet Form and Partly in Periodicals Newly Offered in a Single Volume of Dr. C. F. W. Walther.* Dearborn, MI: Mark V, 2008.

Weber, Ralph E., and Joel R. Poinsett. "Joel R. Poinsett's Secret Mexican Dispatch Twenty." *The South Carolina Historical Magazine* 75, no. 2 (1974): 67–76.

Wedgeworth, Steven. "'The Two Sons of Oil' and the Limits of American Religious Dissent." *Journal of Law and Religion* 27, no. 1 (2011): 141–61.

Weeks, Louis B. "The Scriptures and Sabbath Observance in the South." *Journal of Presbyterian History* 59, no. 2 (1981): 267–84.

Weisenberger, Francis P. *The Life of John McLean: A Politician on the United States Supreme Court.* New York: Da Capo Press, 1971.

Wellman, Judith. *Grassroots Reform in the Burned-Over District of Upstate New York : Religion, Abolitionism, and Democracy.* New York: Routledge, 2000.

West, Ellis M. *The Free Exercise of Religion in America: Its Original Constitutional Meaning.* New York: Palgrave MacMillan, 2019.

West, Nathaniel. *The Ark of God: The Safe-guard of the Nation. A Discourse in Defense of Protestantism.* Pittsburgh: J.T. Shyrock, 1852.

Wheelan, Joseph. *Jefferson's War: America's First War on Terror 1801–1805.* New York: Carroll & Graf, 2003.

Whichard, Willis P. *Justice James Iredell.* Durham, NC: Carolina Academic Press, 2000.

White, Henry Alexander. *Southern Presbyterian Leaders.* New York: Neale, 1911.

White, Richard. *The Republic for Which It Stands: The United States During Reconstruction and the Gilded Age, 1865–1896.* Oxford: Oxford University Press, 2017.

Whitehead, Andrew L. *American Idolatry: How Christian Nationalism Betrays the Gospel and Threatens the Church.* Grand Rapids, MI: Brazos, 2023.

Wilentz, Sean. *The Rise of American Democracy: Jefferson to Lincoln.* New York: Norton, 2005.

Willson, James R. *Prince Messiah's Claims to Dominion Over All Governments; and the Disregard of His Authority by the United States, in the Federal Constitution.* Packard, Hoffman, and White, 1832.

Wilson, Andrew. *Remaking the World: How 1776 Created the Post-Christian West.* Wheaton, IL: Crossway, 2023.

Wiltse, Charles M. "A Critical Southerner: John C. Calhoun on the Revolutions of 1848." *Journal of Southern History* 15, no. 3 (1949): 299–310.

Wintersteen, A. H. "Christianity and the Common Law." *The American Law Register* 38, no. 5 (1890): 273–85.

Wolfe, Stephen. *The Case for Christian Nationalism.* Moscow, ID: Canon, 2022.

Young, Mary. Review of *Indian Policy in the Age of Jefferson,* by Anthony F. C. Wallace, Laurence M. Hauptman, Max Mintz, Carl Benn, Claudio Saunt, and Philip J. Deloria. *Journal of the Early Republic* 20, no. 2 (2000): 297–307.